THE CRUSADE AND END OF INDIRA RAJ

THE CRUSADE
and
End of Indira Raj

S. K. GHOSE

Foreword by
JAYAPRAKASH NARAYAN

INTELLECTUAL BOOK CORNER

First Published 1978

Published by
Intellectual Book Corner
23, Pratap Gali, Daryaganj,
New Delhi-110002

Composed by
Sunil Composing Co.
C-241, Mayapuri, Phase II,
New Delhi-110064

Printed at
Ruby Offset Works
New Delhi-110064

Foreword

I am glad that Sri S. K. Ghose has written a comprehensive history of the movement that ended an authoritarian rule. Sri Ghose was the Patna Bureau Chief of the Press Trust of India for many years. In a sense he was involved in the movement as he was in charge of the overall coverage of the struggle throughout the period it lasted. He watched it from a ring-side berth and has, therefore, been in a position to give many eye-witness accounts. He was in a very advantageous position because most of the leading politicians of the State, both of the opposition and of the ruling party, were his personal friends. Being a member of the Bihar Legislative Council also gave him a unique opportunity to study events from inside. Perhaps very few persons knew as much of the movement as he did. What is more, he followed the progress of the movement as it spread to other States and watched the reactions of those in power and the counter-offensives they launched in Bihar and elsewhere.

What he has written is not just an objective narration of events but also the story of the interplay of forces for and against the movement. I do not know of any other book, so broad in its sweep. His picture has been painted on a big canvas beginning from the police firings in Bettiah on March 16, 1974 and ending in the Lok Sabha and State Assembly elections. It has a strange resemblance to Sanjaya recapitulating the battlefield scenes of Kurukshetra to Dhritarastra.

I am happy to note that he has not lost sight of the human and moral aspects of the movement. His conclusions are his own and I do not want to comment on them. I have known Sri Ghose for more than three decades and consider him to be an outstanding and fearless journalist. He has an incisive and forceful style. Sri Ghose, unlike some other journalists, is very particular about ascertaining truth and never attempts to colour facts for effect. This is well illustrated by his story of how he changed from a critic of the movement to its supporter, as he came to watch and study it from close quarters.

I believe that his book, *The Crusade*, will not only be of interest to the general public but also soon become a guide book for students of history of this period and a source book for scholars.

Mahila Charkha Samiti
Kadamkuan, Patna-800003 JAYAPRAKASH NARAYAN
August 9, 1977

Preface

Three events mark modern Indian history—the Mutiny, Quit India and the movement led by Mr. Jayaprakash Narayan. We are perhaps too near the last to see it in perspective. Having been the Patna Bureau Chief of the Press Trust of India for over 25 years, I was in an advantageous position, pretty close to the participants in the movement, including JP, as well as those in power who were trying to suppress it.

At long last, quite unbelievably, the Emergency was lifted. Then something happened. A dear friend, Phaniswar Nath 'Renu', well-known Hindi litterateur—who had renounced his Padamshree award and a monthly pension of Rs. 300 in protest against the repressive policy of the Government against the supporters of the movement—passed away. I met several of JP's associates at his cremation. Some of them suggested that I should write the inside story of the JP movement, what happened and why. For a long time I hesitated. When my wife came to know of it she accused me that it was my laziness that was preventing me from undertaking this task. The accusation was too true to be good.

The book is more about a movement than about a man, though it is hard to separate the two. My narration, necessarily, seeks to light up the charismatic and contradictory career of one whose courage and sensitiveness has created a more than life-size hero-type. It is also a record, some of which is being published for the first time. Reviled, jeered, tortured, even assaulted, JP would not bend, his lonely voice becoming the voice of freedom and conscience in the prisonhouse, gagged and groaning, that was India. Apparently political in substance, his deeper motivations are utterly human and moral. Perhaps in him we have, what Camus longed for, the saint with a difference.

Behind the account of JP's whirlwind tours, the gentle but firm words of the Lok Nayak, the final victory of the cause from which the lonely hero refused to draw any personal profit, is a thrilling adventure whose end we have not seen yet. Will JP's crusade lead to a total revolution or peter out in the years to come? A crusade is usually for and against something, a person or a programme, a cause. There can be little doubt as to what JP's crusade was ultimately for or against. But the crusade itself has two aspects or dimensions: short-term and long-range, local and transcendental, activist and millennial. For the most part I have tried to be factual and left the subtler analysis of motives and speculations for others better qualified.

In these pages, within my limits, I have sought to convey something of the passion, the excitement and the protest of a wounded nation led by an ailing but undaunted leader, who described himself as a 'wounded soldier'.

I have to thank several of my friends and relatives for helping me to write this book. These include Messrs. Sachchidanand, JP's Private Secretary, S. H. Razi, Convenor of the Bihar Jana Sangharsh Samiti, Krishna Kant Prasad, Chief Sub-editor of the daily *Aryavarta*, Jadu Nath Sinha of the Press Information Bureau, Patna, Jagannath Yadav, M.L.A. (now Parliamentary Secretary), my son-in-law, Ranjan Narayan, my younger brother, Dr. Sisirkumar Ghose of Viswabharati, Santi Niketan, and Krishna Murari Krishna for his excellent photographs.

Labanya Nivas
Patrakar Nagar
Patna-800016
August 1, 1977

SUDHANSU KUMAR GHOSE

Contents

ONE

JP's Finest Hour

It was the evening of March 20, 1977. The place was the Mahila Charkha Samiti, residence of Mr. Jayaprakash Narayan at Kadam Kuan in Central Patna. The hour was 7.30 p.m. It had become evident by then that Mrs. Indira Gandhi and her son Sanjay Gandhi were losing the elections at Rae Bareli and Amethi. Several heads had already rolled. Former Defence Minis er, Mr. Bansi Lal, the Law Minister, Mr. Gokhale and ex-Congress President, Dr. Shankar Dayal Sharma, all were defeated. The socialist leader, George Fernandes, still in Tihar Jail, was winning from Muzaffarpur by a huge margin.

Voting trends in Bihar and Uttar Pradesh indicated that the Janata and its allies were sweeping the polls. In the Congress strong-holds of Rajasthan and Madhya Pradesh, the Janata combine was inflicting a crushing defeat to the Congress nominees. The same wind was blowing in Punjab and Haryana.

Hordes of young men, visiting the Mahila Charkha Samiti, carried an air of muted jubilance, there were no raucous shouts of rejoicing, no exaggerated sense of triumph. Word had gone round from Mr. Narayan's aides that they should be magnanimous in victory, and there should be no unseemly demonstration.

It was rather ironical that JP himself was alone and suffering when the nation was celebrating his victory. The great are always alone.

The youths crowded into the ground-floor room of JP's personal assistants, Sachchidanand and Thomas Abraham, where a transistor had been tuned in to enable them to listen to announcements of results of the election. The solitary telephone in the room was also jammed either with enquiries or with incoming news.

Mr. Jayaprakash Narayan, the founding father of the Janata

Party and the main architect of its victory, was in sedation to relieve him of physical pain. He had undergone an unscheduled dialysis that day and had to leave for Delhi on March 23 for consultations on the formal merger of the parties that had fought the election on the Janata symbol. Post-dialysis, he had an upset stomach and was feeling quite weak. He was not to be disturbed and no visitors were allowed. Only Sachchidanand or Abraham would from time to time tiptoe into his first-floor room to inform him of election results and quietly return to ring up his personal physicians to come to attend on him (unfortunately, all of them were out at the time and could not be contacted).

As I had been called to give my assessment of the election prospects, I happened to be present. I had prepared a typed statement giving an analysis of possible voting trends in Bihar, constituencywise (I had conceded 10 out of 54 seats to the Congress but it drew blank). In view of JP's indisposition, I handed over the typescript of the assessment to Sachchidanand and left. He, however, requested me to come again next morning.

By next morning more results had come in. The Prime Minister as also Mr. Sanjay Gandhi had lost. The Janata nominees were leading by lengths in UP, Bihar, Rajasthan, Madhya Pradesh, Punjab and Haryana. It was clear that in Bihar the Congress was completely sunk.

Since morning streams of visitors were pouring in at JP's residence. Men and women, young and old, came and went up to Mr. Narayan, offered flowers, garlands and bouquets, paid their respects and left. With more results coming in, as the morning wore into noon, it became even more abundantly clear that the Janata and its allies were heading for a decisive majority in the new Lok Sabha.

As Patna Bureau Chief of the PTI (now Samachar) I had known JP for several decades and enjoyed his affection and confidence. When I met him next morning he greeted me with his usual warmth. He was reclining in an easy chair. His left foot was bandaged.

Wherever he had campaigned during his movement, JP used to maintain that if elections were held 95 per cent of the people would vote for the Janata. But I had conceded more seats to the Congress. So I said: "Possibly I have made a fool of myself because it appears the Congress is going to draw a blank in Bihar, Uttar Pradesh, Hariana and Delhi."

JP smiled and confided that though he had expected the Congress to lose heavily, he too had not expected it would cut "such a sorry figure". "What is your reaction?" I asked.

The Lok Nayak, who had performed a near miracle, achieved almost the impossible, quietly replied: "I am happy", and at once added: "It means that a tremendous responsibility has been placed on the shoulders of those who have won. Now they would have to sort out many things."

When I congratulated him and said "it is your achievement", JP suddenly became grave. "It is the mass upsurge that did it. Otherwise a thousand JPs could not achieve it."

The frail warrior, whose one-man crusade had detonated a democratic explosion that blew up a unique type of ruthless dictatorship imposed by Mrs. Indira Gandhi and her son aided and abetted by an infamous coterie by making a mockery of the Constitution and the Parliamentary process, was surprisingly calm and composed after achieving a stunning victory in what was perhaps his last battle. India's Man of Destiny had truly become a *Sthita Prajna* by attaining complete mental equilibrium at the finest hour of his life.

While returning home, I could still hear the echo of his soft-spoken voice "it was the mass upsurge that did it" and wonder at his modesty! But was he not the Crusader who had created that upsurge and added a chapter in the struggle for freedom and man's age-long quest for a just society?

TWO

The Crusader

A tall, lanky, handsome young Indian, who had just crossed his teens, with but a few dollars in his pocket, landed in America in October, 1922, to seek higher education. He worked as a helper in a fruit shop and a garden and as a dish-washer in a hotel for seven long years to earn his keep and to pay for his education. Originally a student of science, after having studied science for three years in an American university, he switched over to arts, to secure a Bachelor's degree. He then studied sociology, especially in Marxian literature and turned a communist. He took his Master of Arts degree in Sociology and presented a thesis on "Social Variation" which brought him instant recognition. But that was nothing compared to the heights to which he rose later. He planned to secure a Ph.D. but circumstances forced him to give up the idea and return home.

That young man was Jayaprakash Narayan, now universally respected and known by the first two initials of his name, J.P. He was born on October 11, 1902, in village Sitab Diara in the district of Saran in Bihar, which has now gone to Uttar Pradesh due to the changing course of the river Sarju. He came of a lower middle class family. His father, Babu Harsu Dayal, was a Canal Officer in the Bihar Government, who had some land in village Sitab Diara, one of whose 'tolas' (localities) is now known as Jayaprakash Nagar. JP received his early education in the local primary school. Later, he passed his Entrance examination from the Patna Collegiate School, winning a Divisional scholarship. He then took admission in Patna College where he studied science and was considered to be a brilliant student. After only one year, he, however, left college, sought the guidance of Babu Rajendra Prasad (who later became the first President of India) and joined the non-cooperation movement launched by Mahatma Gandhi. After the fires of the first non-cooperation movement had subsided, JP passed the I.Sc. examination from the Bihar Vidyapith. He decided, however, not to have his college education controlled by the British Government, which had been described by the Mahatma as a "Satanic Government", and left for U.S.A.

On his way back home from the United States, JP travelled via London where he met several communist leaders, including the late Rajani Palme Dutt. JP had been married early. On his return he went first to Sabarmati Ashram of Mahatma Gandhi where his wife, Sreemati Prabhawati Devi, lived. The Mahatma treated Prabhawati as his own daughter, and naturally JP received the treatment of a son-in-law. JP thus had easy access to Gandhiji who introduced him to Pandit Jawaharlal Nehru. They immediately became friends as both held radical views. Nehru soon invited JP to join the Indian National Congress and work for national independence. He also placed JP in charge of the Labour Department of the Congress and posted him at its central headquarters at Allahabad.

As a Marxist, JP did not believe in non-violence. Yet such was his love and respect for the Mahatma that he joined the freedom struggle under his leadership. In the early thirties, when Gandhiji launched his second non-cooperation movement (the Salt Satyagraha) and all top-ranking Congress leaders went to prison, JP was made the General Secretary of the Indian National Congress and asked to operate from Bombay headquarters of the AICC. He soon earned the reputation of being the "brain of the Congress". He was arrested in Bombay in 1932 and transferred to Nasik Central Jail, where he came in touch with prominent leftists like Mr. Achyut Patwardhan, Mr. Minoo Masani, Mr. Purushottam Tricumdas, Mr. Asoka Mehta and others. It was in Nasik prison that he got the idea of forming a socialist group within the Congress. This group later came to be known as the Congress Socialist Party, which, under his leadership, played a significant role in the country's national and socialist movements. Even Mahatma Gandhi hailed him as the "Master of Indian Socialism" and once declared that "what JP does not know of socialism, no one else in India does". Initially, the party led by JP was backed by Pandit

Nehru. Although Nehru never joined this party, he helped it from outside and maintained close relations with JP and other leaders of the party.

JP had deep regard for Mahatma Gandhi though he himself was then a believer in the cult of violence. He said once: "I bow before the non-violence of Mahatma Gandhi, but it is easier for me to fight with a gun." It was because of his faith in violence that the British Government kept constant watch on his activities and arrested him in 1940 on the charge of opposing British war efforts and kept him in Deoli detention camp in Rajasthan. It was from the Deoli jail that he smuggled out his famous letter giving detailed instructions to his partymen to organise underground revolt against British imperialism. The letter was, however, intercepted and seized by police intelligence men and his plan was frustrated. The British Government publicised the letter in a distorted form and tried to denigrate him in the eyes of the people. But Mahatma Gandhi immediately came to his rescue. While dissociating from his violent plans, the Mahatma condemned the British attempt to malign a patriot like JP. He also pleaded for the abolition of the Deoli detention camp. The British Government later abolished it and transferred JP to the Hazaribagh Central Jail in Bihar.

When the Quit India movement was launched by Mahatma Gandhi in August, 1942, JP was behind prison bars in Hazaribagh. Reports of the mighty upsurge of the people that followed the arrest of Mahatma Gandhi and other national leaders reached him and made him restless. On the night of November 9, 1942, JP along with three other Bihar revolutionaries, Messrs. Yogendra Shukul, Suraj Narain Singh and Ramnandan Mishra, managed to scale the 21 ft. high walls of the Hazaribagh Central Jail and escaped. The news of his escape spread like wild fire despite Government efforts to suppress it and it boosted the morale of the August revolutionaries throughout the country. JP and his comrades went underground and formed a small army of freedom fighters known as the Azad Dasta. Arrangements were also made to train young recruits in the jungles of the Nepal terai. Some of the top men of the Azad Dasta were Achyut Patwardhan, Mrs. Aruna Asaf Ali, Dr. Ram Manohar Lohia and Suraj Narain Singh. Mr. Narayan was its supreme leader. JP also tried to establish contact with the Azad Hind

Fauj of Netaji Subhas Chandra Bose in Burma. The British Government was seriously perturbed and launched a man-hunt for JP and his associates, and requested the Government of Nepal to keep an eye on them. Along with Dr. Lohia and others JP was arrested by the Nepal police and kept in Hanuman Nagar Jail. But before they could be handed over to the Indian police across the border, a column of the Azad Dasta led by Mr. Suraj Narain Singh stormed the jail and after a brief encounter with the guards rescued them. JP became a legendary figure. The then Home Member, Mr. Reginald Maxwell, was after his blood and announced rewards for his apprehension. JP was finally arrested on September 18, 1943, while travelling in a train to Punjab and was lodged in the Lahore Fort. As a prisoner, he was made to lie on ice slabs and subjected to inhuman torture to extract some unworthy confessions from him. But JP did not bend. He was then transferred to the Agra Central Jail. He was released on April 11, 1946, only after Mahatma Gandhi had made it a pre-condition for compromise talks between the Congress and the British Government.

JP was bitterly opposed to the partitioning of the country. So was Gandhiji. While JP wanted to organise public opinion against the Congress scheme of partition, Gandhiji counselled patience and advised him not to agitate and divide the people on this issue. JP submitted, much against his will, to the Mahatma's directive. Later he regretted this as a blunder on his part. In the wake of partition came widespread communal violence resulting in large-scale killings in Muslim and Hindu majority areas. JP and his friends lent powerful support to Mahatma Gandhi and Pandit Nehru in stemming the tide of communal frenzy that rocked the sub-continent.

Nehru's Plight

Few of our countrymen, except perhaps some citizens of Patna with a long memory, know that the late Prime Minister, Pandit Jawaharlal Nehru, had suffered one of the worst indignities of his life in the State Capital of Bihar. The darling of the nation could not even address a public meeting at the Wheeler Senate Hall in Central Patna in the face of an angry and hostile audience. But when Pandit Nehru failed, JP, who had accompanied him, succeeded in saving the situation and denouncing the angry demonstrators for their scandalous behaviour.

It happened on a cold November night in 1946 before the country's partition. Many Biharis living in Calcutta had been the victims of the Calcutta killings in August, 1946, when the late Saheed Suhrawardy was the Chief Minister of undivided Bengal. Then came the slaughter of Noakhali forcing Mahatma Gandhi to go on a peace mission. But Noakholi had set Bihar ablaze. Frenzied Hindu mobs avenged themselves on defenceless Muslim minorities living in the countryside in south Bihar.

That day Pandit Nehru, accompanied by one of his Cabinet colleagues belonging to the Muslim League, Sardar Abdul Rab Nishtar, had toured in a special train parts of south Bihar on the Patna-Gaya line of the Eastern Railway. He had whistle-stopped at several places and addressed small gatherings of Hindu villagers and denounced them for the atrocities. In fact, he had threatened them with dire consequences, including aerial bombing, if necessary. The rhetoric was far from relished by the audience.

About 150 members of an armed Hindu mob had been mowed down by police bullets and hand grenades at Nagarnausa (about 40 miles south-east of Patna) and their bodies removed that day to Patna in open trucks. This had created tension in the town. And when Pandit Nehru, accompanied by Mr. Narayan, went by car to the Senate Hall, he was mobbed as soon as he got down. His jacket was torn, his cap thrown to the ground and an angry youth tried to throw a garland of shoes on him. Undaunted, Pandit Nehru entered the Senate Hall. The doors were immediately closed by the police to prevent further rush of demonstrators. By that time the hall was full mostly with agitated young men who appeared to belong to the Rashtriya Swayam Sewak Sangh.

Only two reporters had been able to get in. Myself, representing the Associated Press of India (which after independence became the Press Trust of India, the national news agency, later snuffed out of existence shortly after the declaration of internal emergency to ensure media control) and Mr. Narayan Gupta of the *Amrita Bazar Patrika*.

Pandit Nehru got up with Mr. Narayan on a table on the built-in rostrum of the hall and started addressing the gathering.

The angry assemblage greeted him with boos and jeers and refused to listen. He was quick to realise their resentment and cause of anger. In a conciliatory effort he said that he was sorry to hear that about 100 to 150 Hindus had also been killed in police firings at Nagarnausa.

Immediately the audience shouted "Pandrah Sau" (fifteen hundred). The hall had been surrounded by that time not only by policemen but also British soldiers armed with rifles and sten guns. They were peeping from outside through the glass panes to see what was happening inside. As ill luck would have it, at that very moment an electric fuse blew up. The sound could be heard above the din. The crowd thought the police or the tommies had opened fire outside the hall. At once many young men bared their chests and started shouting "Shoot us Nehru, Shoot us, what else can we expect from you?" The mass leader Nehru tried his utmost to coax and cajole them to give him a hearing but they remained adament and refused to listen. The perplexed Prime Minister stopped speaking and suddenly there was a lull. I was standing on the right side of Pandit Nehru and the *Patrika* representative, Mr. Gupta, on the left by the side of Mr. Narayan. I do not know why I chose that awkward moment to question the Prime Minister about Mahatma Gandhi's visit to Noakhali and if he would also be visiting Bihar. Pandit Nehru stooped to answer my questions.

The noisy demonstration suddenly ceased. Mr. Narayan, who was bursting with anger at the youths' misconduct, seized the opportunity and started lashing out against the gathering. He said they had disgraced the ancient civilization of India. They had repudiated their religion and traditions by attacking and killing and injuring their weak and helpless neighbours, including even women and children. They had indulged in kidnapping, rape, loot and arson. Did their religion teach them to act like beasts? He said that they deserved no sympathy and no action taken by the Government could be considered harsh enough to quell the communal disturbances and to bring them back to their senses.

The same gathering, which had refused to listen to Nehru, took Mr. Narayan's tongue-lashing in pin-drop silence and dispersed quietly. (Pandit Nehru did not try to address them again.) That night Mr. Narayan proved his superiority even over Nehru.

(The report of this incident was published abroad but not inside the country. Thereby hangs a tale. It was the first occasion when on my return to office I was asked by the then PTI Bureau Chief, Mr. P. M. Balen, to prepare the report and to refer it to our Bombay head office to the Chief News Editor, Mr. P. S. Gopalan, for approval. He suggested that I should not show my copy to anybody but 'creed' it myself. While I was creeding my report, Mr. Norman Clifford, the Delhi-based staffer of the London *News Chronicle*, and an Australian journalist, whose name I do not remember now, came to our office and read it. They had not been able to enter the Wheeler Senate Hall but had come to know that I was inside. Their reports were picked up by the foreign newspapers and that is how the incident got publicity abroad. My report on this incident was never circulated though the other activities of Pandit Nehru that I had covered received wide publicity.)

During those days, the only other occasion when I found JP losing his temper, was at the meeting of the General Council of the All India Railwaymen's Federation held at Danapur in 1949 to decide on the issue of the first ever strike of railwaymen. The communists tried to create trouble when they found the majority inclined to respond to the appeal of the Prime Minister, Pandit Nehru, to stay the proposed strike to give the Government some time to examine the railwaymen's demands. The communists created noisy scenes, misbehaved with Mr. Narayan and insisted on giving a call for general strike. JP, who was the President of the Railwaymen's Federation, denounced them and exposed their role mercilessly. They staged a walk out in protest. Because of the mischief created by the communists at the evening session (they cut off the power supply) it had to be postponed till next morning.

Yet by nature JP is very gentle, one of Nature's rare gentlemen. Because of this he is apt to take a man at his word and quite often gets deceived (for the simple reason that all those who go to meet him are not angels though they put their best foot forward before him). His speeches lack the politician's fireworks. Even from the public platform, he speaks like a college professor addressing his pupils, arguing and analysing facts of a given situation point by point and explaining his stand. When he invites comments, he is prepared to accept criticisms. At least this has been his style for the last two decades. Even on the issue of Bangla Desh after the military crackdown in East Pakistan, although JP felt very strongly on the issue, he never expressed his anger about the indecision of the Government of India. He went abroad to plead the case of East Pakistan in Islamic countries. Though he stayed for five days in Cairo, President Sadat did not, of course, meet him. When he addressed gatherings on the issue of Bangla Desh, one could feel the anguish of his soul.

Socialists Quit Congress

After independence, JP, as leader of the Socialist Party, became increasingly critical of the policies of the Congress and its Government. Sardar Vallabh Bhai Patel took strong exception to the attitude of the socialists and even threatened them with disciplinary action. After the assassination of Mahatma Gandhi in January, 1948, Mr. Narayan, Acharya Narendra Dev and other socialists decided finally to quit the Congress and formed the Socialist Party of India at Nasik. The socialists, who had been returned to the legislatures, resigned. It was at the Nasik conference of the Socialist Party that he raised the question of ends and means and pleaded for the adoption of right means to achieve the noble ends of socialism. Although he still called himself a Marxist, he seemed to be moving close to the Gandhian technique and the philosophy of non-violence. He now wanted to change the constitution of the Socialist Party and turn it into a democratic mass organisation with open membership as distinguished from restricted membership. A year later in 1949 it was at his instance that the Party adopted a new constitution which provided for a mass base with open membership.

Under his leadership the Socialist Party expanded rapidly and soon assumed the shape of a national opposition with promise to become an alternative to the Congress. Apart from his role as a democrat, JP gave socialism a new democratic dimension and content. This was recognised by international socialists who looked upon him as "the founding father of democratic socialism in India", to use the words of the British socialist leader, Mr. Hugh Gaitskill. The first general elections in free India in 1952 turned out to be an unequal fight between a well-entrenched and fully financed Congress Party on the one side and a disunited opposition on the other. The socialists had over-estimated their strength and contested two-thirds of the seats in the country. They thus scattered their strength and resources over a much wider area than they could manage. No wonder they lost heavily. The election results highlighted the need for consolidation of socialist and democratic forces. Due to JP's efforts the Socialist Party and the Krishak Praja Mazdoor Party (KPMP) led by Acharya J. B. Kripalani merged, and the Praja Socialist Party was born. As the PSP became a political force to contend with, Prime Minister Nehru sought its cooperation in the programme of national reconstruction on socialist lines. JP held talks with Nehru at the latter's invitation and submitted a 14-point programme, which Nehru found difficult to implement. This added to the frustration in the socialist rank and file. Some prominent socialists now questioned the correctness of the policy and programme of the Party and a bitter ideological conflict followed leading to mutual recriminations.

The Jeevandani

By now JP's faith in dialectical materialism had been shaken. He looked for a sounder and quicker method of achieving socialism through non-violent methods. He had already rejected the violent methods of communism which had failed to create a society based on socialist values in countries where violent revolutions had taken place. It was at this psychological moment that Acharya Vinoba Bhave appeared on the scene with his programme of land distribution through the Bhoodan movement. Its initial success attracted JP, who saw in it possibilities of non-violent social change through a change in the general will of the people. JP moved closer to the Gandhian philosophy as interpreted by Vinoba. He found in this philosophy a more satisfying answer to the ideological problems of socialism. Ultimately, he announced his resolve to become a Jeevandani and dedicate his life to the service of the people at the call of

Vinoba at the historic Sarvodaya Conference held at Bodh Gaya in 1954 in the presence of President Rajendra Prasad, Prime Minister Nehru, Acharya Kripalani and other national leaders. Jeevandan signalled JP's departure from politics or party politics. Although he continued to be a member of the PSP his interest in the activities of the Party progressively decreased. The fact did not go unnoticed and caused some concern among his erstwhile colleagues.

JP never had a lust for pelf or power. He proved it by becoming a 'Jeevandani' although the highest offices in the land were within his reach. Pandit Nehru had once described JP as "the future Prime Minister of India". Whenever the question "After Nehru, Who?" was raised, invariably it was JP's name that leapt up. When the question of choosing a successor to President Radhakrishnan arose, all eyes looked up to JP. But untouched by the lust of worldly power, JP issued a public statement that the Presidentship should be offered to Dr. Zakir Husain. This would be a proof of India's secularism. Again after the death of Dr. Zakir Husain, national opinion favoured JP for the Presidentship. Even Prime Minister Indira Gandhi was reported to have supported this view. Although there was no formal offer, it was known that JP could have become the President if he had so desired. Again, he made his position clear by issuing a statement that he had "no desire to be a prisoner in the Rashtrapati Bhavan".

Though JP left power politics, he has never failed to raise his powerful voice on national and international issues. He championed the cause of Tibetan independence which was later fully justified by events. It was only when the Chinese attacked and humiliated India in 1962 that it was universally realised that India's acceptance of Chinese suzerainty over Tibet was a serious blunder. He was the first to take up the cause of Bangla Desh. A statement issued by him on March 15, 1971, paying tribute to the heroic people of Bangla Desh was repeatedly broadcast by the newly-freed Dacca Betar Kendra. It was he who helped to establish a people-to-people relationship between India and Bangla Desh.

Dacoits and Naxalites

One of his historic triumphs of moral persuasion was evident in early 1972 when his "change-of-heart mission" in Chambal Valley brought about the surrender of over 400 notorious dacoits whom all the power of State and the police had failed to apprehend and liquidate. JP's signal social service rendered during the terrible famine of 1967 in Bihar will not be forgotten by the people of the State. He formed the Bihar Relief Committee and opened relief centres at the district, block and panchayat levels and covered practically two-thirds of Bihar and brought succour to the starving people. Despite his failing health, he personally toured the famine-stricken areas in the summer heat. But for the tireless efforts of JP, the Chairman of the Relief Committee, many would have died of starvation. This Committee continued to function to render relief to the people during floods and drought. In June, 1974, the Chief Minister, Mr. Abdul Ghafoor, speaking in the Bihar Assembly, threatened to have the accounts of the Relief Committee audited (as if its funds were being misappropriated) if he did not withdraw his agitation.

Between 1970 and 1972 JP had been devoting his time and energy on eliminating Naxalite violence in his Sarvodaya way in Musahari Block in Muzaffarpur district in north Bihar. In the villages of this Block, where the extremists had created a reign of terror with murder and mayhem, the situation returned to near-normalcy mainly through his efforts.

But it was not that JP received bouquets only and not brickbats. For, in course of his long career he has not failed to espouse some unpopular causes. One such was the people's cause in Kashmir. On the Naga question too, JP had to face public resentment. In Nagaland he strongly advocated a peaceful solution rather than a military solution. It was at his suggestion that Prime Minister Nehru agreed to set up the Nagaland Peace Mission with JP as one of its members to explore the possibilities of a peaceful settlement. The Peace Mission was soon able to bring about a ceasefire in Nagaland followed by protracted negotiations between representatives of underground Nagas and of the Government of India. The Naga question has remained unsolved yet. But at least the necessary background has been created in which a solution can be found and permanent peace assured. JP's contribution to peace-making in Nagaland is bearing fruit today. For, soon after assumption of office, the new Prime Minister, Mr. Morarji Desai, expressed his willingness to have talks with the leaders of the underground Nagas and his overture had a favourable response from Mr. A. Z. Phizo, the rebel Naga leader. (Mr. Phizo met Mr. Desai during the latter's visit to London; unfortunately, nothing came out of it because of the Naga leader's insistence on the independence of Nagaland.)

JP fell seriously ill at Muzaffarpur only two days after his 70th birthday. He has never recovered his health, even partially, since then. At the time he had announced that he would retire from public activities from October 11, 1972. The purpose of his retirement, he said, would be to "read, write and think" more about the future than about the past and present. The challenges to democracy and freedom were uppermost in his mind and his thoughts were centering round ways and means to meet them despite his indifferent health. But this was not to be.

The letter that he had written to his associates before his 70th birthday said: "Today, the 11th October, 1971, I have completed 69 years of my life. If I live until then, I shall be 70 on October 11, 1972. I am writing this to tell you of a personal decision that I have taken with the full concurrence of my wife that from October 11, 1972, to October 11, 1973, *i.e.*, for that entire period of 12 months, I shall withdraw myself completely from any kind of public and social work and sever my connections with every organisation with which I am connected now (about 20 organisations)."

In the concluding portion of his letter he said: "What I shall do after the expiry of the period of retreat, I do not know. I know only this that until body and mind keep functioning, I shall continue to serve my country and the world. I know after that, the style of my future work will have to change radically because the present style has proved too wasteful of time and energy, both physical and mental. More than this I cannot say at present about my future which really rests in the hands of God."

He went on his holiday to his village home in Sitab Diara, where, within a month, he developed a carbuncle in his left hand. He left for Varanasi for medical treatment. At Varanasi, he requested his attending physicians to have a medical check up of his wife, Mrs. Prabhawati Devi, who had been ailing for the past one year, but had been trying to hide it from him. The results of the medical check up came as a shock. Prabhawati Devi was suffering from cancer.

Mr. Narayan removed her to Bombay without delay. The rest he himself needed eluded him completety and the days of his mental agony started and have not ceased even after his wife's passing away on April 15, 1973. Throughout his entire married life, Mrs. Prabhawati Devi, who was issueless, had virtually mothered him. Even at most of his public appearances, she used to be at his side. He had remained totally dependent on her for almost everything. He deeply loved and respected his wife. Without her, he became helpless. Before him then was a big void while his health, never sturdy, started worsening.

Then came the agitation in Gujarat. He went there not to involve himself but to restore peace. When he returned to Bihar, he found the student front in turmoil. There would be no peace for him.

Although the Gujarat and Bihar situations appeared similar outwardly, there were fundamental differences between the two. The Gujarat Chief Minister Chiman Bhai Patel sought to placate both factions within his Cabinet forgetting that the spoils of office were limited but the ambitions of partymen were unlimited. But Bihar Chief Minister Abdul Ghafoor was openly hostile to corrupt Ministers whom he humiliated at every opportunity. Even the student agitators of Bihar did not question Mr. Ghafoor's honesty though they denounced his repressive policy as well as his corrupt Ministers.

In Gujarat the agitation had been marked by violence from beginning to end. In Bihar the saintly Jayaprakash Narayan, with his international stature, agreed to lead the agitation after the violent disturbances of March 18, 1974, only after extracting a pledge from the student and youth agitators that they would remain peaceful "notwithstanding the gravest provocation".

In a State of the size of Bihar with a population of about 60 million, with two well-defined groups openly hostile to one another, violence could be sparked off even against the wishes of the agitators by outsiders. JP never tried to hide his dissatisfaction over the violent nature of the Gujarat agitation. He, therefore, strongly advised the people of other States, during his tours, to emulate the Bihar type of peaceful agitation instead of the Gujarat type.

THREE

Explosive Situation

The situation in the country shortly before the Bihar flare-up was described even by an out and out pro-Indira Gandhi mass circulation weekly, CURRENT, as 'explosive'. The cover story of its February 9, 1974 issue carried screaming headlines and described the situation, partly quoting Mr. Mohan Dharia, the then Union Minister of State for Planning, and Mr. Rajni Patel, President of the Bombay Pradesh Congress Committee, thus:

"Seething mass discontent has caused an explosive situation in the country. Galloping prices, non-availability of essential commodities, hoarding, black-marketing and black money have given rise to a political and economic crisis of vast dimensions.

"The Government has singularly failed to rise to the expectations of the people—to provide them with the bare minimum. The ruling party, which won a massive mandate from the people, is cracking under its own weight. Factionalism and groupism have torn it asunder. Congressmen out of power have been challenging Congressmen in power. The lust of power has made them totally oblivious to the disaster ahead.

"Gujarat has provided the spectacle of an internecine war among Congressmen. The worst enemy of a Congressman today is a Congressman. It is balderdash to accuse the weak, disunited, frustrated and rudderless Opposition. The ruling party should own up its responsibility of its sins of omission and commission. Its leaders should show the courage of the Mahatma, they should admit that they have blundered.

"What has shocked the country most is the involvement of the ruling party in giving protection to the Guilty Men, who have played havoc with the nation's economy. The situation has not, we feel, still gone beyond control. If the party in power does not act soon, India will be embroiled in a turmoil . . . .

"Mr. Mohan Dharia, Union Minister of State for Planning, has threatened to resign his office if the situation does not improve soon. He has suggested certain concrete steps to arrest further deterioration in the economy.

"Mr. Rajni Patel, President of the Bombay Pradesh Congress Committee, and of late the target of vehement attacks by his antagonists, has also made confessions. He has expressed apprehension about the explosive situation in Bombay, the metropolis of India.

"Bombay is perched on a powder keg. The ruling party has hardly taken note of the grim warnings which are being hurled at it from the chawls and dens of poverty. It has found a traditional method of facing the challenge—the ruthless and brutal use of force by the most hated element of society—the police."

The situation in Bihar was worse. Rice was selling at Rs. 100 per maund despite a good harvest. This had affected the prices of all other essential commodities. The students had troubles of their own. They found their present predicament unbearable and the future bleak. They knew their teachers were appointed not on merit but on the basis of their caste and political pulls. Many teachers indulged openly in caste politics and rarely taught. These very dishonest people managed to land cushy jobs while the students did not have the wherewithal to buy enough food for subsistence, far less for buying text-books or even exercise-books which had become costly. Hostel accommodation was inadequate and the food served invariably poor. In a girls' hostel in the vicinity of the Patna University itself, water supply was irregular and toilet facilities awful.

The students had been agitating for the redressal of their grievances since December, 1973. There had been demonstrations and gherao of the Vice-Chancellor. Student leaders had also gone on hunger-strike before the Chhajjubagh residence of the Chief Minister, Mr. Abdul Ghafoor (his official residence was at 3, King George Avenue). The Chief Minister had agreed to concede their demands. There was also a Cabinet decision to this effect, which was announced in the Assembly by the Minister of State for Education, Mr. Nitishwar Prasad Sinha. The students alleged that these orders were never implemented.

They felt frustrated and had no faith in the administration. Things were allowed to drift and the student unrest grew. In early March, 1974, student leaders of various universities of Bihar met in Patna and formulated a 12-point charter of demands. The charter included bringing down prices, ensuring supply of essential commodities which had become scarce, cheaper text-books and exercise-books, better hostel accommodation and better food, eradication of corruption, jobs for the educated unemployed, action against hoarders, profiteers and blackmarketeers. The meeting also announced the formation of the Bihar Chhatra Sangharsh Samiti (Students' Action Committee). Those included in it belonged to the youth wings of the Samyukta Socialist Party, the Socialist Party, the Jana Sangh, the Congress(O), CPI and the CPI(M). Soon hijacking of buses and demonstrations in the university area became frequent.

Finding their just demands ignored and, on the contrary, finding armed police in the campuses of the colleges and the Patna University, the angry students gave a call for the gherao of the Assembly on the opening day of its budget session on March 18. The youth wings of the CPI and the CPI(M) dissociated themselves from the call and formed a Bihar Rajya Chhatra Naujawan Morcha of their own. It was an attempt of the CPI to wrest the initiative. A pamphlet issued on its behalf showed that the students' wing of the CPI(M-L) was also in the Morcha. The Morcha charged the Samiti with indulging in shadow-fighting and announced that they would organise a separate demonstration at the Collectorate in Bettiah (subdivisional headquarters town of West Champaran) and also before the residence of Mr. Vidyakar Kavi, the Education Minister of Bihar, on March 16. There was an attempt on that day to storm the Bettiah Collectorate by a mixed mob. This led to police firings in which seven persons were killed. The same evening about 200 members of the Morcha gheraoed the residence of the Education Minister, Mr. Kavi, in Patna. Kavi came out to meet the demonstrators. Immediately an attempt was made to kidnap him. In the melee his jacket was torn. Someone tried to strike a blow on his head with a lathi. But before it could fall on his head, it was snatched away by a police constable. (Kavi said later that a large section of the mob comprised non-students having 'vicious looks'.) Soon brickbatting started and a bomb also exploded. The police intervened, made lathi-charges and burst tear gas shells and dispersed the mob. That very night the retreating members of the mob brickbatted the buildings of the *Searchlight* and the *Indian Nation*, the two English dailies of Patna. The *Pradeep* and the *Aryavarta*, the Hindi counterparts of these two dailies, were also housed in the same buildings.

Then came the fateful day of March 18. It sparked off a Statewide agitation, which soon turned into a mass movement and created a mass upsurge under the leadership of Mr. Narayan. It had its repercussions all over the country and ultimately led to the overthrow of the Congress Government at the Centre led by Mrs. Indira Gandhi even when it appeared to be impregnable after the proclamation of Emergency.

The CPI, the Jana Sangh, the Congress(O), the Socialist Party, and the SSP had earlier announced their decision to boycott the Assembly on its opening day on March 18. The entire area comprising the Raj Bhawan-Secretariat-Assembly complex was heavily barricaded. With several thousand policemen carrying lathis, rifles and light machine guns swarming all over the place, it presented the scene of a battle-ground. The entire area was cordoned off in the characteristic concentration camp style with barbed wires.

Over thirty thousand students and youths of Bihar had come to participate in the gherao of the Assembly. Quite a sizeable number of them had managed to break through the barricades and the police cordons while others were held at bay outside. A delegation of half a dozen Samiti workers headed by the President and General Secretary of the Patna University Students Union, Mr. Laloo Prasad Yadav and Mr. Sushil Kumar Mody, went to Raj Bhawan to meet the Governor, Mr. Ramchandra Dhondiba Bhandare, about half an hour before the commencement of the session. They were allowed to meet the Governor, who received them politely and offered them tea. He did not, however, agree to their request not to go to the Assembly. He told them that as Governor of the State he had certain duties to perform which he could not abrogate.

The distance from Raj Bhawan to the Assembly is about seven furlongs. It is a straight drive from east to west through the western gates of the Secretariat. To prevent the Governor from going to the Assembly a group of Samiti demonstrators squatted before the eastern gates of the Raj Bhawan. The police could have arrested them or removed them physically. But they chose instead to beat them up mercilessly and dragged them away before the eyes of thousands of youths, students and onlookers. The fat was in the fire and mob violence broke out! Showering of brickbats started from all sides and the police too resorted to repeated lathi-charges and tear gassing. The police later alleged that brickbatting had started even before the squatters had been removed. But this was not corroborated by independent eye-witnesses.

Policemen had been deployed in the barricaded area, but the northern and southern flanks of the Secretariat and the Assembly had been left unguarded. The citizens living in the rest of the town had been left to fend for themselves. Shortly before mid-day the house of the Secretary of the Assembly, Mr. Vishwanath Mishra, located outside the southern gates of the Assembly, was set on fire. The police just looked on from the compound of the Secretariat and the Assembly. Within a short while two big buildings housing the head office of the Patna Municipal Corporation, the Police Cooperative Bank building, a petrol pump, several other houses and about forty roadside stalls and hutments were set ablaze.

The disturbances spread. At about 1 p.m. I received a frantic telephone call from the Chief Reporter of the *Searchlight*, Mr. Satyanarain Lal, that a mob had attacked the press and was trying to set it on fire. He requested me to contact the Chief Secretary and the Inspector-General of Police to rush help. I went on dialling both these officers but found the lines constantly engaged. I went up on the roof of the PTI building and saw smoke coming out of the *Searchlight* building. Then I rushed to the nearby Kotwali Police Station. I saw more than 100 armed policemen assembled there. A sub-inspector of police, who was standing there, told me when I approached him, that he knew of the attack on the *Searchlight* (whose building was hardly two furlongs away from the Kotwali). He was sorry he could not send police help from Kotwali because reports had been received that the disturbances were spreading and the Kotwali itself might be raided. He argued that if policemen were sent away to the *Searchlight*, who would protect the Kotwali? He nodded his head and that was the end of the matter.

As I was returning to my office on the Fraser Road, I saw a mob collecting in front of the buildings of the Newspapers and Publications Ltd., publishers of the *Indian Nation* and the *Aryavarta*, located within a stone's throw from the PTI. The gates were closed. Some persons from the mob had succeeded in persuading the *Indian Nation* staff to allow them to enter the premises. The employees of the newspapers smelt a rat when they found one of the intruders was trying to set on fire a bundle of torn newsprint. They were immediately driven away. Soon the mob outside the gates began to swell. A young man drove a hijacked bus and rammed open the iron gates.

By that time over three hundred employees of the Newspapers and Publications Ltd. had assembled inside the compound. They carried lathis, rods and whatever else came handy to offer resistance. It was not merely a question of loyalty to their institution, they knew that if the press was wrecked they would lose their daily bread. They fought frenziedly and beat back the first wave of the mob attack. I was watching the situation from the balcony of the PTI building. While the battle was on, again I rang up the Chief Secretary, Mr. P. K. J. Menon, and this time I could talk to him. I told him that the *Searchlight*, the *Pradeep*, the *Indian Nation* and the *Aryavarta* were under mob attack and that the police were nowhere in sight. It appeared from his response that he had already received the information. He said he was sending help and rang off. There were three more waves of mob attack on the *Indian Nation* and each was beaten off by the employees. The police did not appear on the scene till 4 p.m. when the mob had melted away.

While the attack was on, groups of young men separated and re-formed into two small groups. One attacked the posh Sujata restaurant (said to be partly owned by a Minister, Mr. Baleshwar Ram), broke open its doors (it had downed its shutters earlier) and went about setting fire to it after looting bottles of whisky and snacks. Some even started drinking straight from the bottles. The adjacent petrol pump, the Palm

Tree, came handy. They took out petrol in cans and used it for arson.

Another mob went ahead to the big department store, the D. Lal & Sons. It was not, however, looted because its Manager produced a receipt proving that he had paid a substantial contribution to the agitators. The mob then turned to the PTI building. When I was informed about it, Mr. Indra Kumar, MLC (SSP) and Mr. H. K. Verma, a member of the Bihar Pradesh Congress Committee, were with me. Peeping through the curtains, we saw two Chhatra Sangharsh Samiti youths coming on a motor-cycle. They stopped and started talking to the leaders of the mob. When they learnt of their intention, they at once objected and said: "You can't do this. What will the people say if we do this to the Dada (meaning me), who has never denied us the publicity that we deserve." There was some argument but the mob left and moved northwards. I have mentioned this because it was apparent that the Samiti boys did not have the slightest acquaintance with the mob leaders.

Soon another big department store, Messrs. J. G. Carr's, was raided and plundered. The raiders carried away the booty in costly VIP suitcases (also lifted) and disappeared. Another mob attacked the nearby prestigious vegetarian hotel "Rajasthan", looted it, and set it on fire. All this happened on the Fraser Road, frequented by influential politicians, political "sabjantas" (know-alls) and elite of the town, within a distance of three hundred yards. It was clear that the initiative had passed from the hands of student agitators to hooligans, anti-social elements and other unknown dark forces besides agent provocateurs.

While this was going on on Fraser Road, the Bihar Journals Limited (*Searchlight* and *Pradeep*) on the Patna-Gaya Road, which runs further west from north to south, was also facing waves of mob attack. The employees of the Bihar Newspapers and Publications Ltd. could beat back the mob because its buildings were better protected and surrounded by walls. The defences of the Bihar Journals were comparatively weak. Its building was open to attack from three sides. So, despite the resistance offered by its employees, it ultimately went up in flames. Its machine room was in shambles, its library and stock of newsprint were gutted.

A jeepload of armed CRP jawans arrived before the Newspapers and Publications and opened fire in the air when the mob had already dispersed. The same thing happened with the Bihar Journals. A CRP squad arrived when the whole press was burned down. The jawans got down from their jeep and opend fire on the onlookers standing on the road before the gates of the General Post Office near the Bihar Journals building. An innocent postal employee was killed.

The Chief Secretary had rung me up at 2.30 p.m. and informed me that the Government had given "shoot-at-sight" order on violent demonstrators, looters and arsonists. Yet, why were the police late in reaching the disturbed areas? Why again did the police remain silent spectators when they were concentrated in strength in the Raj Bhawan-Secretariat-Assembly complex while some big buildings, houses and a large number of hutments and roadside stalls went up in flames before their eyes? They even refused to rush to the residence of the Secretary of the Assembly when it was burning near the southern gates of the legislature.

A high Government of India official, who shall remain unnamed, flew into Patna a couple of days later. He paid a visit to me (he was an old friend) late at night and we had a long talk about the situation arising out of the disturbances of March 18.

I asked: "Tell me, my friend, why did the police remain passive onlookers when Patna was burning? Was there a silent mutiny? If so, why?"

"Sh . . . Sh . . . Sh. For heaven's sake, don't even breathe it", was his mock-serious response. He quietly informed me that because of the reluctance of the local police and the dearth of CRP jawans, sorties after sorties had to be flown throughout the night to bring BSF jawans to Patna. Though there was no mutiny as such, there was strong apathy among the Bihar constabulary which made them inactive when the situation showed signs of going out of control Did the policemen on duty before Raj Bhawan deliberately beat up and drag by the hair the squatters before the eyes of thousands of demonstrators and spectators? He did not know. The police, particularly in its lower echelons, is notoriously corrupt. The police constables were themselves victims of two corrupt politicians during two successive ministries. They were sullen and angry.

Be that as it may, because they were luckewarm in going into action, ultimately CRP men had to be sent out to handle the situation on that fateful day rather late. They went into action a little earlier in the vicinity of the secretariat and the Assembly and opened fire on several occasions. But those who fell victims to their bullets were mostly innocent people.

At several places particularly the Municipal Corporation building, the Bihar Journals and the Rajasthan hotel, inflammable material of very high potency had been used, with remarkable speed, to cause the maximum damage. I was myself a witness to it. The Sujata restaurant was set on fire by using petrol from the adjacent petrol pump. Yet the fire died down on its own within two hours. But the Rajasthan hotel, a solid brick building, went up in flames in a trice. So quickly, in fact, that two girls caught unawares, received severe burn injuries. A young woman staying on the first floor finding herself suddenly enveloped in flames jumped down and fractured her hip bone and had to be in plaster in hospital for several months. The use of high potency incendiaries clearly indicated that the arsonists knew their business and were no amateurs.

It is quite likely that some hidden hands ware at work behind the facade of the students' agitation. The question why newspapers and posh hotels and restaurants were the targets of arson has never been satisfactorily answered. One thing was obvious, however. The skilled arsonists were outsiders, the like of whom had never been in Patna. They were not hired men of politicians or Chhatra Sangharsh Samiti youths. The fact that they threatened to burn the PTI building proved it. I have spent almost my entire life in Bihar, forty years of it as a professional journalist and for more than 25 years as Patna Bureau Chief of the PTI. Leaders of all political parties, both the ruling and the opposition parties, including the Naxalite leader, Mr. Satya Narain Singh, have been my personal friends for a long time. It is no secret in Bihar. Quite often it has also landed me in embarrassing situations. The youth and student leaders of every hue have also been very close to me. They wanted, naturally, publicity but did not know how to go about it. I helped them out and they were obliged to me. I had seen and heard the Chhatra Sangharsh Samiti boys preventing the mob that came to burn down the PTI office. The *Indian Nation* and the *Aryavarta* and the *Searchlight* and the *Pradeep* had been giving a lot of importance to the Samiti's agitation. The *Pradeep* had gone to the length of upholding the right of the students to revolt against injustice. Then why were they subjected to attacks?

The Government tried to pass the buck and laid the blame squarely on the RSS, the Jana Sangh and the Anand Marg (though all the three could not be equally involved) and by implication the SSP, which believed in complete "Vani Swatantrata" (freedom of expression). For, four SSP legislators, including Mr. Karpoori Thakur, a former Chief Minister and ex-Chairman of the All India Samyukta Socialist Party, were arrested in one sweep a day after the disturbances on the charge of instigating violence. The accusing finger was also pointed, by implication, to the Tarun Shanti Sena and the Gandhi Peace Foundation. Several of their leading workers were arrested at Muzaffarpur when there was a Statewide flare-up on the occasion of the Bihar Bundh on the next day. The call was given by the Samiti after the Patna disturbances. The opposition parties returned the compliment and held the Government guilty for whatever had happened. They also pointed the accusing finger to the CPI, which quickly denied the accusation.

Mr. Jayaprakash Narayan was mortified over the arrests of Tarun Shanti Sena and Gandhi Peace Foundation workers. But his reaction came a little later. The Tarun Shanti Sena was founded by Acharya Vinoba Bhave for peaceful resolution of people's problems and fighting the forces of violence with non-violent methods. The Gandhi Peace Foundation, as its name suggests, works for peace and not anarchy. Sensible people, who had not lost their heads, in the excitement of the civil commotion, found it extremely difficult to stomach the implied charge that the Shanti Sena and the Gandhi Peace Foundation workers were behind the disturbances.

Mr. Narayan himself, who had nothing to do with the students' agitation at that time, was also not spared. He was accused by Government spokesmen of instigating the students to violence though he had publicly asked them to desist from organising the Bihar Bundh because of the turn that their agitation had taken. They did not pay heed, and mob violence again erupted in different parts of the State in the wake of the Bihar Bundh. The Samiti had given the call for Bihar Bundh in protest against the repressive action of the Government on the Assembly gherao day and the large-scale arrests of youths and students.

The whole State of Bihar was on fire. There were numerous lathi-charges, tear gassing and police firings as a result of which at least twentyfive persons were killed and over two hundred injured. This is according to official versions given at the time. Curfew was clamped in a dozen towns. In Patna there was day curfew as well as night curfew with a brief break in between. It took about a weak for the situation to return to normal. There was a growing realisation among students that they had unwittingly walked into the trap of anti-social elements and also offered themselves as pawns in the game of political parties out to settle their ancient scores.

The Chhatra Sangharsh Samiti included youths who were not students. It was also called for some time as Chhatra Yuva Sangharsh Samiti. Some members of its Steering Committee included Jagannath Yadav, a college teacher, Mithilesh Kumar Sinha, a lawyer, and some others like Basisth Narain Singh, Sivanand Tiwary and Raghunath Gupta were leaders of the youth wings of the Congress(O), the Socialist Party and the SSP. But in the end the name Chhatra Sangharsh Samiti stuck.

The violent confrontation led to introspection and the Samiti tried hard to keep its agitation peaceful. This was reflected in their weeklong programme of satyagraha launched on March 30 when they observed Statewide fast from sunrise to sunset at street corners in improvised camps. They now put forward, for the first time, a new demand—the resignation of the Ministry. Placards bearing this demand hung on roadside clotheslines, excellent impromptu mass media, started wafting in the pre-summer breeze carrying the message far and wide.

An uneasy quiet prevailed. Mr. Jayaprakash Narayan had not yet decided to lead the movement though he had been hurt and angry over the police violence and indiscriminate arrests of students and youths, including workers of the Tarun Shanti Sena and Gandhi Peace Foundation. He issued a statement in the fourth week of March which gave clear indication which way his mind was working. He said: "If the Government has not discovered by now who the real culprits are and continues to bark up the wrong tree and defame the Gandhi Peace Foundation and the Tarun Shanti Sena, poor Jayaprakash and the section of students who are pledged to peaceful means, it will never succeed in bringing violence under control."

Mr. Narayan's stand was: the Government must learn to discriminate between organised and planned violence, such as burning of the *Searchlight* building and other acts of arson and looting of shops and small violence such as brickbatting or setting fire to stray vehicles in anger or retaliation or in misconceived militancy. He held that there was no evidence that the Government was making any such distinction, with the result that the real culprits were going scot free and others, including the innocent, were being punished. His allegation sounded true because, besides hooligans, some mushroom student and youth organisations had sprung up in the wake of the disturbances and these elements were responsible for loot, arson and extortion. To escape the arms of the law these mushroom organisations were trying to curry favour with the government by posing as lackeys and good boys. What was worse, they were getting encouragement from the politicians in power.

At this stage the Samiti youth leaders started approaching JP for guiding and leading them. At first JP was not interested in the ouster of the Ghafoor Ministry. The Chief Minister, Mr. Abdul Ghafoor, had gone to his residence at the time and met him, held out an olive branch and tried to come to an understanding. He failed to satisfy JP, who had earlier given a certificate to him publicly for his honesty. Later he angrily withdrew that certificate as the Government continued with its repressive policy.

At this point JP had made up his mind to fight corruption, maladministration, blackmarketing, profiteering, hoarding and other social and economic evils. The situation started getting complicated because in spite of the efforts of the Samiti not to get involved with political parties, the Socialist Party, the SSP, the CPI(M), the Socialist Unity Centre and the Rovolutionary Socialist Party decided on a programme of action to organise meetings in the villages, blocks and towns between April 1 and

April 5 to demand an end to "the repressive policy of the Government", withdrawal of the Border Security Force, the Central Reserve Police and of prohibitory orders promulgated under section 144 Cr. P.C. in all districts of the State. The Samiti workers were also fanning out in the villages to keep the agitation avowedly along peaceful ways. Leaders of the legislature groups of the Jana Sangh, the SSP, the Sccialist Party and the Organisation Congress also decided to defy section 144 Cr. P.C. in Patna and to hold a public meeting at Gandhi Maidan on April 9. The Samiti also announced its decision to launch dharna all over the State before Government offices and court arrest.

To cap it all, the Tripathi faction of the State Non-gazetted Employees' Federation announced its decision to gherao the Patna Secretariat, the collectorate and subdivisional courts from April 8 to April 11 to press its demands for the supply of essential commodities at subsidised rates, payment of medical and house rent allowance and increase in dearness allowance. With all its outward calm Bihar had become a bundle of livewires spluttering sparks on all sides and round about were the powder barrels of injustice, hunger and poverty.

FOUR

JP Leads Silent Procession

Samiti leaders had been visiting JP since March 21 and urging him to lead them. Always JP insisted that they must pledge themselves to remain peaceful and they agreed. It was announced on April 7 that next day JP would lead a silent procession of Sarvodaya workers and youths and students "to demonstrate to the government and the people their peaceful intentions and that they were against forces of violence which indulged in destructive activities and arson".

JP issued a statement advising those who did not form a part of the procession to throng both sides of the roads along the route of the procession without interfering with the traffic. He also advised them not to raise any slogans. He said: "I want to make it clear that this movement is not in favour of or against any party. It is meant for your good, the good of society, the good of Bihar and the country. The students and youths are in the vanguard of this movement."

Next day the Bihar Assembly was adjourned *sine die* without passing the customary vote of thanks to the Governor for his address to the joint session of the legislature on its opening day (March 18) amidst noisy scenes over the externment of Mr. Raj Narain on April 6. The same evening the Governor prorogued the budget session of the State Legislature.

Mr. Narayan came out on the streets and led a huge silent procession of students, youths, women, sarvodaya and social workers in the afternoon of April 8. The processionists, including JP, who was in a jeep, had their lips sealed with saffron or pieces of dark cotton cloth. Many also had their hands tied behind their backs. Central and western Patna came out on the streets to watch the progress of this unique procession and flower petals were showered from housetops as it wended its way from the Congress Maidan in Kadamkuan, where JP's residence is located, via Station Road, Fraser Road, Gandhi Maidan Road, Ashoka Rajpath, Govind Mitra Road and the Ramkrishna Avenue before returning to its starting-point and dispersing peacefully.

Several hundred women, including girl students, formed the vanguard of the procession. It was followed by workers of the Sarvodaya Mandal, the Tarun Shanti Sena, the Gandhi Peace Foundation, students and youths carrying placards "Haamla Chahe Jo Bhi Ho, Haath Hamara Nahi Uthega" (whatever the provocation, we won't raise our hands in retaliation). When it reached the Patna Central Jail, a large number of youths, arrested in connection with the agitation, gave silent salutes to JP from the roof of the prison.

On the following evening, addressing a mammoth meeting at Gandhi Maidan, Mr. Narayan called upon the youth to be prepared to sacrifice all for ending the political, economic and social evils and rampant corruption. He said that what he was leading now was not an agitation but a movement. He felt mere change in the Ministry would not do any good to the country. The ruling party as well as the opposition parties had failed to serve the cause of the people. The situation was going from bad to worse. The whole set-up had to be overhauled by involving the people in the task of rebuilding the nation. He thus briefly indicated what he would later expound and elaborate as "Sampurna Kranti" or Total Revolution.

JP maintained that the prices had been soaring because of the faulty economic policy of the Prime Minister, Mrs. Indira Gandhi. Unless she changed her policy, the prices would not come down. He said the Planning Minister, Mr. D. P. Dhar, was a good diplomat but he would give him a 'big zero' for his planning.

Mr. Narayan regretted that the Prime Minister should have abused him. At first he felt he should not say anything as she was like his daughter. But then he thought that if he did not speak, he might be misunderstood by the people. Moreover, he could not sit idle when hunger was stalking the land and allow the situation to drift.

Mrs. Gandhi did not like Mr. Narayan's support to student

and youth agitators and airing his views on corruption. Some Congress members of Parliament from Bihar had met the Prime Minister and condemned Mr. Narayan. For her part she had remarked: "I know there are persons, who stay at places like that of Mr. Ramnath Goenka but preach gospel to us." This obiter dictum had received wide publicity in the press.

At a public meeting at Bhubaneswar, she had declared that the people were with her and not with JP; that was why he was trying to involve the Sarvodaya workers in the Bihar agitation though Acharya Vinoba Bhave did not approve of it. (Did she herself persuade the Sant to disapprove it? What else ptompted Vinoba to burn all the correspondence she had with him?)

Mr. Narayan had dismissed Mrs. Gandhi's claim to represent the people on the basis of the U.P. election results as nonsense. He had also said: "My humble submission to Mrs. Gandhi is not to presume to teach me and other Sarvodaya workers where our duty lies and not to use her proven skill in trying to drive a wedge between me and Acharya Vinoba Bhave (ultimately she did succeed) and thus split the Sarvodaya movement. There is complete understanding between me and Acharya Vinoba Bhave and we know the limits of agreement and disagreement. While there is a vast area of agreement between us there is a tiny area not so much of disagreement as of difference in approach to certain problems. There is absolutely no difference in matters of principle. Anyway, it is not for Mrs. Gandhi but for Acharya Bhave himself and the Sarva Seva Sangh to guide the Sarvodaya movement."

As to her slighting remark about staying as a guest of Mr. Ramnath Goenka in Delhi, Mr. Narayan said: "No whole-time social worker, who has no independent source of income, can live without the help of personal friends who have the necessary means. If Indiraji's measuring scale were applied universally, Mahatma Gandhi would be found to be the most corrupt of all because his entire entourage was supported by his rich admirers."

Mr. Bibhuti Mishra, a Congress MP from Bihar, tried to twist JP's remark and accused him of describing Mahatma Gandhi as a corrupt man although JP had said nothing of the sort. Mahatma Gandhi, when he was alive, did stay at Birla Bhavan at Delhi. Would Mrs. Gandhi have denied the Mahatma the right to preach his gospel? Her anger had made her forget that people, who had dedicated their lives to some worthy cause, did not have the advantage of men and women in power to stay at Raj Bhawans, Inspection Bungalows or State Guest Houses. Should such a person be forced to put up under the open sky or under the shade of a tree if he had willing friends to provide him with accommodation and amenities of life? Moreover, there was a lot of difference between men in power amassing wealth without the least sense of shame and people living farthest from the seats of power having no means of livelihood working for some noble cause living on the charity of their friends. This was sidetracking the issue of corruption with a vengeance. It certainly did not help ease the seething discontent in the country created by corrupt politicians.

If the elders had compromised, the youths had revolted. It was a rebellion of a different kind never witnessed before in India. It could not be crushed by bullets or bayonets. There was a much simpler and peaceful method of quelling it. All that the rulers had to do was to be honest themselves and to punish the corrupt instead of filling the jails with youths fighting for a righteous cause.

FIVE

Appeasing JP

Did the High Command of the ruling party, which meant the Prime Minister, Mrs. Indira Gandhi, relent? It did not. On the contrary, it went on committing one folly after another. All this culminated in the declaration of the internal emergency. It was then that the non-communist opposition parties sought to combine under the guidance of JP to challenge Mrs. Gandhi's Government. Initially, however, Mrs. Gandhi went through the motions to appease JP when he entered the arena and took up the task of leading the Bihar movement. At her behest the Congress High Command directed all the fortyfive Bihar Ministers and the Chief Minister, Mr. Abdul Ghafoor, to submit their resignations and to hand them over to the AICC Observer for Bihar, Mrs. Maragatham Chandrasekhar. At first there was a lot of humming and hawing among the Cabinet colleagues of Mr. Ghafoor (who were openly demanding his ouster) as they did not know who would be retained and who dropped. But in the end fortyone Ministers—four were out of town—handed over their resignations to Mr. Ghafoor, who in turn, passed them on to Mrs. Chandrasekhar on April 10, the day JP left for Calcutta on his way to Madras for a medical check up.

The same afternoon, Mrs. Chandrasekhar flew back to Delhi with the resignations and handed them over to the Congress President, Dr. Shankar Dayal Sharma, who immediately started consultations with Mrs. Gandhi. Mrs. Chandrasekhar, who had been sent to Bihar to assess the situation and to collect the resignations, had apprised both Mrs. Gandhi and Dr. Sharma that in spite of differences within the Bihar Party, Congressmen were united in meeting any challenge from "right reactionaries and fascist forces".

While confabulations were going on among the Congress high-ups in Delhi how to drop a large number of Ministers without losing face, the Ministers likely to be affected were on the point of revolt and opposed the move to "purge" the Ministry. They met on April 14 at the residence of Mr. Budhdev Singh, a Minister of State, under the Presidentship of the Finance Minister, Mr. Daroga Prasad Roy, where angry speeches were delivered against the move and the consensus was that dropping of Ministers would tar their public image as the people would take it that those purged were all corrupt. Why pick on a few?

A seven-member delegation of the anti-purge Ministers went to the residence of Mr. Ghafoor and told him to convey their feelings to Mrs. Chandrasekhar, who was airdashing to Patna that day. The Chief Minister said he would comply with their suggestion though he declined to disclose his own stand. After Mrs. Chandrasekhar had called on him, Mr. Ghafoor told me (PTI) that he had informed her that so far as he was concerned, he would comply with whatever directions the Congress High Command thought fit to give. "I have told her that I do not maintain double standards", he said.

He said Mrs. Chandrasekhar had explained to him that the Ministers to be dropped need not be considered corrupt because they had tendered their resignations to the Congress High Command on the pattern of the Kamaraj Plan. Mr. Ghafoor made it clear that neither his views had been sought on the subject of reconstitution of the Cabinet nor had he volunteered any opinion. On April 17, Ministers likely to be dropped threatened to resign and demanded that Mr. Ghafoor should seek a vote of confidence from the State Congress Legislature Party.

The impact of Mr. Narayan's stand was dramatically demonstrated in the Lok Sabha on April 11. A 25-yeay-old young man, Ratan Chandra Gupta of Jharia (Bihar), managed to enter the Visitors' Gallery and started shouting "Bhrastachariyon Ko Phansi Do" (hang the corrupt), "Jayaprakash Narayan Zindabad" and "Inquilab Zindabad". He was immediately nabbed by the watch and ward staff, who recovered from his possession a cracker and a pistol. The House convicted and sentenced the youth to one month's rigorous imprisonment in the Tihar jail despite protests from members of the opposition.

JP, who was at Delhi on that day, made it clear in a statement that he would not accept any office, however high, nor rejoin power and party politics. He drew a distinction between politics as broadly understood and power and party politics. He said: "The very day in 1954 (when he became a Jeevandani) when I announced my withdrawal for the rest of my life from party and power politics, I had made it clear that I shall continue to take part in the politics of the nation. I have no intention of discontinuing this."

The statement was issued as a rejoinder to an unwise statement made at the time by the SSP leader, Mr. Raj Narain, at Lucknow that in his view JP should become the President of India. A perplexed Mr. Narayan said: "I do not know why even well-meaning friends are bent upon humiliating me every now and then. Sometimes I am to be the Rashtrapati, at other times I am to lead the opposition parties.

"It seems that those who are occupied with power and party politics understand only party, power, position and elections. They seem to be incapable of appreciating that any one standing outside of this can serve his country and his people and feel sufficiently rewarded not to be casting covetous glances at high office. Party and power politicians also seem to be incapable of understanding that there is politics of a larger and broader meaning than the politics of party and power. No citizen of a modern society can opt out of such politics because even his daily bread has become a political issue.

Addressing the All India Conference of Citizens for Democracy at Delhi on April 14, Mr. Narayan described the happenings in Gujarat and Bihar as the first signs of the people bestirring themselves at long last to resist misrule and corruption at high places. He felt a concrete pattern emerging. This was a welcome sign as far as it went and he had no doubt that students and youths would be in the vanguard of all such resistance movements. The paralyse-the-government movement had already been launched in Bihar on April 9.

SIX

Gaya Firings

At Gaya, Satyagraha led to police firings. According to official reports, at least eight persons had been killed and fifteen injured in three separate police firings on April 12. Unofficial versions said at least fifty to one hundred persons had been killed and many more injured. These versions were also quoted in the Lok Sabha in the course of a four-hour debate on Gaya firings on April 19.

The police said they had fired to disperse riotous mobs but independent witnesses had a different story to tell. A 16-hour curfew was clamped from sunset to 10 a.m. next day after violence broke out in Gaya. The police alleged that about two thousand youths, students and a batch of women had gheraoed the government offices in the district headquarters town and then moved on and attacked the Kotwali, the telephone exchange and the head post office. The demonstrators had also allegedly set a police van on fire.

Mr. Ali Hyder, Convenor of the Gaya Jan Sangharsh Samiti, who is a very simple, honest and dedicated worker, told me that the trouble was provoked by a police sergeant who had manhandled, abused and humiliated some women squatters and then, when they protested, had some young boys beaten up. A lawyer, a relative of mine, told me that the 16-hour curfew had been imposed only to remove bodies of persons killed in police firings for surreptitious disposal at night.

The reports of the firings and alleged police brutalities created tension in many towns of north and south Bihar, where the movement to paralyse the government was intensified and processions taken out and rallies held in defiance of section 144 Cr. P.C. The lawyers of Gaya boycotted the courts in protest till April 22. No doubt there had been police excesses in Gaya.

Even prominent office-bearers of the Gaya District Congress Committee led by their President, Mr. J. K. Palit, went on batchwise protest fasts in relays before the statue of Mahatma Gandhi. Government's credibility reached a new low when it even denied a shoot-at-sight order given by the District Magistrate of Gaya, Mr. B. B. Lal. But Mr. Lal himself confirmed it at a press conference. Thousands of citizens of the town had heard the order announced on mikes.

Mr. Dilkishore Singh, a Congress member of Rajya Sabha from Bihar, was deputed by the BPCC President, Mr. Sitaram Kesari, M.P., to make an on-the-spot enquiry at Gaya to find out the truth. Mr. Singh visited the places where the police firings had occurred, saw the injured in the hospital, met representatives of lawyers, doctors, teachers, students and party workers. He also took statements from people whose houses in lanes and bylanes had allegedly been entered and ransacked by the police and women inmates assaulted or humiliated after the firings.

Dilkishore told me in an interview on April 30, which received countrywide publicity, that the situation in Gaya had been mishandled and that the tragic incidents could have been "easily averted with greater tact". He said: "What happened appeared gruesome. The mass of evidence I have collected only emphasises the need for doing something to restore the confidence of the people of Gaya. Many sober and responsible persons have told me that the tragedy could have been averted with greater tact. I am inclined to agree with them."

Dilkishore is a lawyer. He had already reported his findings to the BPCC President. He said: "Each and every person I had met had heard the announcement of the shoot-at-sight order issued after the clamping of curfew on April 12. Everyone also felt that the continued deployment of the BSF and the CRP was a source of constant irritation and provocation. I tried to contact the local officials many times but could not get any statements from them in the absence of the District Magistrate, Mr. B. B. Lal."

An unofficial three-member Citizens' Enquiry Committee had also been set up by Mr. Jayaprakash Narayan, who himself released its findings which held the Gaya firings "unprovoked, unwarranted and unjustified". It examined 150 witnesses at

Gaya after holding an on-the-spot enquiry and came to the conclusion that the firings had been resorted to more out of vengeance than necessity. There was no danger to private or public property, such as the Post Office or the Kotwali, as alleged by the Government. The Enquiry Committee was of the opinion that the large number of deaths by police firings were caused on the one hand by the wrong decision of the Executive Magistrate, Mr. A. K. Sinha, to hand over charge to the BSF with blanket orders to shoot as they liked, and on the other, by the ineptitude of the Subdivisional Officer, Mr. M. K. Kassim, in controlling the BSF. It also held one BSF Naik guilty of "deliberately murdering four persons and stealing money, wrist watches and gold rings from the persons of the dead and injured".

It found that under the cover of curfew and the shoot-at-sight order, the BSF and the CRP men in particular unleashed a reign of terror on the city, breaking open several houses, detaining unwary stragglers arriving by night trains and humiliating and misbehaving with ladies. It was also firmly of the opinion that many more persons had been killed in the firings than those admitted by the Government.

The Committee maintained that the movement of the students at Gaya, which had received popular support, had been peaceful, thoroughly disciplined and non-violent. It held that an embittered administration embarrassed by the success of the movement had sought "to teach the demonstrators a lesson" through lathi-charges, firings and other police excesses.

The Prime Minister was worried despite the brave face that she put up. She had not been able to make up her mind on the reconstitution of the Bihar Ministry though resignations of the Ministers had been procured. On April 15 she made a frontal attack on what she described as "the disruptionist aspects" of the agitation in Gujarat and Bihar, which had also spread to Maharashtra.

In the light of what happened when she promulgated internal emergency fourteen months later, it was an interesting speech. Inaugurating the annual meeting of the Indian Chamber of Commerce and Industry, she conceded that though the pace of the democratic system was slower it had greater capacity for self-correction than any other system. She spoke of continued attempts to undermine democratic sanctions and institutions and said that some short-sighted cynics or even corrupt groups had aligned themselves with those wanting to demolish the foundations of orderly society and constitutional behaviour.

She had a dig at Mr. Narayan without naming him and said even those who swore by non-violence indulged in activities which encouraged disruptive forces. She held that in a democratic society there should be a partnership based on mutual understanding, a spirit of give and take. Only then could a democratic system be built and nurtured and national unity fostered amidst diversity and disparity. Stating that peaceful methods and democracy were essential for the nation's survival (she had not a word to say about the police brutalities in Bihar), Mrs. Gandhi emphasised the need for faith in the good sense and discrimination of the people (she herself lost that faith when she proclaimed emergency), who would ultimately reject these forces (the people rejected her, her son and her party when they got the opportunity).

The echo of the Gaya police firings was heard on April 19 in the Lok Sabha when it was the subject of a four-hour debate during which opposition parties squarely blamed the Congress Party for the unrest in Bihar and some other parts of the country. They maintained that the incidents in Gaya were a reflection of the general situation in the country and demanded a judicial enquiry. Some members also demanded imposition of President's rule in Bihar.

I have quoted the findings of the on-the-spot enquiry held by Mr. Dilkishore Singh, a Congress MP from Bihar, to show with what ease blatant falsehood could be reeled out in the Lok Sabha on this issue even by a venerable person like the Union Home Minister, Mr. Uma Shankar Dikshit, obviously on the basis of information supplied by the Bihar Government. Mr. Dikshit bypassed altogether the demands for judicial enquiry and imposition of President's Rule and stuck to the official version of the Gaya incidents and the figures of casualties. He even denied the shoot-at-sight order given by the District Magistrate of Gaya, which had been confirmed by Mr. Dilkishore Singh as well as the Citizens' Enquiry Committee.

The Home Minister conceded that the situation in the country was indeed serious but indulged in unctuous shibboleths and asked members of every party to search their hearts and sincerely try to do something to ease the situation. He said the Government alone should not be blamed for the rising prices, shortages and prevalent corruption. He felt the Government should not be castigated particularly for shortages and soaring prices because these were due to factors beyond its control. He also implored the opposition not to malign Congress politicians as a whole as corrupt lest they lost their credibility (he forgot that his own partymen were voicing this charge against the Ministry in Bihar).

Mr. Dikshit also asserted that before the police firings in Gaya all the rules in the Police Manual had been followed (meaning thereby that before resort to firings, due warnings had been given and there had been lathi charges followed by tear gassing). Mr. S. M. Banerji asked: "Why are you then shirking a judicial probe?"

Mr. Dikshit retorted: "This is an utterly fallacious argument. First there is a falsehood (that between fifty to one hundred persons were killed) and then there is the demand for judicial enquiry."

According to his information, he alleged, two political parties were involved in preparations for "something very serious" at Gaya on April 12. When the CPI members wanted him to name the parties, he declined. He added, however, that the CPI was not one of the parties. He asserted that there had been no police excesses. Mr. Dikshit neither yielded to the demand for judicial enquiry nor did he care to visit Gaya.

But the "disruptive forces" about whom the Prime Minister, Mrs. Gandhi, had mentioned in her inaugural address at the annual conference of the Indian Chambers of Commerce and Industry and thundered "we must pool our energies together to meet this challenge", continued to worry her. There was reason for anxiety. Eminent litterateurs like Padamshree Phanishwar Nath Renu, Akademy Award winner poet Nagarjun, well-known artist Damodar Ambastha and a large number of college and school teachers and lawyers had started joining the JP-led movement. The non-communist political parties were already supporting the agitation, which by mid-April was showing signs of spreading outside Bihar. The Jana Sangh leader, Mr. Atal Bihari Vajpayee, courted arrest with four hundred party workers, including MLAs, by holding demonstrations before the Madhya Pradesh Assembly at Bhopal. To make matters worse, Mr. Mahamaya Prasad Sinha, a former Chief Minister of Bihar, resigned his membership of the Bihar Assembly as well as of the Congress Party at a time when a section of Bihar Ministers, who had been forced to tender their resignations to the Congress High Command and were apprehensive of being dropped, were also on the point of revolt and threatening resignation from the Party.

Unmindful of the threats of even partymen, the Prime Minister, who had not abandoned her stick, now dangled the proverbial carrot before the activists of the Bihar agitation. At her behest the Congress High Command finally decided on April 18 to drop as many as thirtyfive Ministers, Ministers of State and Deputy Ministers from Ghafoor's Ministry. Twelve out of twentytwo of them held Cabinet rank, nineteen were Ministers of State and four were Deputy Ministers.

Besides Ghafoor, the following were retained: Daroga Prasad Roy, Chandra Sekhar Singh, Shreemati Ramdulari Sinha, Kedar Pandey, Lahtan Choudhary, Narsingh Baitha, Dr. Jagannath Mishra, Sidui Hembrom and Dr. Ram Raj Prasad Singh. Umesh Prasad Verma, Simon Tigga and Ramashray Prasad Singh were promoted as full-fledged Ministers from Ministers of State. Mr. Suresh Ram, son of the Union Defence Minister, Mr. Jagjiwan Ram, was also proposed to be inducted as a Minister but he declined obviously on the advice of his father who had not been consulted.

Dr. Shankar Dayal Sharma, the Congress President, explained that those who were being dropped were not necessarily corrupt. The reconstitution of the Ministry was an internal matter of the Congress. The changes had been made to retain some for carrying on the administration while others had been relieved of office for—an old recipe or rationale—utilisation in organisational work.

The dissidents led by Mr. Ram Lakhan Singh Yadav, MLA, and Mr. Nagendra Jha, MLA, joined hands with the axed Ministers. Their spokesman said the reconstituted Ministry was not going to fool anybody because "some architects of corruption" had been retained. Mr. Ram Lakhan Singh Yadav said: "It would do no good". Mr. Nagendra Jha commented that he did not expect anything from the pruned Ministry. Mr. Jai Narain, MLA, another dissident leader, said: "It is old wine in a new bottle."

Since the dissident Congressmen themselves had such a poor opinion of the reconstituted Ministry, it was idle to expect Mr. Narayan or the Chhatra Sangharsh Samiti to be taken in by this gimmick since they knew that at least three of the retained Ministers were facing charges of corruption (amassing wealth disproportionate to their known sources of income) before the Lok Ayukta.

Mr. Narayan said in a statement that the swearing in of the reconstituted Ministry would only strengthen the demand for the dissolution of the Assembly, as it was not at all expected to provide a clean and good government. He said the Congress High Command should act in good time and with good grace to save itself from the humiliation it suffered in Gujarat.

Meanwhile, the month-long students' agitation continued and more and more women started participating in it. Besides students and youths, on April 29 women went on 12-hour fasts in at least one hundred places in Patna. The fasts were organised before the residences of some Ministers considered to be corrupt.

On the previous day members of the Patna High Court Bar Association had taken out a silent procession and gone to Raj Bhawan to demand the resignation of the Governor, Mr. R. D. Bhandare. They were, however, not allowed to enter. Earlier in the day the Patna District Bar Association had taken out a similar procession.

Mr. B. C. Ghose, President of the High Court Advocates' Association, told newsmen that the Association wanted the Governor, instead of presiding over a rotten and inefficient government, to rise to the occasion and resign in view of the failure of the administration on all fronts, which could not even control the runaway prices. He said only such action could awaken those who ruled from Delhi and presided over the destiny of Bihar, and for whom corruption had become a way of life.

The Cabinet reshuffle drama only gave a further impetus to the Samiti to intensify its dharna agitation. Reports received from different parts of Bihar indicated that Samiti volunteers were offering dharna before government offices in the blocks, subdivisional and district headquarters towns peacefully. The same was going on in the State capital. The administration was virtually paralysed due to the double-pronged attack on the Ghafoor Ministry—the movement of the youths and students from outside and the dissident Congressmen working from the inside for its ouster.

On April 21 the Action Committee of the Chhatra Sangharsh Samiti announced that the emphasis of its struggle hence forward would be on securing the ouster of the Ministry. It said in a statement: "We demand the resignation of the Ministry because large number of youths were killed by this government when they went to the legislature on March 18 to demand bread for the masses. We feel this government is responsible for the present ills like high prices, corruption and unemployment." It also called upon the people to join the movement to force the guilty, inhuman Ministry to quit.

The same evening, in support of this demand, a silent procession was taken out by women led by the widow of Batukeshwar Dutt, associate of martyr Bhagat Singh.

Earlier that day the Government gave indications that it was prepared to bend a bit. The Finance Minister, Mr. Daroga Prasad Rai (a former Chief Minister), told a press conference that the government had already conceded most of the demands of the students. He added: "But we are still prepared to have a dialogue with the student leaders and concede their other genuine demands in spite of financial stringency. We also invite them to come forward with some concrete suggestions for the eradication of corruption and holding the price line. Let me also inform them that we have already decided to purchase 50,000 to 1,00,000 tonnes of wheat from some of the surplus States to meet the food crisis. With the same object in view we have also requested the Union Government to increase our monthly quota of wheat."

Mr. Rai conceded that it was a fact that dharnas, relay fasts and demonstrations were going on before government offices, but claimed that "government work has not suffered much" because of it. He also agreed that the overall situation in the State was peaceful.

Only on the previous day the Health Minister, Mr. Kedar

Pandey, was humiliated by a large group of Samiti demonstrators. They stopped his car while he was proceeding to Srikrishna Puri and offered him a garland of shoes and a set of bangles and a packet of vermillion. Mr. Pandey, the only Minister who had never shied away from the students despite their attempts to secure resignations through coercive methods, struck to his guns ignoring the insult and went on arguing with them. Meanwhile the police arrived on the scene. Mr. Pandey had the good sense to avoid trouble by sending the police back. The young men appreciated his gesture and allowed him to proceed.

After the police firings in Gaya, the Samiti had launched a programme of "Maut Ki Ghanti" (ringing the bell of death) in all the towns of the State. To signify the sounding of the doom knell of the Ministry, they asked housewives to beat utensils at a given signal at night. Although this became quite popular, it proved to be only an amusing feature or side show, a comic relief. People had also started taking out processions driving pigs, donkeys and dogs with labels carrying the names of Ministers round their necks. (JP, when he came to know of it, publicly denounced it.)

Mr. Narayan left for Vellore on April 23 to have his enlarged prostrate gland operated.

SEVEN

Programme of Action

Mr. Jayaprakash Narayan spelled out some do's and dont's for the participants in the movement before his departure. He said they must eschew violence in word and deed whatever the provocation might be. Raising of abusive slogans must stop. The slogans must be such as to appeal to the people and explain the objectives of the struggle. If there was to be condemnation of anything, it must be in dignified language. No one should be forced to do anything against his will and fasts, gheraos and dharnas must not assume coercive character. The families of Ministers, legislators and businessmen must not be harassed or ill-treated.

Releasing the programme, Mr. Narayan said that the first week of May should be devoted to building up and strengthening of the organs of the struggle. The second week should be devoted to the objective of voicing the demand for the resignation of the Ministry and the dissolution of the State Assembly. The third week should be observed as anti-corruption week in which sons and daughters of corrupt persons, including Ministers, bureaucrats, businessmen, hoarders and profiteers, should be persuaded to observe a 12-hour fast in their homes to impress upon their elders to tread the narrow but straight path of virtue and not to indulge in dishonest practices. One day should be devoted by the youths and students for taking pledges not to indulge in any corrupt practices. The fourth week should be observed to highlight the need for a complete overhauling of the present education system to link academic learning with manual labour and training in skills needed in farms and factories. The first two days of June should be devoted to review the progress of their work and plan for the future.

Mr. Narayan told reporters he expected to return after five

weeks. He suggested the creation of an effective people's machinery to exercise control over the bureaucracy and members of the Assembly and Ministers. He maintained that under the present system the people had no control over the so-called public servants or their own elected representatives. He said his idea of 'partyless government' appeared utopian to some people but no one could deny the need of an instrument to control the vagaries of the elected representatives and of the bureaucrats. He condemned the delisting of the *Searchlight* for its outspoken criticism of the Government. It only showed the government's utter disregard for the freedom of the press.

He thanked women, lawyers, doctors, teachers and other sections of the people for their participation in dharnas, fasts and other programmes of action related to the movement. He also thanked non-communist opposition parties for their co-operation with the movement but pleaded with them to work in a non-partisan spirit and not to try to utilise it for their political ends.

He also announced that he was appointing four prominent Sarvodaya workers Messrs. Ram Murti, Narain Desai, Man-mohan Choudhary and Tripurari Saran to direct and guide the movement in his absence.

JP's departure did not slacken the movement though some novel features were introduced by the Samiti. For instance, it initiated a programme of a two-hour Janata curfew in selected areas of Patna and other towns between 9 a.m. and 11 a.m. at a given signal. This action had no meaning. It only caused harassment to the people and quite often led to the arrest of those enforcing it. Many Mukhiyas of Gram Panchayats of Gaya, Rohtas, Nawadah and Aurangabad districts resigned in support of the movement subject to the approval of Mr. Narayan on his return from Vellore. A section of the journalists of Patna also started observing fasts before their respective institutions to signify their sympathy with the students' struggle. Samiti volunteers continued their programme of dharnas, fasts and satyagraha before government offices. They also launched this programme before the residences of Ministers and members of the Assembly.

Mr. Narayan issued two statements from Vellore while convalescing after his operation in May, 1974. The first, issued on May 14, gave detailed reasons why the Bihar Assembly should be dissolved and the state placed under President's Rule for a brief spell till the holding of fresh elections.

Appealing to the members of the Assembly to resign, he said: "In 1972 you received your mandate from the people and became their accredited representatives. But you cannot be unaware of the radical change in the situation in Bihar that has taken place in these two years. Even though the Congress Party secured a majority at the elections, it has failed to give the people a stable government. Personal ambitions and rivalries of Congress leaders and MLAs have been responsible from the beginning for bitter infighting which for months at a time has brought the functioning of the government to a standstill. Even today the Ministry is beset with internal dissensions and external pressures from the so-called dissidents. This has created a sense of insecurity in the present government paralysing its functioning. All this has deeply affected the people's interests which have been steadily deteriorating.

"Thus the party which the last general elections in Bihar put in power, has failed totally to deal with any of the serious problems facing the State. Prices have been steadily rising, scarcity of essential commodities has become the rule, hoarding, blackmarketing and profiteering have been going on without check or hindrance, the academic institutions are paralysed and the lives of thousands of young men are being wasted.

"As for corruption, no serious attempt has been made to deal with it except at some lower levels. It has been my view from the beginning that corruption cannot be rooted out or even curbed and controlled, unless corruption at the Minister's level is effectively dealt with. In spite of several reshufflings of the Ministry, quite a few of the powerful Ministers, who are generally believed by the people to have been deeply sunk in corruption, continue to share in the spoils. There can be no credible means of eradicating corruption at the top.

"The major opposition parties in the Assembly have lent their support to the present movement from the outset. Many of their leaders and members have been sent to prison. So, if you opposition MLAs continue to stick to your seats in the Assembly, you not only expose your erstwhile support as being hollow, but also become a party to all the wrongs perpetrated by the Bihar Government. Therefore, it is in the interest of all of you, whether of the Government or of the opposition, and in the interest of good, clean and efficient government that you seek a fresh mandate."

As far back as May, 1974, Mr. Narayan had advised the students' non-party democratic organisations and other watch-dogs of democracy to ensure that the next elections when they came should be free and fair. He wanted them to educate the voters and enlighten them so that in deciding their own fate they could act intelligently without being influenced by money, caste, creed, etc.

In his second statement, issued on May 22, Mr. Narayan warned that we would soon have a dictatorship if the loss of faith in democracy deepened and persisted. He said the "mass upsurges" in Gujarat and Bihar might be unconstitutional but not anti-democratic. What could the people do when constitutional methods and the established democratic institutions failed to respond to their will or to solve their pressing problems? "Therefore", Mr. Narayan said, "it is a healthy and welcome symptom of our democracy that the people, the real masters, should rise and take recourse to unconstitutional but powerful means to assert themselves and bend the powers that be to their will". He reiterated the need for forging permanent organs of the people's power from the villages to the constituency and to the State level to do away with the ills besetting the country. He maintained that the nation's electoral law was full of defects and loopholes. The need for its reform had been recognised and pressed for the past so many years but the party in power at the Centre had never considered it necessary to do anything about it.

Even under the present electoral system, defective as it was, the unlimited use of money, large-scale impersonation, use of force to prevent the weakest sections from exercising their franchise, abuse of the electoral machinary, hoodwinking of the people by attractive and false promises, etc., had robbed the elections of much of their value and eroded the people's faith in them.

After JP's departure for Vellore, the Samiti organised state-wide 12-hour fasts on April 30 to press for the resignation of the Ghafoor Ministry and the dissolution of the Assembly. It was reported that the response to the call was encouraging and that in many houses of the sympathisers of the movement ovens were not lighted and the inmates went without food during the day. Most of the hotels and restaurants in the towns remained closed till sunset. A Catholic priest of Bettiah, Father Cordeiro, observed a 48-hour fast and did not even drink water. He spent the time in total silence covering his mouth with a piece of black cotton cloth. He demanded payment of compensation to the families of the victims of the police firings in Bettiah on March 16, judicial enquiry into the police firings in Patna, immediate launching of a dehoarding drive and bringing down prices. At several places silent processions were taken out by youths carrying urns containing symbolic bones and ashes of the victims of police firings in different parts of the State.

On May 4, the Health Minister, Mr. Lahtan Choudhary, was gheraoed when he went to village Mahisi in Saharsa district without knowing that a two-hour Janata curfew was on. The demonstrators asked him to resign and when he refused, he was roughly handled and forced to return.

May 7 had been fixed by Mr. Narayan as the deadline for the resignation of the members of the Bihar Assembly. On that date 18 out of 24 Jana Sangh members led by Mr. Bijoy Kumar Mitra and six out of seventeen SSP members led by Mr. Karpoori Thakur, a former Chief Minister and ex-Chairman of the All India SSP, resigned. Mr. Mahamaya Prasad Sinha, the lone Congress member to quit the Assembly, had announced his resignation much earlier (till the first anniversary of the agitation on March 18, 1975, only 42 had resigned).

In his covering letter to the Speaker of the Bihar Assembly, Pandit Harinath Mishra, Mr. Thakur warned the government that if the Ministry failed to resign, his party would set up a parallel government. He said his party was not only in favour of the dissolution of the Assembly but also of the Lok Sabha.

The warning fell on deaf ears. On the contrary, the government promptly announced that it would take steps to hold by-elections to fill up the vacancies caused by such resignations (though it never did).

The nationwide railwaymen's strike commenced on May 8 and the Government was hard put to contend with it while the agitation for the dissolution of the Assembly and resignation of the Ministry was already going full steam. In fact, the very day on which the railwaymen's strike commenced, the Chhatra Sangharsh Samiti organised a Patna Bundh to press its demands. On the same day again, the Lok Sabha adopted a Bill amending the Constitution to prevent resignation of legislators obtained under duress. The Bill provided that the resignation of a legislator shall not be accepted by the Speaker or the Chairman if he was satisfied after making an enquiry that the resignation was not voluntary or genuine.

While the programme of dharna before government offices in the State continued, from May 10 in Patna the Samiti workers concentrated their activities also on the MLA flats in observance of the "Assembly Dissolution Week". Relay fasts, demonstrations and torchlight processions around the Legislators' Club area formed part of the programme. Besides MLA flats, batchwise hunger-strike was also organised before the residences of 25 legislators, including Ministers.

Barring minor stray incidents, the agitation, by and large, was peaceful. Unnerved by its success and the popular response it was getting, the Bihar Pradesh Congress Committee decided to jump into the fray. The BPCC directed its District Committees to hold counter-demonstrations, processions and meetings from May 12 and allotted different districts to different Ministers. This naturally led to trouble.

On May 11 several hundred women belonging to the Patna Nari Mandal, which was supporting the JP-led movement, headed by Dr. Veena Srivastava, a college teacher, gheraoed the Patna Station of the AIR. They demonstrated for an hour shouting slogans decrying the role of the AIR for carrying on only government propaganda and maligning the youths and students for continuing their struggle for a better order.

Came May 12. The counter-processions taken out by the Congress led to a serious clash in Monghyr town, where a dusk to dawn curfew had to be clamped. Seventyfive Congressmen, including the Union Deputy Minister for Education, Mr. D. P. Yadav, were injured, some seriously, and hospitalised. There was tension in Monghyr town following the burning on the previous night of the office of the Chhatra Sangharsh Samiti, which had given the call for Monghyr Bundh, in protest, the next day. Vehicular traffic was nil and the shops and bazars were closed since morning. In the midst of the Bundh the Monghyr District Congress Committee took out a procession led by Mr. D. P. Yadav and Mr. Chandra Sekhar Singh, Industries Minister of Bihar, and Congress legislators of the district. When the procession, taken out from Tilak Maidan, reached the Chowk area, hundreds of students and youths waiting there raised counter-slogans. The latter far outnumbered the processionists. They also appeared to be spoiling for trouble. There was a skirmish and soon the processionists were surrounded and attacked. Some prominent Congressmen, who obviously believed in discretion being the better part of valour, left their comrades in the lurch and quietly slipped away to the police station with the main body of the armed escorts. This was said to be the reason why so many Congressmen were easily beaten up.

A similar procession at Siwan, led by the Finance Minister, Mr. Daroga Prasad Rai, was greeted with showers of brickbats. Several Congressmen, including Mr. Rai, received minor injuries. On May 13, the second day of the counter-agitation, there were more clashes. Two of them occurred in Gaya town. During the clash a Congress MLC caught by youths was forced to wear a garland of shoes and paraded in the streets. He was later rescued by the police. The Samiti was observing Black Day at Gaya on that date and had taken out a procession, which clashed head-on with another procession led by the Local Self Government Minister, Mr. Ramashray Prasad Singh. On the same day a Congress rally addressed by the Irrigation Minister, Dr. Jagannath Mishra, was gheraoed and brickbatted at Darbhanga. At Bettiah and Muzaffarpur tension mounted over processions and counter-processions but actual clashes were somehow avoided. In other parts of Bihar Congress processions were not interfered with.

All the while the Prime Minister, Mrs. Gandhi, was keeping a close watch on the situation. Out of temper when a delegation of dissident Congressmen met her on May 23 and demanded change of leadership in the State Congress Legislature Party, she packed them off with the warning unitedly to face the challenge of the agitation, else she would have to take some drastic step against them. A dissident Congress leader of Bihar, Mr. Jai Narain, said in an interview in Delhi that the Prime

Minister and the Congress High Command seemed to be more worried over the intensification of the agitation than our feelings on the issue of leadership.

By this time Mrs. Anjali Dutta, the widow of revolutionary Batukeshwar Dutta, had also joined the agitation. She led a torchlight procession taken out by the Patna Nari Mandal on May 27 to press for the dissolution of the Assembly. The Union Home Minister, Mr. Uma Shankar Dikshit, the Railway Minister, Mr. Lalit Narain Mishra, and Mr. Yashpal Kapur M.P., airdashed to Patna on May 28 and told a joint meeting of the State Congress Legislature Party and Congress members of Parliament from Bihar not to take the agitation lightly but to face the challenge with determination. Mr. Dikshit said they should understand that the main object of the JP-led agitation was not merely the ouster of the Bihar Ministry and the dissolution of the State Assembly but the overthrow of the Congress Government headed by Mrs. Gandhi at the Centre. He also made it clear that no matter what happened, the Bihar Assembly would not be dissolved.

EIGHT

Firing by Indira Brigade

JP returned from Vellore to Patna on June 2. The agitation had continued during his absence and many youths, besides leaders of non-communist parties, had been jailed. Most of the jails were full and several jail officials had declined to take any more prisoners.

By the beginning of June, Patna was divided into 10 police zones and six sectors, each manned by senior magistrates and police officers for the "maintenance of law and order". Three new police stations were also opened in Kankarbagh, Jakkanpur and the Secretariat area.

By then 46 companies of the Border Security Force, 4,600 jawans of the Bihar Military Police, besides several thousand CRP men had been deployed all over the State, particularly in the "sensitive" areas. All these zones and sectors of Patna functioned under senior magistrates with full powers "to use force according to the needs of the situation". Armed policemen were deputed for manning the town police outposts. Mobile police patrols headed by magistrates were also in action.

The then Defence Minister, Mr. Jagjiwan Ram, during a visit to Patna on June 1, told reporters that "Bihar won't be allowed to go the Gujarat way". All the while the youths arrested and lodged in the Patna Central jail launched dharna demanding quick disposal of their cases, removal of corruption in jail and supply of better food. Youth leaders Jagannath Yadav, Ram Janam Sinha and Arun Kumar Verma declared from inside the jail that their dharna was a part of the bigger agitation continuing outside.

On his return to Patna JP was given a tumultuous welcome at the airport by 20,000 youths and large number of opposition leaders like Messrs. Krishna Ballabh Sahay (who died in a car accident on his way to Hazaribagh the very next day), Raj Narain (defying a ban on his entry to Bihar), Mahamaya Prasad Sinha, Satyendra Narain Sinha, Ramanand Tiwary, Basawan Sinha and the Sarvodaya leader, Acharya Ram Murti. The sky was rent with cries of "Vidhan Sabha Bhanga Karo" (dissolve the Assembly), "Jaya Prakash Zindabad", "Bhrastachar Mitana Hai, Naya Bihar Banana Hai" (we have to remove corruption and build a new Bihar).

Mr. Narayan declined to say anything to waiting pressmen at the airport except that "my health is all right but I have been advised by doctors to take three months' rest". The wound caused by the incision for the operation had not fully healed and was still oozing. Because of this JP had to wear a dhoti tied as a Lungi. But, as subsequent events would show, there was to be no rest for him.

On June 5 a mammoth march to Raj Bhawan from Gandhi Maidan was scheduled to be organised to present to the Governor over one crore signatures of citizens of Bihar demanding the dissolution of the Bihar Assembly. (The CPI organised a huge procession on June 3 to demand summoning of the Assembly.) Although Chief Minister Abdul Ghafoor expressed his worry over JP's health and deprecated the idea that his followers should want him to lead the Great March in such gruelling heat, Mr. Rajdeo Singh, Inspector General of the BSF, told reporters on June 3 that the Bihar Government had given a "free hand" to his force to deal firmly with the situation created by the proposed massive demonstration if it led to trouble.

Mr. Singh declared: "We shall teach a lesson to the goondas if they raise their heads. We shall deal firmly but fairly to prevent arson and loot." (Actually it proved to be one of the most peaceful processions in Patna). Next evening a flag march of 3,000 jawans of the BSF, the CRP and the BMP armed with rifles, bren guns, sten guns and machine guns was organised by the government "to serve as a warning to anti-social elements and to assure peaceful citizens".

While the State Government was itching for a showdown, the Prime Minister, Mrs. Indira Gandhi, was giving peace feelers to JP. Her emissary, Mr. Yashpal Kapur, MP, met JP on the eve of the Great March. The talks were, as was only to be expected, fruitless. JP did not like the carrot-and-the-stick approach, especially when discontent was mounting over the denial of the legitimate demands of the Chhatra Sangharsh Samiti formulated in the month of March and the repressive policy of the Government. (The dissolution of the Assembly was not, by the way, one of the original demands of the Samiti.)

On the eve of the Great March a large number of train, steamer and bus services were cancelled to prevent the demonstrators from coming to Patna (but mass-scale ticketless travelling had been winked at to ensure the success of the CPI procession on June 3). Yet on June 5 since morning thousands and thousands of people started assembling at the Gandhi Maidan. How they came and from where was a mystery. Within a couple of hours after midday, the whole of Gandhi Maidan was transformed into a sea of humanity. The March started at 3.30 p.m. in scorching heat led by Mr. Narayan in a jeep covered with khaskhas heavily sprinkled with water, which soon dried up. Youths took their turns to protect JP from the heat by fanning him with palm-leaf fans. A truck carrying huge mounds of signatures of citizens demanding dissolution of the Assembly formed the vanguard of the procession, escorted by hundreds of policemen. Armed police pickets were also posted at strategic points all along the route. It was a weird spectacle, as full of nobility as of foreboding.

When the procession was returning from Raj Bhawan, fire was opened (eight rounds) from the Bailey Road flat of a Congress MLA, Mr. Phulena Rai, by members of an organisation known as the Indira Brigade. JP escaped but a police driver and sixteen members of the procession were injured. The police led by the City Superintendent of Police, Mr. P. C. Haldar (now Chief Intelligence Officer, Central Intelligence Bureau, Bihar), at once swung into action and arrested 17 persons, mostly young men, from the flat of Mr. Phulena Rai, who could not be traced. The police also recovered from the flat 1 DBBL gun, 2 single-barrel guns, 5 pistols, some ammunition and large number of liquor bottles besides some pornographic pictures. The arrested persons were: Triyug Singh, Rajendra Singh Bismil, Sheo Narain Singh, Arvind Singh,

Mundrika Singh, Maguni Singh, Rajinder Singh, Suresh Singh, Sita Ram Singh, Dhiraj Singh, Nandan Prasad, Ram Kishore Singh, Nathuni Singh, Kriyanand Pandey, Chandip Kumar and Awadh Kumar Singh.

The District Magistrate, Mr. Vijay Shankar Dubey, sent the injured to hospital. The same night the Commissioner of Patna Division announced an *ad hoc* grant of Rs. 200/- each for the injured. Despite the grave provocation, the processionists remained peaceful and the District Magistrate thanked them for their forbearance.

Although the Pradesh Congress bulletin used to publicise the activities of the Indira Brigade, the PCC General Secretary, Mr. Ramanand Yadav, disowned it totally the very next day and condemned violent activities in which its members were indulging. The Congress President, Dr. Shankar Dayal Sharma, also issued a similar denial in Delhi and promptly suspended Mr. Phulena Rai from membership of the party. He was in such a mighty hurry to drop Phulena Rai that he did not even issue a show cause notice.

Notwithstanding the denials, the fact remained that during the past two years not one but three Indira Brigades had been formed in Bihar. The first was formed by Mr. Jagdish Narain Choubey M.L.C. (Congress), who died recently. The *BLITZ* of Bombay published a story on it with the photograph of Mr. Choubey. When this paper tiger became moribund and soon died a natural death, a second was formed under the leadership of a Patna Advocate. This too became somnolent and soon went out of existence. Then came the third. This Brigade was well-heeled and liberally financed by a powerful Minister, who not only hated Mr. Ghafoor but also Mr. Narayan because the Samiti boys had made a special target of him as the most corrupt politician of the State.

The headquarters of this Brigade, responsible for the shooting, was located at first in Room No. 7 of the Patna Dak Bungalow adjacent to the PTI building. The members openly wined, dined and womanised. They also had about a dozen taxis at their disposal on a wholtime basis. They utilised these taxis to tour the State to carry on a campaign both against Mr. Ghafoor and JP's agitation. A bomb exploded in their room accidentally in the month of May. The occupants at once fled but one of them was caught by a peon of the PTI and an onlooker and handed over to the police. The Senior Superintendent of Police, Mr. Gopal Acharya, and the City S.P., Mr. Haldar, reached the scene within minutes. On opening the room all that they could find were several empty liquor bottles neatly arranged over an empty attache case. I was present when they made the search. The Brigade men never returned to the Dak Bungalow again.

After the flag march by jawans of the BSF, the CRP and the BMP on June 4, two cars carrying the banners of the Indira Brigade appeared on the Fraser Road. The occupants gesticulated and shouted "CIA Ka Kutta (CIA's dog) Jaya Prakash" and other anti-JP slogans. From the balcony of the PTI, I saw and heard them shouting. Capt. Suraj Prakash Singh, General Secretary of the Gaya District Congress Committee, who was with me, at once issued a statement denouncing them.

Next time they surfaced, on June 5, the Indira Brigade became world news. Mr. Phulena Rai was suspected by the police to have gone into hiding in the house of a Minister. Five days later the police seized and attached his property in Champaran district. Mr. Rai suddenly appeared in the Bihar Assembly on June 11 and made a brief statement that he had gone to his village home on June 5 after attending the House and that he knew nothing of the shooting incident. He then went out of the House accompanied by some Congress legislators and surrendered himself to the District Magistrate, who was waiting outside. He was arrested and sent to jail. The cases against Mr. Rai and all other suspects, who had been charge-sheeted, were dropped during the emergency by the then Chief Minister, Dr. Jagannath Mishra, reportedly at the behest of the Union Government.

The procession returned to Gandhi Maidan after the shooting incident and held a rally. It was at this rally that Mr. Narayan was named "Lok Nayak" (supreme leader of the people). The whole maidan reverberated with thunderous cries of "Lok Nayak Zindabad".

Addressing the rally, JP called upon the people to stop payment of taxes to the Government as it had lost their confidence. He also directed the students to ensure the closure of the colleges and the universities of Bihar by boycotting their classes and examinations for a year and to participate actively in the agitation (the colleges and universities were to open from mid-July).

He announced that from June 7 onwards demonstrations and picketing would be held peacefully before the gates of the Assembly to prevent the legislators and Ministers from attending the legislature. He warned the MLAs to resign within a week or face peaceful gherao of their residences. He said the students and youths would continue to fill the jails till the demand for the dissolution of the Assembly was conceded. It was at this rally that JP called upon the Chhatra Sangharsh Samitis and the Jana Sangharsh Samitis to build their organisations from the Block to the State level to prepare the ground for the victory of their nominees at the time of the next Assembly and Lok Sabha elections.

(The Congress Parliamentary Board took JP's call for preventing members to attending the Bihar Assembly as a challenge and discussed it at an extraordinary meeting held at Delhi on June 6. It directed all Congress MLAs of Bihar to attend the Assembly session without fail, notwithstanding picketing and gherao. It called upon not only Congress legislators but also all Congressmen of Bihar to boldly to face the challenge posed by JP's agitation. The CPB resolved that there was no question of conceding the demand for the dissolution of the Assembly.)

JP also denounced the existing members of the Assembly who had refused to resign and asked the people to ensure their defeat at the polls (when the Lok Sabha elections were held in March, 1977 the Congress drew blank in Bihar). He also made a passing reference to the shooting incident and asked the youths not to get provoked. Though tired in body and mind after the strain of leading the procession, JP addressed the rally for nearly two hours. All the while several doctors stood by at his side to stop him in case he showed signs of collapse from fatigue.

By this time 13 out of 24 Jana Sangh MLAs and seven out of seventeen SSP MLAs had resigned. The Jana Sangh had also expelled its remaining 11 MLAs from the party. Mr. Mahamaya Prasad Sinha a former Chief Minister in the United Front Government, was the only Congress MLA to resign at the call of JP. (No wonder he later trounced his CPI rival in Patna in the Lok Sabha election by a margin of over 2,50,000 votes. Mr. Ramavatar Shastri, his CPI rival, had been returned successively for the two previous terms from this constituency. Both Mr. Shastri and the Congress nominee, Mr. R. P. Sinha, forfeited their security.)

On the day of the Great March, the Bihar Assembly had met in an atmosphere of gloom and uncertainty. The entire area within half a mile radius of the Assembly was heavily barricaded and guarded by contingents of armed constables and jawans of the BSF and the CRP. As days passed the barricades went on extending while Ministers, who claimed to be representatives of the people, sought the safety of the armed constabulary. Patna started having a fore-taste of "barricaded democracy".

NINE

Satyagraha & Vinoba

As announced by JP the satyagraha before the Assembly commenced on June 7 and 53 satyagrahis, including 24 Sarvodaya workers, were arrested on the first day. The satyagraha was offered in batches. The first batch of 24 Sarvodaya workers arrived at the Assembly gates at 7.45 a.m. and were promptly nabbed (it was a Friday when the Assembly sits from 9 a.m.). The second and third batches of satyagrahis were arrested between 9 and 9.30 a.m. The last batch included Mr. Bijoy Kumar Mitra, a Jana Sangh leaderand an ex-Minister.

JP's decision to launch the agitation for Assembly dissolution was not liked by Acharya Vinoba Bhave, who described it as "a mistaken step". This was the version of Mr. V. P. Sathe, a Congress MP, who claimed to have discussed the matter with the Sant. Mr. Sathe said in a statement issued at Nagpur that the Sant had told him categorically that problems like price rise and corruption could not be solved by dissolving the representative bodies of the people and paving the way for President's rule. He said Acharya Bhave proposed to discuss the matter with JP at the time of the Sarva Seva Sangh Conference scheduled at his ashram on June 18. Till then he would only watch the situation. Ultimately there was a split in the Sarva Seva Sangh itself over the issue of JP's agitation and the participation of Sarvodaya workers in it.

Later events proved that Acharya Bhave did not really like the agitation. For, when the emergency was declared a year later, he hailed it as "Anushashan Parva" (era of discipline). Previously he had warned the President of the Sarva Seva Sangh, Mr. Siddhraj Dhadda, against involving Sarvodaya workers in the anti-Government agitation launched by JP and told him "Aap Haar Bhi Jayange Aur Maar Bhi Khayange" (you will not only be defeated but also be beaten up).

The first phase of the agitation concluded with the end of the satyagraha before the Assembly from the third week of July and the second and more intensive phase of statewide agitation was launched from August 1 when the scene shifted from the Assembly to the districts, blocks, panchayats and Assembly constituencies. Though not spectacular, the first phase proved to be quite effective despite the fact that it could not bring about the dissolution of the Assembly. A section of the youthful agitators had a feeling that they had not achieved much and were, therefore, itching for a more showy form of agitation.

Since Mr. Narayan took upon himself the responsibility of guiding the agitation, it remained, barring stray cases, peaceful. He personally used to administer a pledge to the satyagrahis sent out to the Assembly to remain peaceful in the face of all provocation. The satyagrahis dutifully went to the Assembly gates, shouted slogans and courted arrest.

Between June 7 and July 12, when this satyagraha was called off, over 3,400 satyagrahis had been arrested. During this phase though the Centre looked askance at the agitators, the local administration did not treat them harshly. The magistrates and the police politely asked them to board the waiting buses, where they were provided with lunch packets to ensure that they did not go hungry, and then whisked off. During the last three days of the satyagraha, they were taken into custody but returned to their home towns and released (the satyagrahis came from various districts to participate in the satyagraha). There was no alternative for the government but to release them because neither the Patna Central Jail nor the Phulwari Camp Jail nor even the district jails, which also were full (because the agitation was continuing in district towns too) could accommodate them. The government also appeared to be considerate because the satyagrahis did not create trouble.

The satyagraha proved too tame to satisfy some hot heads bent upon mischief. Fortunately, these were isolated instances. In patna, Mr. Ramesh Jha, MLA (Congress), a former Minister of State, was gheraoed and manhandled at Kankarbagh (south Patna) and his security guard, who pulled out his revolver, was assaulted. This incident angered the Chief Minister, Mr. Ghafoor, so much that he declared in the Assembly that if there was repetition of such incidents, he would not hesitate to send even the tallest the agitators (meaning JP) to his "Aasli Mokam" (real home or jail).

Mr. Jha undertook a fast demanding a personal apology from Mr. Narayan, who was then out of town. JP did not oblige him but he telegraphically condemned the action of the youths who had misbehaved with Mr. Jha. In Raxaul a mob of agitators demonstrated before the Champaran District Political Conference organised by the Congress and allegedly attempted to set fire to the cars of some Congress leaders and officers (what these officers were doing there was never explained) and threw away the food cooked for 3,000 delegates. At Muzaffarpur the record room of the Langat Singh College was burnt down. There was also arson at the Ram Dayalu Singh College in the same town. There was some trouble at the Goenka College at Sitamarhi too.

Though the Chhatra Sangharsh Samiti youths were being blamed, it was doubtful if they alone were responsible. For, the Education Minister, Dr. Ram Raj Prasad Singh, admitted that records had been burnt in colleges where funds had been misappropriated. This gave a totally different colour to the cases of arson. Obviously those guilty of embezzlement were trying to take advantage of the situation to burn the records and throw the blame on the agitators.

During this period four other Congress MLAs were manhandled for their refusal to resign. They were Messrs. Mohammad Hussain Azad and Nizamuddin (at Kishanganj), Shyam Narain Pandey (at Arrah) and Raghunath Jha (at Sitamarhi). That a section of the youths was fretting was also apparent from a call given by them for Patna Bundh on July 15 though Mr. Narayan's programme of action nowhere suggested resort to Bundhs. In fact he had specifically stressed that efforts should be made to cause the minimum inconvenience to the people.

Although it was not perceptible on the surface, the peaceful agitation had, during its first phase, hurt the Government financially. The State's overdrafts with the Reserve Bank of India had reached an all-time high and stood at Rs. 60 crores when the weekly permissible limit of O.D. was only Rs. 7.40 crores. The RBI had understandably been too tolerant and obviously turning a blind eye. But the moment it decided to stop the ODs, the government employees and all institutions which depended on the government for their sustenance on grants and aids were likely to be in the soup.

The Bihar Government's establishment charges alone at the time came to about Rs. 12 crores. The government reply to a question in the Assembly stated that the gap between Government's daily income and expenditure had increased tremendously. This situation had developed because the entire machinery of the government was engaged in tackling the law and order problem created by the agitation. The agitators might not be disturbing the peace, but the government had to remain alert round the clock. Whether the militant section of the agitators realised it or not, the agitation by remaining peaceful without being showy had started sapping the strength of the government at its weakest spot, namely, finance. (Subsequently it was claimed by Government that its revenue had actually doubled!)

After the programme of satyagraha had been launched, the Central Congress leadership was in a fix. One section suggested a dialogue with JP and the Union Home Minister, Mr. Uma Shankar Dikshit, twice talked telephonically with JP in the second week of June and expressed his desire to come down to Patna for detailed discussions. JP did not encourage him because he suspected the sincerity of the Congress leadership.

The hard-liners in the Congress wanted confrontation. They got a report circulated from Delhi that JP's objectives were not limited to Bihar. They maintained that JP's sole purpose was to cause maximum embarrassment to the Prime Minister, Mrs. Indira Gandhi, who was then facing a tough economic situation (her own creation) and to fan the discontent among the people. They held that Mr. Narayan's was a political challenge which had to be met squarely.

An unnamed Congress High Command source declared: "If we could cope with the much bigger challenge posed by the Syndicate in 1969, how can we submit to JP's pressure tactics?"

Replying to the debate on the Governor's address in the

Bihar Assembly, the Chief Minister, Mr. Ghafoor, on the one hand urged Mr. Narayan to withdraw his agitation and on the other threatened to have the accounts of the Bihar Relief Committee (whose Chairman was JP) audited. The innuendo was that the accounts of the Relief Committee were not in order and that JP was responsible for it. Mr. Ghafoor maintained that by spearheading the agitation JP had washed away all the credit he had earned for his heroic role in the freedom struggle.

TEN

Why Dissolution ?

The demand for the dissolution of the Assembly and the resignation of the Ministry was not contained in the original 12-point demand of the students formulated in the month of March. It had been subsequently added because of the repressive role of the "corrupt government" to suppress a democratic agitation.

Mr. Narayan referred to it in a signed article in the weekly "Everyman" after he gave his call for satyagraha in which he said that he had been compelled by events to support the demand for dissolution of the Assembly and the resignation of the Ministry even though he knew it would not solve the State's problems. (This was an indirect reply to Acharya Vinoba Bhave's comment.)

He said this demand was added only (a) when political and administrative corruption in the State showed no sign of abatement; (b) when the peoples' interests suffered because of infighting among Congress lagislators; and (c) the Bihar Government stumbled from one misdeed and failure to another in dealing with the peaceful movement of the students and people of Bihar.

Had the Assembly, he said, censured the government for its inefficiency, corruption and mismanagement of the peoples' affairs and helped to establish a better government, the situation would have been very different. As it happened, the repeated reshuffling of the Ministry hardly improved anything and the fact that the MLAs were found to be more busy with their factional fights than with serving the people made matters worse.

Whenever the youths and students strayed from the path of peace, JP did not hesitate publicly to condemn such action.

When four legislators were manhandled outside the Assembly on June 12 (the issue was raised in the House), JP condemned the action and apologised (in a letter) to the Speaker, Pandit Harinath Mishra, for the incident, though his own reports were that outsiders were responsible for it.

The submission of petitions containing signatures of over one crore citizens of Bihar to the Governor on June 5 demanding dissolution of the Assembly had worried the State Congress leadership. Efforts were, therefore, made to counter it and the Youth Congress was utilised for the purpose. But all that the Youth Congress could do was to submit a petition opposing dissolution purported to have been signed by 33,000 citizens of Chotanagpur Division.

Mr. Narayan told a press conference on June 17 that a point of no return had been reached as far as the demand for the dissolution of the Assembly and the resignation of the Ministry were concerned. However, he added, if the Assembly was dissolved the programme of paralysing the Government and the no-tax campaign might be suspended.

When I asked if he would be prepared to have a dialogue with the Congress leaders since they seemed agreeable to end corruption, Mr. Narayan said they were neither serious nor sincere because they had allowed the Santhanam Committee's report on corruption to gather dust without taking any action on its suggestions to root out corruption from administration.

He said: "I am ready to have talks with the Congress leaders at Delhi or with Mr. Ghafoor. I shall ask only one question: 'Are you going to drop the corrupt Ministers'? I know they won't. Then what is the point in having a talk?"

"Everybody knows", JP added, "that huge sums are collected for the Congress election fund. If I talk to the Congress leaders, I shall have to raise it and within two minutes the talks would fail".

He said: "Recently in Orissa rupees twenty lakhs was spent in the election of Mrs. Nandini Satpathy. But did anybody care to enquire from where the money came?"

Partyless Democracy

For Sometimes JP had also been advocating his idea of

partyless democracy. This had unnerved even leaders of political parties supporting his agitation. They felt that he wanted to put the clock of history back and secure the disbandment of all political parties. Some of them even challenged his theory while the CPI and the Congress ridiculed it.

Mr. Narayan explained at a press conference that by partyless democracy he meant that the people should have an effective control on their representatives in the legislature. He said there should be a strong peoples' committee in every constituency to see that their elected representatives served their interest. He felt the people were wide awake now and what was happening in Bihar was a mass upsurge. Whichever party came to power, it must be under the control of the electorate.

On June 18, Mr. Morarji Desai announced full support of his party Congress(O) to the JP-led agitation. Addressing a public meeting in Patna he also called upon his party MLAs to resign. He declared: "The end of the present corrupt regime brooks no delay." He also visited the Patna Central Jail and met the youths arrested for participation in the agitation.

Three days later, Mr. Narayan said at Allahabad that if the Bihar agitation failed, it would mean the end of democracy in the country. He said the entire country was on the verge of an explosion. If the mass upsurge in Bihar failed as in Gujarat after initial success, the people would be left without any hope. He also suggested Bihar type of agitation in UP. (JP was never enamoured of the Gujarat type agitation which began with a violent bang and ended in a whimper.)

The Congress leaders started accusing him, however, of undertaking tours "to set the country politically ablaze". In his inaugural address at the All India Youth Conference at Allahabad on June 22, Mr. Narayan said that any one could see that the country was already ablaze. The fire was already under the "chairs of power". It was undeniable that the people were groaning under the burden of soaring prices, rampant corruption and callousness of the rulers.

ELEVEN

Closure of Colleges

JP's call for the closure of colleges and universities of Bihar (scheduled to open in mid-July) for one year had unnerved a sizeable section of students and their guardians, some of whom had pleaded with him to exempt those who wanted to attend their classes and to appear at the university examinations. The students of technical institutions and medical colleges were also unhappy about it. The medical students had pointed out that besides studying and attending their classes they had to do ward duty in the hospitals and to attend to the patients.

But JP stuck to his stand and declined to withdraw his call to students to sacrifice one year of their career in the larger interest of society. He told a largely attended students' meeting at the Patna Law College on June 29: "I realise that those students, who are not with the movement and are concerned only with their career and personal interest, will lose a year. But I want these students and their guardians to consider if the larger interest of education and of the student community as a whole and the still larger interest of the State should be subordinate to their personal interests.

"Are not these students and their guardians also aware of the rampant corruption in the State and are they not too being crushed under the weight of ever-rising prices? Are they not also victims of misrule? Do they not also realise the futility of the present educational system? Do not these students too face the fearful prospect of unemployment? Do not they and their guardians also want a basic and fundamental change in the whole system of education? Are they too not opposed to the existing social and economic inequalities, exploitation and injustices?

"This is not the time, particularly for young men, to be idle spectators. They must plunge into the struggle. Examinations are important no doubt, but at certain moments of history there are other things more important than examinations and degrees."

Mr. Narayan also made it clear that he was not exempting even medical, engineering and technical colleges from his appeal for one year's closure.

Though he never resiled from his stand, Mr. Narayan later mellowed and did not insist on preventing students from appearing at the university examinations after the colleges opened. There was some contradiction in JP's stand with that of even leading activists of the Chhatra Sangharsh Samitis. These young man had been clamouring for the opening of the colleges and universities after these were closed following the disturbances of March 18. They felt that the agitation would gather momentum and strength only if the colleges and universities were opened because many students, who had left for their village homes, would return and participate in the movement.

Whether this expectation was correct or not is anybody's guess. But they had too much respect for the Lok Nayak to voice such views before him. Several of them, however, confided their feelings to me, and I believe, to others as well.

There was also trouble and police firings at Jamshedpur and Begusarai on July 18 after the colleges opened. Despite all the faults of the Kedar Pandey Ministry, it had one achievement to its credit. And that was its success in totally eliminating the use of unfair means at examinations. Mr. Pandey had done away with the autonomy of the universities and government had taken them over. His successor government decided to turn a blind eye to copying, passing of chits, impersonation *et al* at the examinations. This was the easiest way to bypass JP's call. The move succeeded to a great extent because there was rush to appear at the examinations since the majority of the students did not want to let go this golden opportunity to pass the examinations without tears. The situation became so ludicrous that many university teachers refused to undertake invigilation work because by trying to be strict they invited trouble upon themselves.

When the examinations began, there were some cases of

brickbatting and attempts to obstruct students willing to attend their classes and to sit for their examinations at several places on the very day JP returned to Patna on July 18 after a brief sojourn outside the State. Since he insisted that the agitators must remain peaceful, they became helpless and more and more students started appearing at the examinations. Official sources alleged, however, that at Begusarai and Jamshedpur, the agitators had resorted to violence to prevent examinees from appearing at their examinations. They also alleged that at Jamshedpur the police had been attacked with bombs and bows and arrows. The next day, on the basis of his own sources of information, Mr. Narayan blamed the police, agent provocateurs and the CPI, which was actively opposed to his agitation from the start, for whatever had occurred at Jamshedpur and Begusarai (both pockets of influence of CPI).

Mr. Narayan had known me for over three and a half decades. Naturally he had confidence in me. He also believed that as the local Bureau Chief of PTI, I was in a position to take an objective view of the overall situation. He used to call me occasionally for my appraisal of the situation. He wanted the "harshest" assessment. On one such occasion I had submitted to him that his blanket call for the closure of colleges was a mistake because barring those who were active participants in his agitation others would attend their classes and appear at the examinations though a section of them might join in processions and some other forms of demonstration from time to time. The majority of them would not, however, give up their studies for full one year. Besides, it would antagonise many guardians. There was another danger. The students might fight students since the youth wings of the Congress and of the CPI were already hostile. I had also pointed out that by allowing the students to use unfair means at the examinations the Government had already played a big mischief.

Mr. Narayan kept silent for a few seconds and then said that he was no longer insisting on preventing willing students from attending their classes or appearing at examinations. He said this when I pointed out that Mahatma Gandhi had given a similar call in the early twenties and JP himself had left his studies to join the non-cooperation movement. The Mahatma had not, however, asked those who responded to his call to prevent students intent on prosecuting their studies. They were not subjected to coercion but left undisturbed.

I also pointed out that the Mahatma did not allow the participation of minors in his movement. This needs explaining. After he had given his call for boycott of colleges and universities, JP also asked senior High School students to participate in the movement and suggested that even primary and middle school students could be utilised for a limited purpose like shouting slogans. Here JP was unyielding. He smiled and said: "They are Banar Senas" (monkey brigades which fought on the side of Rama against the demon king Ravana).

In retrospect one may still feel that the use of school students was possibly not justified. It is a debatable point but one could not expect JP who was aiming at "Sampurna Kranti" (total revolution), which meant total involvement of the people, to turn down willing cooperation from unspoilt youngsters for a systemic change in society, which, *inter alia*, meant abolition of the dowry system, casteism and all other social evils besides political and economic evils. With that end in view, he perhaps thought it was better to catch them young since cold and calculated mature adults, indulging in party and power politics, had done nothing over the years to make him feel enthusiastic about them.

Mr. Narayan's call had also scared a large section of college and university teachers, including those sympathetic to his movement several of whom had courted imprisonment. If the colleges and universities were to remain closed for one year about 20,000 employees, including teachers, would not get their salaries and starve with their families.

But he never withdrew his call. He stuck to his principle though he did not push matters too far. JP, who had asked the students to leave the colleges and universities and to "plunge into the agitation and to actively participate in it", later somewhat changed his stance to ensure that their studies did not suffer. He came out with a lengthy statement prepared by him and a number of educationists titled "New Dimensions in Bihar's Education". Unfortunately, this important document received little publicity in the newspapers for want of space. Even excerpts from it should help to set the record straight.

New Dimensions of Education

The statement said *inter alia*: "The first and the most urgent requirement is a programme of studies for those students who have responded to the call to devote a whole year to the movement, even at the cost of a year's formal attendance in colleges or university . . . Though . . . they have withdrawn from attendance to conventional institutions, they have not withdrawn from studies . . . They could, on their own or with such aid as may be devised pursue academic learning of at least the same level as their comperes in college and university, and add to it more relevant studies that relate to their learning to the pressing issues of the day. In addition, they will also be engaged in the political programme of the movement. It should be possible to integrate this three-fold activity in such a way that the students who have come away from their classes give themselves a richer education than the ones who stayed on.

"As a first step towards the implementation of this new education programme it is necessary to obtain certain information from the students concerned. This educational programme would require the cooperation of college and university teachers. I appeal to them for their cooperation and as a first step, to kindly answer the questionnaire below. While I make this appeal I am aware of the atmosphere of fear pervading the colleges and universities of Bihar. This pervading fear has already seriously eroded the dignity and worth of the noble profession of teaching and irretrievably damaged, if not destroyed the academic independence of the university. This fear has also abridged the personality of the individual teacher. Even more than the currently authorised and forced corruption at examinations has this general climate of academic demoralisation blighted the future of education in Bihar.

"But need there be this fear? Are not the teachers, principals and Vice-Chancellors being afraid of a mere shadow, a ghost? Do they not realise that if they unite to save their profession and the future of education and summon up enough courage and just cry a collective BOO! In the face of the ghost, it will melt away into nothingness. Happily, there is at least one Vice-Chancellor (Mr. Devendra Prasad Singh of Bhagalpur University) who has stood for the honour and dignity of his office and person, and quite a few teachers and principals who have stood their ground and refused to be accomplices in the degradation of their profession and of education. Some of them had paid the price in terms of prison and suspension from or loss of service. All honour to them. But what about the rest? This historic moment calls for an answer. If they act together, the entire student community of Bihar will stand behind them and no one will dare touch a hair on their head. May their conscience and professional honour guide them.

"I know that some university teachers' associations are controlled by persons whose political affiliations dispose them to be opposed to the present movement. But the question before them is not whether they are for or against this movement, but whether they too stand for the independence, dignity and honour of their profession and their university?

"While I do hope to receive the cooperation of college and university teachers, it is necessary to enlarge the teaching resources of this new programme. Accordingly, I appeal also for the cooperation of retired college and university teachers and such retired high school teachers as may have post-graduate degrees. I further appeal for the cooperation of such students with post-graduate degrees as may not have found any employment yet and thus may have a good deal of time at their hands.

"Being actively concerned now with basic changes in the present educational system, I have been meeting quite a number students and teachers so as to be able to understand the existing of system better. The most vital conclusion to which I have been driven is that the first requirement of a better and more meaningful education is the presence among young men and women a sincere desire for knowledge and skills. I have been appalled to find that only a small percentage of our students today are charged with such desire. The rest want nothing more than a degree, which is prized not for its educational but commercial value. A degree for most students is a mere passport to employment. Guardians and parents too have the same attitude towards education and degrees. The exceptions amongst students and guardians do not alter the general picture.

"Such being the true picture, no educational reform of a basic nature is possible unless either (a) degrees are abolished or (b) degrees are delinked from employment. Neither of these is going to happen in the next few months. They form more appropriately a part of the long-term educational project that the movement is attempting to work out. Here I am concerned with the immediate task of providing educational assistance to those students who have responded to the call of the movement and who would be wanting to go back to their colleges whenever the Pradesh Chhatra Sangharsh Samiti directs: possibly after the dissolution of the Legislative Assembly.

"I have every hope that this educational programme will assist the non-cooperating students to equip themselves sufficiently well to be able, whenever they return to college in accordance with the decision of the Bihar Pradesh Chhatra Sangharsh Samiti, to begin from the point they would have been at had they continued at college. Should an examination be due when they return to college, this programme should enable them to sit for it without, or at the most, with a brief preparation.

"As a high degree of dedication and high norms of conduct are expected from these students, I do hope that they will not indulge in the corrupt practices that the Bihar Government itself has recently encouraged, sanctioned and enforced.

"This assumes that the requirement of a minimum percentage of class-room attendance will be waived in the case of these students, who at present form about 80 per cent of the college and university students of Bihar. (JP's information was not correct because attendance was fairly good even if the tall claims of the Government were to be discounted.) Not only would such a requirement be an unnecessary formality, it would also be an affront to the students who for the first time since independence are fighting for issues of vital national importance and making such heroic sacrifices. In fact, it would be impossible for the authorities to enforce the attendance rule because they would be faced with the opposition of almost their entire student community.

"The university authorities would have also to take into account the fact that the present movement is itself an intensive school and those engaged in it are receiving an invaluable education of which group discussion and training camps are just a part. In addition, this programme will help them to study in some depth 'the passing issues of the day'. To begin with, discussion papers on corruption, inflation, unemployment, etc. (the very evils this movement is fighting against), will be circulated for group discussion. Questions raised at these discussions and not answered there may be sent to persons or institutions to be specified later.

"Lest this programme should be mistaken for the alternative plan of a more relevant and satisfying education, let me stress again that it is intended to do no more than help the students who may be either actively or passively engaged in the movement to resume their academic careers, within the existing systemi tself, without loss of time or studies. While doing this the present programme is intended also—as explained above—to enrich their education with additional studies and the experience gained from the movement."

Blue-print for Action

Although the achievements of the peoples' struggle spearheaded by the Jana Sangharsh and Chhatra Sangharsh Samitis had so far been considerable, JP felt it was not enough. He felt that wherever the Jana Sangharsh and Chhatra Sangharsh Samitis had been organised, the struggle had achieved some success. In his view the movement was still disorganised. He wanted it to be fully organised throughout the State from the village to the State level because his aim was total revolution. In consultation with leaders of the Sangharsh Samitis and Sarvodaya workers, he drew up a detailed programme by expanding his programme of June 5. He prepared its blue-print in Calcutta and released it in Patna after the programme of satyagraha before the Assembly was called off.

He directed that Sangharsh Samitis (both Jana and Chhatra) should be formed without delay in every Panchayat, block, subdivision and district to work for "total revolution" peacefully. Only active participants in the struggle should join these Samitis and their convenors must not belong to any political party. They should be independents. He stressed that this was a must. He also directed that similar Samitis should be formed in every constituency so that they would be able to play an important role when the elections were held. He insisted that there should be at least one Jana Sangharsh and one Chhatra Sangharsh

Samiti for every booth functioning under an apex organisation in every constituency, whose convenor also must be an independent and not a partyman. These Samitis should function as sentinels of democracy. The Panchayat, Block and Zilla Samitis would awaken the political consciousness of the people and espouse their cause. In the constituencies they would select the candidates for contesting the elections. If their nominees after being returned failed to serve them, the Constituency Samitis would have the right to recall them and replace them. JP said this was necessary to build up "Lok Shakti" (the peoples' power) for the success of democracy. The Samitis should also offer satyagraha wherever necessary, and carry on the no-tax campaign vigorously to paralyse the government and bring about its collapse.

From August 1 the movement should aim at completely paralysing the government by ensuring suspension of work in all government offices and non-payment of taxes. The Samitis should see to it that not a paisa was paid by the villagers towards land rent, water rent, etc. Agricultural loans should not be repaid. The non-cooperation of the people with the government should be total. In the cities and towns excise shops should be vigorously picketted by satyagrahis because excise was a big source of government revenue. Addicts should also be persuaded to give up taking drugs and alcohol as it was ruinous for them. Satyagraha should also be offered before government licensing agencies as these were another source of government revenue. Cooperation of the government employees should be sought for paralysing government work in the blocks, subdivisions and districts. It should be explained to government employees that the agitation was meant for their good as it sought to replace the present rotten system with a better system of administration.

JP exempted from the purview of this programme courts, banks, railways, post and telegraph offices, supply and rationing offices and the like as these concerned the everyday life of the people. This exemption was necessary because the Samitis should not do anything which cause unnecessary inconvenience to the people. For the same reason, he also exempted the Patna Secretariat for the time being, particularly because visitation of floods had already been reported.

Other tasks given to the Samitis by JP included: (1) prevention of profiteering, blackmarketing and hoarding from the village to the State level; (2) careful watch on the functioning of the ration shops and government distribution agencies to ensure that they functioned properly (he felt women were best suited for this task); (3) holding of processions and demonstrations in the constituencies to put pressure on members of the Assembly who had not resigned; and (4) peaceful gherao of the MLAs in their village homes at the conclusion of the session of the Assembly on July 12 (gherao of family members of MLAs, however, was banned). He suggested that at least fifteen public meetings should be held in every constituency where resolutions should be passed demanding the resignation of MLAs and copies sent to the Governor and the headquarters of the Samiti in Patna.

He also outlined a special programme for the observance of Lokmanya Tilak's birthday on August 1, "The August Revolution Day" on August 9 and the Independence Day on August 15. He said: "Tilak's birthday should be observed by fasting for the whole day and holding public meetings in the evening where the people should take pledges not to indulge in any corrupt practice themselves and to raise their voice against corruption wherever it existed.

August Revolution Day (the day on which the Quit India resolution was passed) should be observed by taking out *prabhat Pheries* in every town and village in the morning and holding public meetings in the evening to explain the purpose of total revolution. JP said that though freedom had been achieved 27 years ago, its fruits had not reached the masses yet. It could be achieved only when a society free from exploitation and repression was established. This, he has always held, was the main object of the movement. The resignation of the Ministry or the dissolution of the Assembly was not the end but only one of the means or stages. Stress was being laid on this means only because the Ministry and the Assembly were proving to be a hurdle to achieving the end. He made it clear that when he had given the call for closure of colleges and universities for one year, he did not want it to be a holiday. He wanted that the revolution he aimed at was to be brought about within this period.

JP concluded by saying: "We have started our journey on a new road to peaceful revolution. . . There is no greater power than the power of the people. It is our duty to arouse that dormant power. Our only hope lies in it. The future of Bihar, nay that of India, lies in the consolidation of the organised power of the masses. We are ordinary people but we have undertaken a Herculean task. We have to take every step with patience and courage. The future is ours. I am confident of our victory."

TWELVE

Examinations : A Farce

The Chhatra Sangharsh Samiti had not remained a silent spectator to the encouragement given by the Bihar Government to the largescale use of unfair means in the university examinations. On July 21 nineteen students, including Sushil Kumar Mody, General Secretary of the Patna University Students' Union and a member of the Steering Committee of the Samiti, were arrested by the police for launching a fast before the Bihar National College in Patna in protest against the encouragement given to intermediate examinees to use unfair means. Mody was detained under the MISA and the others on the charge of attempting to commit suicide by fasting!

On August 1, in observance of Tilak Day, JP addressed a mammoth public meeting at Patna City at Gandhi Sarovar in the midst of a downpour. He reiterated his demand for the resignation of the Bihar Ministry and the dissolution of the Assembly. He also pointed out that the Government had reduced the university examinations to a farce. He charged the government of encouraging the students to use unfair means. Examinees were being even allowed to carry their answer books home to get the answers written there. He produced a bunch of such answer books collected by members of the Samiti from the residences of some of the examinees.

Next day addressing another huge gathering in the midst of heavy rains at Chukker Maidan in Muzaffarpur, he called upon the voters in every constituency to hold meetings and pass votes of confidence against their representatives who had not resigned till then. He also asked the youths to gherao the residences of the MLAs and secure their resignations. He complimented students who had refused to attend their classes or appear at the university examinations despite the alluring bait thrown by the government.

On August 4 the CPI(M) leader Jyoti Basu announced at a press conference at Jamshedpur support of his party to the demands of Mr. Narayan, including the dissolution of the State Assembly. He said his own party was not able to participate in the agitation because parties like the Jana Sangh and the Congress(O) were associated with it. He maintained that the voters had every right to recall corrupt legislators from the Assembly. But he differed with JP's call for boycott of colleges and universities for one year. Rather the students should attend the colleges and organise campaigns to paralyse the government. But he advised the students not to attend the colleges and universities till the police were withdrawn from their campuses.

Although the Bhartiya Lok Dal formed subsequently lent full support to JP's movement, initially one of its main constituents, the Swatantra Party, was divided over the issue when it met at New Delhi on August 5. The President of the Swatantra Party, Mr. Piloo Mody, told reporters that the party had authorised him to dissolve it and merge with the proposed Bhartiya Lok Dal to be launched on August 29.

Mr. Minoo Masani, a former President of the Swatantra Party, told a separate press conference that JP's non-party movement and not the BLD could be the national alternative to the Congress.

Picketing of liquor shops was resorted to by Samiti volunteers from the beginning of August all over the State. Processions were also taken out exhorting the people not to pay entertainment tax for going to cinema houses. The picketing was so successful that many liquor shops remained closed for days together. So much so that by August 21 an official spokesman was forced to admit that it was causing on an average loss of rupees two lakhs in excise revenue every day. Picketing of excise shops also led to an amusing side effect—increase in illicit distillation of country liquor in the tribal areas of Santhal Parganas.

The Samiti volunteers also launched dehoarding operations. To take the wind out of the sails of the agitators, the Congress Working Committee directed partymen all over the country, particularly in Bihar, to undertake dehoarding drives. The result of the Congress drive, not unexpectedly, was poor. But the Samiti drive too created problems because of the overzealousness of its workers who wanted to make a spectacular show. They could catch but few big hoarders. On the other hand, they created trouble for many retailers. To gain papularity, they forced retailers to sell foodgrains at rates lower than the prices at which they had bought from the village Mandis. Long queues of consumers soon exhausted the stocks of the retailers whose shops had been raided by the volunteers. After that the retailers refused to bring fresh stocks because they could not be expected to sell at a loss. The overzealous dehoarders realised their mistake and stopped this practice. The prices however, did not come down in the towns.

Prabhat pheries (early morning exhortations to the people through songs by small groups of youths) and processions were taken out in Patna and elsewhere on August 9 in observance of August Revolution Day, which was also observed as Martyrs' Day. In Patna the main procession taken out by the Chhatra Sangharsh Samiti terminated at the Martyrs' Memorial before the Secretariat where seven young men had been killed in police firing in August, 1942. A public meeting was held there and resolutions were passed demanding the resignation of the Ministry and dissolution of the Assembly. Mass fasts from sunrise to sunset were also organised in observance of the Day all over the State.

For the first time in 27 years students and youths (supporting the agitation) boycotted the official celebrations of the Independence Day on August 15. They held parallel celebrations in various parts of Bihar. Fifteen students were arrested in Patna while holding such a celebration at the Martyrs' Memorial. At Hazaribagh the national flag was hoisted at a parallel celebration by a poor 85-year old farmer, Manki Mahto. With tears in his eyes he said in halting language that year after year he was finding the lot of the poor going from bad to worse due to Congress misrule. He said the youths had done the right thing by launching a struggle under the leadership of Mr. Narayan.

The State Congress then decided to launch its counterattack. The Union Railway Minister, Mr. Lalit Narain Mishra, alleged at a meeting of the Bihar Pradesh Congress Committee held on August 18 that the agitation launched by Mr. Narayan was part of an "international conspiracy to weaken the socialist nations". He also said that the agitation was an open attack on the democratic functioning of the government. He warned Bihar Congressmen not to treat it lightly because its real aim was overthrow of Congress Governments in the States as well as at the Centre. The PCC President, Mr. Sitaram Keshari, MP, also spoke in the same vein.

The PCC adopted a resolution moved by Mr. Ram Lakhan Singh Yadav, MLA, which described the JP-led agitation as part of a conspiracy to usher in fascism in the country. It said the forces behind the movement were afraid of social, economic and other development efforts, which were hurting the vested interests. Mr. Radha Nandan Jha, MLA alleged that before the agitation was launched a CIA agent had undertaken a three-day tour of Bihar. Whether they themselves believed in these allegations may be doubted. But there is no doubt that they were afraid of the movement and their *raison d'etre* in danger.

THIRTEEN

Confrontation with Delhi

At JP's call on August 23rd. Black Day was observed. It included a 12-hour mass fast in protest against the "repression let loose on peaceful satyagrahis by the government". JP himself led the fast before he left for Lucknow by the evening train. A procession was also taken out in the evening by Samiti volunteers wearing black arm-bands. When they attempted to hold a public meeting, they were lathi-charged by the CRP. Four of them were arrested.

The next day, inaugurating the Uttar Pradesh Youth and Student Conference at Lucknow, JP challenged the Prime Minister and the Congress President, Dr. Shankar Dayal Sharma, to hold a referendum on the issue of the dissolution of the Bihar Assembly. He said Bihar was on fire. How long would the people tolerate tyranny? If the movement in Bihar remained peaceful and became successful, he added, it would lead to peaceful revolution in other parts of the country also.

JP declared: "I have no doubt what the verdict of the people of Bihar will be at the next elections, be it to the Assembly or to the Lok Sabha. I hope I shall be alive to witness it."

He advised the youths and students of Uttar Pradesh not to go in for the Gujarat type of agitation but to launch a Bihar type of peaceful agitation.

The pace of the agitation in Bihar, however, slowed down because north Bihar was devastated by one of the worst floods affecting a population of six and a half million people. Large parts of south Bihar on the other hand were affected by acute drought necessitating the declaration of Chotanagpur Division as a "scarcity area". The floods, of which there were several visitations, continued in the month of September. The army had to be called out to help in relief and rescue operations after mid-September.

Congressmen, however, did very little to provide relief except issuing statements. The pro-changers and no-changers were more preoccupied with infighting than with relief. JP undertook tours of the flood-devastated areas several times and called upon Jana and Chhatra Sangharsh Samitis to undertake relief work in the month of August itself long before the army's help was sought by the government. He suggested the rural workers of the Samitis to arrange for the supply of drinking water and to render any other relief they could organise. He wanted medical students to render medical relief and the engineering students to help in the construction of houses of flood-sufferers after the recession of floods. He also deputed a three-member team to assist the Jana Sangharsh and Chhatra Sangharsh Samitis in flood relief work.

It was decided, however, to intensify the struggle from October 2, the birthday of Mahatma Gandhi. The decision was taken at a meeting of the consultative committee of the representatives of political parties supporting the movement. JP attended it. The programme drawn up by the Committee envisaged general strike, bundhs, and dharna before government offices. The aim of the programme was to paralyse work in all government and semi-government offices and institutions. The representatives of the SSP, the Jana Sangh, the Socialist Party and the Congress(O) decided to make necessary preparations for the intensified struggle.

The programme envisaged more and more involvement of small farmers, landless workers, harijans, adibasis, muslims and women in the struggle. It laid down some socio-economic objectives like land to the landless, fair wages for agricultural labourers, lowering of land rent and water rates and ending usurious money-lending by mahajans in the villages. The Jana and Chhatra Sangharsh Samitis were directed to build up their organisations from the Panchayat Upwards.

JP gave a call to the people to enrol as satyagrahis for the movement to paralyse the government to be launched from October 2. Subsequently, a call was given for a three-day Bihar bundh commencing October 3.

The Union Home Minister, Mr. Dikshit, reiterated on

September 3 the Government of India's decision that in no circumstances the Bihar Assembly would be dissolved. Replying to a 4-hour debate on the Bihar situation in Lok Sabha, he observed that it was JP who had "confused the situation".

Replying to Mr. Dikshit's charge at a public meeting in Patna City on September 9, JP said he would be prepared to call off the agitation if the Government came to terms with the students and arrived at an agreement.

That day the entire opposition had walked out of the Lok Sabha in protest against the Home Minister's unsatisfactory reply on the continuance of external emergency promulgated on December 3, 1971, though the Prime Minister had stated sometime ago that there was no war emergency any longer. Mr. Dikshit had taken the stand that the emergency provisions were being used only to deal with economic offenders. The walk out was staged after Mr. S. N. Mishra (Cong.) and Mr. Atal Bihari Vajpayee (Jana Sangh) had angrily protested that the reasons given by Mr. Dikshit were strange because the external emergency was declared in the context of external aggression from the side of Pakistan. Long after that cause had been removed, the Government was putting forward the plea of economic offences. The opposition strongly suspected it would be used against political workers.

Mr. Narayan foresaw that the reluctance of the powers that to be end the external emergency was merely a prelude to something more serious. But at that stage even JP could not foresee the promulgation of internal emergency to crush the movement. He had been speaking against the continuance of external emergency at public meetings but he could not believe or perhaps realise that Mrs. Gandhi would throw all democratic norms to the winds and turn a dictator. He did, of course, expect to be arrested and detained. In fact, he frequently referred to his impending arrest. His supporters were already being arrested in large numbers. The jails of Bihar had virtually been stuffed with prisoners, who had to sleep by rotation and queues before the toilet were never-ending. The feeling was growing that he would have to carry the confrontation to Delhi.

A statement issued by JP in Patna gives vent to these forebodings: "The Bihar struggle is no longer a State issue. It has acquired an all-India importance and the country's fate has come to be bound up with its success or failure. At the moment when the Bihar struggle is about to enter a decisive phase and particularly in view of the fact that it is not confronted with the tottering government of Bihar but with the power of Delhi itself, the support of other States would take a more decisive form and its direction too should be towards Delhi."

"The dissolution of the Bihar Assembly", he added, "has become a categorical imperative of the struggle not only because it is with the Assembly's implicit and explicit support that the present corrupt, inefficient and oppressive Ministry has been functioning, but also because the Congress High Command has reduced the Assembly to an unnecessary burdensome costly farce. The chief function of a legislature is to legislate. But the Bihar Assembly has abdicated its legislative powers and handed them over to the executive, which has been ruling with the help of ordinances. Even taxes have been levied by ordinances. The rule by ordinances reached the limit of ridiculousness when the very day the Assembly was prorogued no less than fourteen ordinances were promulgated.

"The Ministry and the Assembly would have disappeared from the scene months ago in view of the overwhelming demand of the people. That they have not gone yet is due to the fact that the Centre, and the Prime Minister in particular, has made this an issue of prestige. This is like cutting the nose to spite the face, because the longer this Ministry and the Assembly lasts, the lower and still lower will the prestige of the Congress sink."

"The students and peoples' struggle in Bihar", JP said, "is poised for a decisive offensive to be launched on October 2. It is only right that the date should be Gandhiji's birthday because in reality the Bihar movement aims at completing the revolution that Gandhiji's assassination had abruptly left unfinished. In the past 27 years the country has been led by the powers that be in Delhi farther and farther away from the path and the goals of the Father of the Nation . . . The struggle in Bihar is attempting to bring the country back to the path from which it has been led astray.

"Though the aims of the movement can be realised only in a peaceful total revolution *i.e.* when basic social, economic, political and cultural changes are brought about in society, the exigencies of the struggle have so dictated that resignation of the Bihar Ministry and dissolution of the State Assembly has become its immediate goals after which it would be possible for the students and the people to concentrate on the long-term ends of the struggle."

FOURTEEN

Bihar Bundh Violence

During the unprecedented three-day Bihar Bundh commencing October 3 life in most parts of the State was completely paralysed. Buses, taxis, cycle-rickshaws and tandems remained off the roads. The shops and markets were all closed. The trains did not move on the Eastern and North Eastern Railways in Bihar because of large-scale squatting on railway tracks, removal of fish plates, tampering with tracks and disruption of tele-communications. Train services of the North East Frontier Railway were also seriously affected. Only the South Eastern Railway remained unaffected.

Work in government offices from State to the Block level came to a grinding halt. In Patna in the old Secretariat attendance of employees, other than officers, was negligible. It was slightly better in the new Secretariat. Life remained normal only in Singhbhum district, and partially normal in Ranchi district. In both these districts the Youth Congress was active and commanded influence because it had been fighting for popular causes without caring for the frowns of the government and the party bosses. It too had been campaigning for the removal of corrupt Ministers and bureaucrats.

JP described the Bundh as "remarkably successful and peaceful". Considering the size of the State, the number of violent incidents were much less than what he had feared. He also pointed out that even during Mahatma Gandhi's time it had not been possible wholly to prevent violence.

The Chief Minister, Mr. Abdul Ghafoor, said that the people had closed their shops and establishments not out of love for the agitators but out of fear. JP's reply to it at a press conference was that "Ghafoor is either living in a fool's paradise or wants deliberately to believe in made-up stories".

But mob violence did erupt in different parts of the State resulting in police firings at Patna City, Ekma, Masrakh, Dighwara, Tribeniganj, Bidhupur, Patahi, Sasaram, Bhavanipur, Gidhaur, Narpatganj and two other places. At least a dozen persons were killed and many injured, according to official reports. Patna City (east Patna) was the scene of the worst disturbances. Repeated tear-gassing, lathi-charges and firings from riot guns (for the first time in Bihar) failed to dislodge a 10,000 strong mob which had taken control of the Patna City railway station and made movement of trains impossible by squatting on the tracks. Sections of the mob also set on fire the east cabin and the nearby Begumpur post office. Four persons were officially reported to have been killed (riot guns having proved ineffective because rubber pellets had been used heavy rifle fire was soon resorted to and at least sixty injured) Strong rumours spread in the town that many more had been killed and this led to mounting tension. Mr. Jagbandhu Adhikari, MLC, General Secretary of the State Jana Sangh, put the figure of deaths as high as 50 on the strength of information supplied by his party workers. (An unofficial committee set up by JP in its report held after that at least 10 persons had been killed and 200 injured in Patna City.)

Mr. Narayan himself declined to give figures of casualties on the basis of insufficient data. But when he went to Patna City to address a public meeting on October 10, he went round the scenes of disturbances and discouraged the circulation of idle rumours and said that it was no good saying that many people had been killed and that their bodies had been disposed of in ponds and ditches. He said if more persons were killed, their relatives should be able to say how many were missing. Such information should be collected and submitted to a team of lawyers appointed by him to enquire into the police firings.

(I have been an eye-witness to several police firings. From personal experience I can say that the figures of death generally tend to be exaggerated because it is not possible to distinguish which victim has been killed and which injured. What happens is that when people shot down start falling, the police dump them on trucks or vans before the eyes of hundreds of people. Naturally even eye-witnesses tend to err.)

This does not mean that the police do not spirit away bodies of the dead to keep the figure of the number of persons killed low though, to my knowledge and in my long experience, this has not happened in Bihar. But it does happen in other States like, say, West Bengal. On the night of the Patna City police firing, one of my classmates, who held the rank of a Commissioner, telephoned me to enquire if it was true that many had been killed and that the bodies had been removed and disposed off. I was annoyed and I told him: "You have been in charge of several districts as well as a Division. There have been police firings in your jurisdiction. How many bodies did you get disposed of surreptitiously?" He replied that to the best of his knowledge he knew of no such case in Bihar and added: "Of course, I have never ordered removal of bodies for surreptitious disposal to keep the figures of firing deaths down."

Another old friend, a retired high-ranking police official of West Bengal, who was with me at the time and was listening to our talk on the telephone, felt amused. After I replaced the receiver, he turned to me and said: "I congratulate you on browbeating your friend. But your assumption is, unfortunately, wrong. In West Bengal the police have been adepts in clandestine disposal of bodies for a fairly long time." I was taken aback when he named a highly respected politician of that State, long since deceased, who first started ordering the disposal of bodies on the theory "no bodies, no evidence". To this day I do not know if he was pulling my leg or if he was serious though I do not think he was lying.

Mob violence also led to the imposition of curfew in at least six towns, including Patna City, where it was imposed at 1 p.m. on October 5 and lifted on October 8. It was relaxed only for a few hours every day till the situation became near-normal.

The main targets of mob fury were the Eastern and North Eastern Railways. In the muffasil areas violence broke out as the consequence of gheraos of block offices or police stations but it was not planned as in the case of the railways. Dynamite was used in attempts to blow up bridges near Barauni and Falgu. In Barauni timely detection prevented explosion and damage. At Falgu, in Gaya district, the dynamite did not explode as it had not been properly packed. On the Eastern Railway signalling equipment were damaged at 34 stations, eight signal posts uprooted and telephone wires cut in almost all sections in Dinapore Division. Telephone cables of the Posts and Telegraph Department on the Grand Chord section were also cut at many places. Several railway cabins were set on fire. The most disturbed area from the point of view of the Eastern Railway's Grand Chord section was Rohtas district.

On the North Eastern Railway the tracks had been tampered with or uprooted at 105 places during the three-day Bundh. The Pasraha-Maheshkhunt section was the worst affected. On the third and last day of the Bundh the railway track had been uprooted at 22 places in this section. Other badly affected spots listed by a spokesman of the Railway were Narayanpur in Chapra section, Thana Bihpur in Mansi section and Teghra in Barauni section. On this section many railway cabins were also damaged.

But even the worst critics of Mr. Narayan did not suggest that he had instigated the violence. In fact before leading a procession of satyagrahis to offer dharna before the Secretariat on October 5, JP reminded his followers that "whatever be the provocation, we shall not lift our hands in retaliation". Ironically enough at that very moment the Patna City railway station was under siege by a huge mob which had already set fire to the east cabin and a nearby post office and indulged in heavy brickbatting.

Mr. Ghafoor alleged that the movement was no longer under Mr. Narayan's control and that it had passed into the hands of disparate elements who had rallied under his banner only to serve their own ends by using him as a cover. This was only partly true and, therefore, misleading. JP was still in control. This was clearly proved on June 5 when the Indira Brigade opened fire and yet there was no retaliation from the huge JP-led procession. But as JP himself had pointed out that in a State of the size of Bihar violence could not be avoided everywhere. He had also pointed out that even Mahatma Gandhi could not achieve complete non-violence in the movements he had launched.

He had on the other hand charged that wherever violence

had occurred, it had been provoked by the Government in conspiracy with the CPI, a conspiracy, which, according to his information, had been hatched in the presence of Mr. Ghafoor. To this Mr. Ghafoor's reply was: "It is strange that the CPI, whose central leaders went in a delegation and met the Prime Minister in Delhi recently and demanded my head on a charger, should conspire with me all the while attacking me personally in the strongest possible language and demanding my ouster. The CPI has its own axe to grind against me personally. Everybody knows it. Only JP does not."

As to the peaceful nature of the agitation, Mr. Ghafoor sarcastically observed: "How peaceful it was, newspaper reports have already recorded. It was so peaceful that tele-communications were cut, fish-plates removed from railway tracks, cabins set on fire and even dynamite used for disrupting rail communications. Many railway and police stations and block offices were attacked. There was also large-scale arson. At Begusarai the telephone exchange was raided by masked men carrying fire-arms who set it on fire."

Top Congress leaders alleged that the movement had passed into the hands of the Ananda Marg and the RSS. Mr. Narayan himself found nothing wrong with the association of the RSS with his movement though he disclaimed any knowledge of the participation of the followers of the Ananda Marg.

The question still remained, who were actually fanning or committing violence? JP held the Government, the CPI and agent provocateurs responsible for it. But these were not the only elements operating behind the scenes even if the charge was partly true.

Mr. Satya Narain Singh, leader of one faction of the Naxalites, was in sympathy with JP's movement and had met him more than once. I know this because Satya Narain used to visit me at odd hours if and when he found an opportunity by eluding the police. Though a diabetic, he looked like a Chambal Valley dacoit. But he was very gentle and, for a revolutionary, sweet-tongued. He was also well-read in extremist literature and had a remarkable knowledge of current affairs, both national and international. His leanings then were definitely pro-Mao Tse Tung. From his talks it was clear that JP was not prepared to take his help unless he promised to eschew violence completely. Though he was fully convinced that power could come only through the barrel of the gun, he used to tell me: "For us it is not a question of violence or non-violence. It all depends upon the exigencies of the situation." He respected JP for his total faith in non-violence, but, I think, he preferred to decide for himself the exigency of a given situation. Satya Narain and his group might not have been openly in the thick of the agitation but it was not altogether improbable that they were operating on its periphery.

Satya Narain came to me on October 6 and issued a statement congratulating the people of Bihar for the successful "heroic Bundh". He said: "It is our firm conviction, however, that the Congress Government, which represents big landlords and big capitalists and serves foreign imperialism would never understand the language of peaceful satyagraha. We are sure the large masses of the people will inevitably draw correct lessons for further intensification of their struggle to oust the Indira regime lock, stock and barrel."

There was another group of young hot-heads. On June 25 a self-styled "Armed Revolutionary Students' Organisation" circulated a pamphlet in Bihar rejecting the peaceful agitation led by JP and threatening to launch armed struggle to "dislodge the corrupt Ministry and demolish the establishment".

While placing on record their regard for JP, they declared: "We differ from the non-violent means adopted by Mr. Narayan because we know Mrs. Indira Gandhi's dictatorship would crush all democratic forms of struggle." Their stand was controversial but their foresight prophetic.

The Bihar Government ignored this pamphlet, a news item about which had also been published in a section of the local press, as the outpourings of some eccentric youths. But a year later after the promulgation of the emergency a frantic search for a copy of this pamphlet was launched by teams of Central Intelligence men. They visited every news agency and newspaper office several times, questioning and prodding and trying to find if it could be traced in our files. No newspaper or news agency office can maintain for long the originals of all the stuff that come to its office for coverage unless they are of a controversial nature about which questions might be raised in future or the material is such that it might become evidence in a court case. After some months these are thrown away in the normal course. The search proved, however, that the threat had been taken quite seriously and an attempt was being made to trace those who circulated it by detecting the press which had printed it.

Bihar Government spokesmen, including the Chief Minister, Mr. Ghafoor, used to poohpooh the scope and extent of the agitation quite often. But the Central Congress leaders did not take it so lightly. The sudden airdash of the Congress President, Dr. Shankar Dayal Sharma, on the last day of the three-day Bundh, proved their concern. Dr. Sharma said on his arrival in Patna that the Congress would fight the agitation in Bihar "tooth and nail". He alleged that it was being led by the RSS, the Ananda Marg and anti-democratic forces who were out to disrupt democracy in India and were playing into the hands of those who wanted to de-stabilise the established government. He described the movement as "anti-national and anti-people". "The attempt to disrupt communications exposes the evil designs and the anti-people nature of this movement", he said.

At JP's suggestion 24-hour relay fasts were organised by batches of satyagrahis before the Bihar Assembly gates for 11 days commencing on October 7. About 1,200 satyagrahis participated in these fasts. The satyagrahis included JP, Mr. Siddharaj Dhaddha, President, All India Sarva Seva Sangh, Mr. Mahamaya Prasad Sinha, Mrs. Sarala Bhadoria, MP, Mr. Satyendra Narain Sinha, MP, Mr. Basawan Sinha, socialist leader, and Mr. Jagbandhu Adhikari, MLC, General Secretary of the State Jana Sangh.

FIFTEEN

Patna Chalo

JP announced on October 14 a four-fold programme of action after watching the situation, two of which were continuing actions while two were new. The programme to paralyse administrative work in Government offices from Block to district levels was to be continued. Courts would be allowed to function. Government offices and departments directly concerned with the people's welfare would also be allowed to function for as long as might be necessary. The programme to keep liquor shops and depots closed would also continue. Taxes were not to be paid.

Wherever the movement had gained enough strength, the programme of people's administration would be implemented. People's administration would function at village, Panchayat and Block levels or at any of the three levels. All the adults in a village would constitute the Gram Sabha. Village representatives would constitute the Panchyat Jana Sabha. One elected representative or Mukhiya from each Panchayat would constitute the Block Jan Sabha, Gram Sabhas and Jan Sabhas would elect Sanchalaks (directors) to be responsible for different types of work. All elections, as far as possible, would be held by consensus. JP was laying the foundation of the society which would help bring about "Sampurna Kranti" or total revolution.

In the first phase, the main task of the people's administration would be boycott of police stations and organisation of Gram Shanti Dals for the prevention of crimes, distribution of essential commodities at fair price, building up of a proper atmosphere in the village for equal treatment to Harijans and prevention of their eviction from homesteads, and attempts to increase employment opportunities. The people's administrations were to take up other programmes to serve the people according to local needs. No one was to be punished or humiliated in any way. Social boycott might, however, be imposed. Youth would be given prominence at every level and adequate representation given to women, Harijans, muslims, adibasis and the poor in general. People's administration would function with the help of voluntary contributions but taxes might be paid to it if so decided by consensus.

He gave a "Patna Chalo" call for a massive demonstration of people's power on November 4 in Patna to force the Ministry and Assembly to go. He wanted lakhs of men and women from all over the State to march to Patna and gherao the residences of Ministers and legislators. The gherao was to start at 12 noon on November 4 and end on the morning of November 5.

JP said if the State Assembly was not dissolved even after the demonstration on November 4, steps would be taken to call a People's Assembly. Legislators, who had resigned their seats in deference to the people's demand, would represent their respective constituencies. In the remaining constituencies convenors and two representatives each from Panchayat Chhatra and Jana Sangharsh Samitis elected by consensus, as far as possible, would constitute a constituency council. They would select their representative. He said the details of the programme to call a People's Assembly would be announced later (this he could not do as the confrontation with Delhi led to the promulgation of internal emergency to crush all opposition to a ruthless regime).

On October 18 the Coordination Committee of the political parties supporting the movement declared in a resolution at a meeting held in Patna that it had enough evidence in hand to indicate that there was a high level conspiracy between the leadership of the ruling Congress and the CPI in Bihar under direct instructions and guidance from their respective central leadership to create situations of violence to defame and, if possible, to disrupt the peaceful people's struggle. It claimed that many instances of violence and sabotage by the CPI had come to its knowledge, the latest being the discovery in the house of a CPI worker in Patna City of a large store of dynamite and other explosives and material for manufacturing bombs. It was curious, said the Committee, that no action had been taken against him by the police.

The Committee cautioned the people to be on their guard against this conspiracy. It maintained that peaceful militancy of the people would be the only fitting reply to those who thought that a people's movement could be subverted through violence and sabotage.

Counter-Offensive

It was becoming clearer and clearer every day that the confrontation of the movement was no longer with the Bihar Ministry but with the Central Ministry. The Congress Working Committee itself underscored this by taking a "firm decision" to launch a nation-wide counter-offensive. The CWC, which met in Delhi on October 15 under the chairmanship of its provisional President, Mr. Debkant Barooah, declared in a unanimous resolution that the Bihar type movement was a threat to parliamentary democracy in the country.

Mr. Barooah, who had been Governor of Bihar before he resigned to become a Central Minister, flew into Patna on October 28, met partymen and sought to make Bihar itself a launching pad for the Congress counter-offensive. He declared after the CWC meeting that "the CPI and all other progressive parties, which believed in parliamentary democracy, will be associated with the counter-offensive". He maintained that the Bihar movement led by JP posed a grave danger to the functioning of parliamentary democracy and the working of the Constitution not only in Bihar but also in other States.

On the same day, Chief Minister Abdul Ghafoor alleged in Patna that the agitation was being run on the Chilean pattern to overthrow the government of duly elected representatives of the people. He did not elaborate. Inaugurating a two-day State Anti-Fascist Conference, he said that to call the movement a students' agitation was a "big fraud" because several political parties were operating under its cover "to achieve something else". He also accused the students of indulging in violence while paying lip-service to *ahimsa* (non-violence). He complained that during the three-day Bihar Bundh no less than 285 violent incidents had occurred involving the use of bombs and crackers in 35 cases.

Mr. Ghafoor said if JP withdrew the agitation and stuck to Gandhian ideals, he would be prepared to resign. If not, Mr. Narayan could carry on the agitation for hundred years without achieving his object of dissolution of the Assembly. He said he had thought during the initial stages of the movement that JP genuinely wanted some reforms. So he (Mr. Ghafoor) had requested JP to support him in fighting corruption. But as the movement continued and spread it became clear to him that what JP wanted was the ouster of the Prime Minister, Mrs. Indira Gandhi. The gaff was meant to discredit JP, which has been always the official Congress policy.

Speeches delivered at the Conference were highly critical of Mr. Narayan. The Secretary of the All India Anti-Communal Committee, Mr. D. R. Goel, went to the length of suggesting that the movement was being financed by the CIA because Mr. Narayan was the Vice-President of the Congress for Cultural Freedom, which, he alleged, was a CIA-sponsored body.

(The charge was maliciously false because the movement was financed by donations from the public. JP used to be presented with fat purses at public meetings wherever he went. In fact, the problem of money had become so acute that he had to undertake more tours than his health would permit.)

JP's response to the tirade against him and his movement was an open threat made at a public meeting at Biharsharif that if the Assembly was not dissolved by December 3, the birthday of Dr. Rajendra Prasad, he would be obliged to carry the agitation to Delhi, the seat of despotism.

Mr. Barooah, on the other hand, busied himself with chalking out the party strategy to counter and contain the agitation. He directed, on October 23, all Congress units in various States to organise meetings and rallies as part of their counter-offensive.

On October 27 the Prime Minister, Mrs. Gandhi, solemnly warned the people against attempts to undermine their faith in free elections, communal solidarity and socialist policies. The warning was contained in a message to a seminar on "Socialism, Democracy and the Public Sector" held in New Delhi. Its main purpose, however, was to discuss JP's movement and to decry it. In an easy-to-identify reference to JP, the Prime Minister said that his agitation was being backed by elements which were openly communal and anti-socialist. She said a concerted propaganda had been let loose to paint a picture of all-pervading corruption in the country.

Mrs. Gandhi went on to say: "All those who feel concerned for secular and socialist democracy should unite to withstand this onslaught and to make the people realise that the real motive of the agitation is to take advantage of the people's economic hardships in order to undermine their faith in free elections, in communal solidarity and socialist policies. We are committed to the eradication of all social and economic evils and injustices. To this end we must rededicate ourselves."

On the previous day the Union Cabinet had taken stock of the Bihar situation. Though the public posture of the Central Government was that the movement of Mr. Narayan had died down, the Central leaders were fully aware from reports received from their own sources and party MPs that the administration was at the point of collapse in various parts of Bihar and that the government was continuing mainly on the strength of the concentration of policemen, the BSF and the CRP.

On the same day three of JP's associates, all well-known Sarvodaya workers, Acharya Ram Murti, Thakur Das Bang and Mrs. Sarala Bhadoria were externed from Bihar. The externment orders were served under the Defence of India Rules and made effective for 60 days. Similar orders were ready to be served on Mr. Siddhraj Dhaddha, President, All India Sarva Seva Sangh, and Mr. Narain Desai but these could not be executed as they had accompanied JP on a three-day tour of Rajasthan.

Mr. Narayan described, rightly, the externment of Sarvodaya leaders as the "last desperate act of a government that has lost all moral sanction". He asked the people to keep their heads cool and march ahead in their peaceful struggle. He also announced that if an externment order was served on him, he would defy it.

To the supporters of the movement, his advice was: "Our immediate task is to demonstrate once again the people's will and the people's power at Patna on November 4. To the success of the task, we should all engage our energies. The people should, if necessary, walk miles to congregate in Patna on that day."

Addressing a public meeting at Jaipur on October 25, JP had warned the Government of India that if it failed to solve the problem of soaring prices and mounting unemployment, his movement would engulf the whole country whether he was alive or dead. He had ridiculed the Congress Plan of counter-offensive and questioned if it had the necessary strength to launch it. He had said that although the Congress and its ally, the CPI, might indulge in some violence, there was no danger of "civil war" in the country.

(This possibly had reference to a syndicated article written by the well-known journalist, Mr. Prem Bhatia, in which it had been stated that the Congress leaders in Delhi feared that the JP-led agitation had the ingredients of a civil war because of his threats to set up parallel administrations at all levels in Bihar if the State Assembly was not dissolved by December 3 and the apprehension that the Congress counter-offensive itself might heighten the existing tensions.)

On October 28, in Patna, the Congress President, Mr. Barooah aired his old suspicion that "foreign hands were behind the Bihar agitation". He told Bihar Congressmen that since "the forces of reaction and disruption" had chosen Bihar for their anti-democratic offensive the Congress had decided to combat it in Bihar. Curiously enough, despite his militancy and his stress on the need for counter-offensive, he still sought to belittle the agitation by declaring that the agitators had chosen Patna, the State Capital, for their onslaught because all the media of publicity were concentrated there and to give the impression that the agitation was Statewide. He also maintained that the agitation had failed on three major counts: (1) only 36 out of 318 MLAs had resigned till then in response to JP's call; (2) the call for the boycott of college and universities and examinations did not evoke appreciable response; and (3) the no-tax campaign had failed because Mr. Ghafoor claimed that the collection of taxes had actually doubled.

Mr. Barooah announced at a meeting of Congress workers that the Party would take out a big procession on November 16 and hold a rally to counter JP's agitation. (Not to be out-done, the CPI announced that it would organise a huge procession and rally on November 11 to demonstrate that the people had no sympathy with the JP-led movement.)

Two days later, JP held out the threat at a press conference at Ludhiana that he would organise a gherao of Parliament itself if the Union Government failed to introduce electoral reforms recommended by the Electoral Reforms Committee after it submitted its report. (The Committee members were then touring the States to ascertain the views of the people on the subject.)

SIXTEEN

Beleaguered City

The Bihar Government, obviously under instruction from the Centre, initiated measures almost on a war scale a week before the scheduled November 4 massive gherao of the Bihar Assembly and the residences of Ministers of MLAs. JP had called upon the people to march to Patna to participate in the gherao. Barricades built in West Patna, particularly the Raj Bhawan, Secretariat, Assembly and MLA flats complex were extended to other parts of the town. Thousands of BSF, CRP jawans and State constabulary were pressed into service to guard all strategic points. Barricades were put up even on both sides of the main line of the Eastern Railway from Danapur in the west to Futwa in the east for a distance of 20 miles. Large number of check-posts were set up to prevent the ingress of demonstrators from outside. By gherao eve Patna had the appearance of a beleaguered city.

While JP was giving a call at Delhi on October 31 to the people to prepare themselves for total revolution, Mr. Nanaji Deshmukh, General Secretary of the All India Jana Sangh, was served with an externment order from Bihar for the second time in four months (he defied it). Mr. Madhu Dandvate, MP, when he arrived by plane to Patna on the morning of November 4, was served with a similar externment order at the airport itself.

The day Nanaji was served with externment order, JP, speaking at a function on the occasion of the celebration of the 99th birth anniversary of Sardar Vallabh Bhai Patel, urged non-communist opposition parties to forge a united front if they were serious about ending Congress misrule. He said, in the UP elections the Congress had been returned to power by polling only 32 per cent of the votes while 68 per cent of the votes cast against it had been wasted on the opposition parties. He stressed that the sufferings of the people could not be mitigated unless the opposition parties united under one umbrella.

The next day on November 1, JP's talks with the Prime Minister, Mrs. Indira Gandhi, lasting 90 minutes, failed mainly on the issue of dissolution of the Bihar Assembly. JP told waiting pressmen after his talks: "No agreement has been reached." He said no further meeting was expected and he was leaving for Patna. He said he had discussed various issues like corruption, inflation, rising prices, electoral and educational reforms, besides the dismissal of the Bihar Ministry and the dissolution of the Assembly. Mr. Jagjivan Ram was also present during the last half hour of the talks. JP announced that the agitation would continue.

The same day in Bihar the police launched a statewide drive to check trains, buses, trucks and steamers to prevent the journey of "unauthorised persons" to Patna. Pamphlets were airdropped from planes warning the people not to participate in the demonstration. Thousands of suspects were detained by November 3 at various check-posts and many arrested. The Government asked the Divisional Commissioners to open camp jails to house those arrested in connection with the proposed gherao and the Patna march. Spotter planes went up the air carrying top officials to watch the movement of people by river and road. Several hundred country boats on the Ganga were seized while river police started patrolling the Ganga and the Gandak on motor launches. Yet thousands of people from different parts of Bihar managed to converge on Patna carrying their own food to participate in the great gherao. Many came on foot from the neighbouring districts. Chhatra Sangharsh Samiti sources said that, eluding the police, more than 50,000 people had been able to come by the night of November 3. The Jana Sangharsh and Chhatra Sangharsh Samitis were hard put to accommodate them. Most of them had to be lodged in maidans under the open sky. Those who could not stand the cold were housed in a school building from where they were promptly evicted by the police.

On November 3, Mr. Narayan went round Patna in a jeep to see for himself the warlike police *bandobast*, which, he said, had never been witnessed even during the worst days of British Raj. He did not address any public meeting. A sticker pasted on his jeep carried the exhortation: "March to Patna and join the gherao." On the previous day on his arrival at the Patna airport, JP had said: "We shall have to wait with courage and patience. I am in no hurry nor are my boys. The agitation would continue with renewed vigour and determination."

On November 3, on the gherao eve, all trains on the main line of the Eastern Railway were cancelled from midnight. Steamer services were also suspended. A Patna-bound steamer, which had already left Pahleza Ghat, was recalled under orders of the District Magistrate of Saran. All up and down trains on the Patna-Gaya line were also cancelled. Police patrolling of the barricaded main line of the Eastern Railway was introduced.

A call for the Delhi Bundh had also been given on November 4 by the Delhi Rajya Chhatra Sangharsh Samiti in support of JP's agitation. Over one thousand Jana Sangh and RSS workers were arrested on the Delhi Bundh eve. On the same day Congress and CPI workers assembled at the Gandhi grounds in Delhi and took a pledge "to fight the forces of right reaction now engaged in subverting democracy and undermining the country's solidarity". They shouted: "Tell JP Delhi will not observe Bundh", "Fascism Murdabad" (down with Fascism), "Bihar Assembly will not be dissolved".

Private shops and establishments, however, remained mostly closed on the Delhi Bundh day but all the State emporia remained open. As if to flaunt the organisers of the Bundh, the Prime Minister, Mrs. Indira Gandhi, went round the fashionable Connaught Place and made some ritual purchases at the Khadi Gram Udyog Bhawan. She also visited some State emporia on the Irwin Road. At the Kashmir Government Emporium she selected a costly Kashmiri shawl but put it aside saying she would be buying it in a few days.

SEVENTEEN

JP Lathi-Charged

The picture in Patna was totally different. The town was virtually under seige. Policemen carrying lathis, rifles, bren guns, sten guns and light machine guns could be seen everywhere. Since the early hours, police jeeps roared and rumbled through the streets to strike terror in the hearts of the citizenry. Armed policemen took up positions at all strategic points. They also surrounded the Gandhi Maiden, the lungs of Patna, to prevent any assemblage of demonstrators.

By sunrise information had reached the Jana and Chhatra Sangharsh office that the Government had decided to be tough and orders had been issued that in no circumstances the demonstrators should be allowed to reach the Gardiner Road where the MLA flats were located and beyond which stood the buildings of the Assembly, the Secretariat and the Raj Bhawan. According to one official source some 200 magistrates and 60,000 BSF and CRP jawans and members of the Bihar constabulary had been deployed in Patna on that morning. JP's own estimate was, of course, much higher.

A spotter plane carrying high officials kept air-to-ground communications and flew daylong sorties to pass on information regarding crowd formations and movements with necessary directions for controlling them.

At 10 a.m. JP came out of his Mahila Charkha Samiti residence in Central Patna and boarded a jeep and led the waiting processionists. A large contingent of policemen accompanied the marchers. By the time it had come near the Bihar National College and was approaching the Gandhi Maidan, the crowd swelled. The police sought to break it up by making a lathi-charge in the rear. The procession, however, went ahead with JP in the lead. As it was nearing the north-eastern fringe of the Gandhi Maidan, the Additional District Magistrate of Patna, Mr. Jamuna Prasad Verma, who was waiting there with a posse of policemen, ordered the processionists to disperse. When they refused, he announced on the mike: "I declare this assembly unlawful. I also declare all those who are in this assembly to be under arrest." JP ignored the threat and entered the Maidan.

Two PTI staffers, S. K. Chatterji and Hargouri Saran, who had been assigned to cover the march, rang me up one after another, that JP had been declared to be under arrest. I asked them if he had actually been taken into custody. But they did not know, because there was a lot of confusion on the scene as students and youths started swarming into the Maidan from all sides breaking barricades and eluding the lathi-wielding police while JP was moving ahead. They rang off to watch further developments.

I was in a difficult position. I could not sit on such a big newsbreak to wait for details or confirmation. I also knew I would be "logged" at the head office desk at Delhi (logging means, for those who do not know, the recording of the time of transmission of a major news item from its centre of origin with the initials of the reporter giving the news, the editor vetting it and the operator creeding it, to ascertain how fast it travelled to the main desk).

For an agency man speed is the essence of news. For him every minute is a deadline. I had to take a decision at once and I decided to take the risk and issued a "snap" (an item carrying this marking gets priority over all other messages under transmission at centres through which it has to pass). Actually there should not have been any risk at all in normal circumstances because a developing story is tied up into neat "leads" for morningers and evenengers (morning and evening newspapers) after enough follow-up materials come in. The one sentence "snap" issued at 10.35 a.m. read:

"The Sarvodaya leader, Mr. Jayaprakash Narayan, was declared arrested this morning when he approached one of the barricades on the fringe of the Gandhi Maidan in an open jeep (more) PTI."

The news travelled with litghtening speed and was broadcast by the AIR within minutes. It also led to a lot of trouble (for me as well as the Additional District Magistrate, Mr. Verma, who never got the permission from the higher authorities to detain Mr. Narayan though more than 3,000 arrests were made in Patna that very day).

Soon both our reporters as well as some other eye-witnesses to the incident leading to the ADM's announcement dropped in. They confirmed the announcement about the declaration of the arrest of JP and others who formed part of the "unlawful assembly". They said, however, that JP had proceeded towards the State Bank of India (located on the western side of the Maidan) with a large crowd following him and that he had not been actually arrested till then.

Just as I was going to give a follow-up making it clear that JP was still free, I received an angry telephonic call from the Chief Minister Abdul Ghafoor. He remonstrated: "Who has told you JP has been arrested? I know your sympathies are with JP but I never expected you to concoct news to embarrass us when we are already facing so much trouble. Do you know I have been receiving frantic telephone calls from the Prime Minister's residence to explain how this news has been flashed by the PTI? Cancel it at once. He has not been arrested. I say so."

I tried to explain that we had not said that JP had been arrested. We had merely carried the announcement of the ADM, which had meant by implication that JP had beed declared to be under arrest. I said the announcement had been heard by hundreds of people. But he was in no mood to understand the subtle semantic difference between "arrested" and "declared to be under arrest" and went on repeating "cancel it, cancel it" and rang off.

In the end I had to "kill" the story and issue a substitute making it clear that JP had not been detained. I do not know what transpired at Delhi but the next morning the News Editor of the PTI, Mr. P. S. Kasvekar, an old friend with whom I had worked in 1945 on the Reuters desk of the Associated Press of India at Bombay, flew into Patna to "assist" me. He always treated me like his elder brother. Had our relationship been known, he might not have been sent.

To continue with the story. Meanwhile JP had moved towards the State Bank of India building followed by a huge crowd, chased by lathi-brandishing policemen. Many tear-gas shells were burst and repeated lathi-charges made in the rear of the procession to break it up, without avail. JP led the procession towards the Fraser Road on his way towards the Gardiner Road (the MLA flats area which had been made out of bounds for the demonstrators).

I watched the procession from the Dak Bungalow corner of the Fraser Road as it moved westwards followed by policemen brandishing lathis. More and more young men broke through the barricades and joined it ignoring the lathi-waving policemen. Soon JP reached the MLA dispensary facing the Income-tax building where the road turns towards Gardiner Road. As the Rubicon was about to be crossed, repeated lathi-charging and teargassing started. JP took out a handkerchief to protect his eyes from the bursting fumes. In a trice lathis wielded by CRP men started showering on JP and his supporters encircling him. JP was hit. He fell down and had a fainting fit. Nanaji Deshmukh, two Chhatra Sangharsh Samiti boys and two Bihar CID men deputed for the security of JP were seriously injured in trying to protect him.

Many other demonstrators were also injured and more taken into police custody. The processionists had no doubt defied the prohibitory order under section 144 Cr. P.C. but they had been peaceful throughout. Even the police did not charge them with having thrown a single brickbat. Their only crime was defiance of the government order that was in force in the town. Did somebody conceive of the idea of finishing off the frail leader with a few well-directed lathi blows and then explain it away as accidental than risk a nation-wide unrest by sending him to jail? (The 'accident' theory was later advanced by no less a person than the Prime Minister, Mrs. Gandhi, herself.)

Within a minute JP regained consciousness and got up and, leaning on the shoulders of Samiti boys accompanied by Mr. S.N. Mishra, MP, proceeded, limping, on foot, from the MLA dispensary. After he had moved a few paces, the strain proved too much and he sat down on a bare cot on the roadside and took a few minutes rest. When I met him there along with some reporters, quiet and grave, he gave a call for Patna Bundh the next day and Bihar Bundh on the day after. This was his protest against the barbarous behaviour of the police.

(Late that night, he exempted from the purview of the Bundh water and power supply, the press, doctors and hospitals, medicine shops and hotels and restaurants.)

The BBC in its broadcast that evening mock-seriously commented that if the Britishers had used the same methods, they could have easily ruled India for another hundred years!

While he was relaxing, JP was examined by Dr. R. V. P. Sinha, a leading surgeon of Bihar, who advised him to return home to have medical care and complete rest. But JP stubbornly refused. He got up and moved towards the Assembly through a narrow side street along the southern flank of the MLA flats. All the while he was followed by a large number of demonstrators. He again showed signs of fatigue and sat down on a chair in front of the residence of Mr. Daroga Prasad Rai, the Finance Minister and a former Chief Minister. As he was sipping a glass of water, the District Magistrate, Mr. Vijay Shankar Dubey, arrived on the scene with a large posse of armed policemen and informed JP that he would not be allowed to proceed any further. He also said that he was going to arrest his followers. JP offered himself for arrest. But the DM kept silent. Soon several hundred demonstrators, who were in the middle and tail end of the street, were arrested and whisked away in waiting buses. The lane was then swarming with excited youths. It was physically impossible for the police to arrest all of them. The assault on JP had also scared them against making any more lathi-charges. Who had ordered the lathi-charge on JP was never found out. The District Magistrate, to the best of my knowledge, did not order it.

There was a stalemate. An empty bus was standing before the gates of Mr. Daroga Prasad Rai's house. Obviously, it had been commandered to carry demonstrators taken into custody. Along with Nanaji Deshmukh and Shyamanandan Mishra, JP boarded the bus to offer dharna before Daroga Rai's house and announced he would not budge till he was arrested. The demonstrators gheraoed Rai's residence and sat on dharna because gherao of Ministers' residences was part of that day's programme.

JP was again examined by Dr. Suresh Prasad of the Indira Institute of Cardiology and two other Government Doctors and given the same advice tendered earlier by Dr. R. V. P. Sinha.

JP thanked them but declined to move though he had developed a pain in the chest on the previous day and had been examined by two heart specialists.

(Subsequently when the question of the lathi-charge on JP was raised in Parliament by some opposition members, the assault was described as a plan to murder him. The charge was hotly denied by the Government.)

It was a fact that a couple of weeks before the Patna lathi-charge an attempt had been made to strangle JP during his visit to Ludhiana. While he was moving with a crowd of admirers, a hefty Sardar suddenly held him in an iron embrace from behind and pressed his sides. JP cried out in pain. The man, suspected to be a hired assassin of an infamous politician who subsequently became a member of the notorious 'caucus', fled and disappeared before he could be apprehended.

JP himself had narrated the story to us. JP had been pressed so hard that a rib fractured and it still caused him mild pain. Again in December, 1974, his motorcade was attacked by a gang of hoodlums while he was proceeding from Delhi to Kurukshetra, but fortunately he escaped unhurt.

When along with a group of newsmen, I met JP in the evening, he looked completely exhausted. But he seemed determined to court arrest. He showed us the marks of injury. There was a wan smile on his face as he pointed to the injuries and said "Vinash Kale Biparit Buddhi" (perverse reasoning is the forerunner of doom). He would repeat that phrase, with deadly effect, at the time of his arrest just before the imposition of the internal emergency.

But the magistracy and the police refused to arrest him and he was forcibly returned to his house in the same bus at 10 p.m. (He had not taken any food since morning.) On alighting from the bus, he told a large gathering of his followers that he had never seen such naked barbarism in 50 years of his political and social life as had been witnessed in Patna that day. He said such shameless cruelty had not been seen even during the British days.

"If I remain alive, I shall bring those responsible for it to their senses", he said. (This was JP's stand while there is talk in high places today of forgiving and forgetting those guilty of worse atrocities during the emergency.)

Mr. Narayan declared that this struggle was not between the people of Bihar and the Government but between the people of India and the Prime Minister, Mrs. Gandhi, and it would continue. Though he was weary and exhausted, JP immediately rushed to the spacious botanical garden in west Patna to meet several thousand demonstrators arrested during the day as they had been kept there in the open as the jails were already packed beyond capacity.

A little background of the Finance Minister, Mr. Daroga Prasad Rai, before whose residence JP had offered dharna for the whole day, may not be out of place here. Mr. Roy had not been in his house throughout the period of the dharna.

In June, 1974, a week after the firing on JP's procession by the Indira Brigade, replying to the five-day budget debate in the Assembly, Mr. Rai had attacked JP for his role in spearheading the students' agitation. He described it as a stab in the back, quoted Shakespeare and cried out like Julius Caesar "Et Tu Brute"! He did not fall, however, as Caesar had done, because he was made of sterner stuff. Mr. Rai might also have remembered that after Caesar fell, the Romans had cried: "Liberty! Freedom! Tyranny is dead!"

The speech appeared to have been only half-rehearsed. For, he forgot to say something more than was expected of him. When he was about to resume his seat, he was prodded by the "lean and hungry-looking" Chief Minister Abdul Ghafoor (both of them belonged to JP's home district Saran). Mr. Rai immediately whipped out a pocket edition of Julius Caesar and started reeling off quotations. This time he reversed his role from that of Caesar to Brutus. What he said in effect was: "Not that I love JP less, but that I love Bihar, nay India more."

On November 5, there was Patna Bundh and Bihar Bundh on November 6. Both the Bundhs were peaceful. On the morning of Bihar Bundh a large number of lathi policemen headed by the Subdivisional Officer, Mr. Nagendra Nath Tiwary, surrounded the house of Mr. Narayan. This caused a commotion in the locality. One of the two private secretaries of JP, Mr. Sachchidanand, rang me up to say that no officer had cared to inform Mr. Narayan or his staff why his house had been surrounded by policemen. He said if JP was being put under house-arrest, the authorities should say so.

I immediately telephoned the Chief Secretary, Mr. P. K. J. Menon, and asked him if JP was being kept under house-arrest? He replied: "Government is merely providing additional security for Mr. Narayan in view of what had happened on November 4, Mr. Narayan is not being put under house arrest." Soon after my talk with the Chief Secretary, policemen, who had taken up positions around JP's residence, were withdrawn.

What happened on November 4 in Patna became the subject of an adjournment motion tabled in the Lok Sabha on November 11 by the leader of the Congress(O) group, Mr. Shyamnandan Mishra, who had been with JP on that memorable day. He charged the Central Government with masterminding the entire operation with the precision of a martinet. They did not realise that they had only helped the movement to gather more strength. In a voice chocked with emotion, he declared that if the Government chose to continue with its policy of brutal repression the battle of Kurukshetra might be re-enacted. He demanded withdrawal of BSF and CRP, whose posting in such large numbers had made Bihar look like a State under occupation of foreign troops.

The Home Minister, Mr. Brahmanand Reddi, wanted 'proof' that JP had been the victim of a murderous assault. The Prime Minister, Mrs. Gandhi, had earlier maintained that JP had been hit 'accidentally'. The Bihar Chief Minister, Mr. Abdul Ghafoor, maintained much later in the Bihar Assembly on December 5 that JP had been hurt "in a melee". Both Ghafoor and Mrs. Gandhi stoutly denied that JP had been hit by police lathis. Mr. Ghafoor maintained that though JP had threatened to physically throw out Ministers and legislators, he (Ghafoor) had taken measures to ensure Mr. Narayan's safety.

No one thought of mentioning the medical report on JP's wounds. A copy of the report, which I had procured, said: "JP had received one abrasion of one inch into half inch over his left collar bone, another abrasion of $1'' \times \frac{3}{4}'' \times \frac{1}{2}''$ over his right ankle. All the injuries had been caused by some hard blunt substance." This demolished the "accidental" and "melee" theory altogether.

JP issued a statement on November 14 on the lathi-charge on him. He said the Prime Minister's theory that it was "accidental" had no foundation because he alone had not been hit. Five others—Nanaji Deshmukh, Ali Hyder, Convenor of Gaya Jana Sangharsh Samiti, Rabindra Jha, a student, and two security men provided for his safety by the Bihar Government, had been injured in attempting to protect him. The student had been trampled upon by a CRP jawan and had vomitted blood. JP asked why so many men should have been injured in trying to save him if no order had been given to hit him? He said whether it was accidental or not should be better known to the Central Government because it was the CRP jawans who were wielding the lathis.

After JP's statement, the Home Minister, Mr. Reddi, offered a tardy apology next day in the Lok Sabha. He said: "Now that JP has chosen to say that he was hurt, I say we are sorry." This apology came at the end of a 40-minute heated debate in which opposition members alleged that there had been a definite plan to murder JP or at least seriously cripple and incapacitate him.

Mr. Samar Guha (Socialist) warned the Government not to forget that a similar incident in respect of Lala Lajpat Rai had given rise to martyrs like Bhagat Singh and his band of revolutionaries. After all that had happened, Mrs. Gandhi said in New Delhi on November 9 that a movement like the one in Bihar posed a threat to the stability of the country and the government would meet this challenge (as if it was not doing it already). She told a meeting of Congress members of Parliament that the party by itself did not want a confrontation. But if it was compelled, both the party and the government would have to take up the challenge.

The Congress President, Mr. Barooah, expressed similar views when he flew into Ranchi where there was a Bundh on November 10. He was greeted with black flags by Samiti boys, who had called the Bundh in protest against the lathi-charge on JP and the demonstrators led by him. Mr. Barooah told Congressmen that the party was firm in its resolve to "crush the enemies of democracy".

Despite the Bundh, a procession was taken out by Congressmen and Youth Congress workers with heavy police escorts. After the Congress procession had gone ahead another much bigger procession was taken out by JP's supporters carrying black flags. They paraded the streets of Ranchi shouting anti-

Congress slogans demanding the dismissal of the Bihar Ministry and the dissolution of the State Assembly.

Speaking at a public meeting organised by the Ranchi District Congress Committee that evening, Mr. Barooah alleged (amidst continuous interruptions and waving of black flags and shouting of slogans denouncing his party) that members of the Grand Alliance, which had been defeated at the last elections and rejected by the people, had regrouped under the leadership of JP and were out to finish democracy by snatching away the right of the people to elect their own representatives. Mr. Barooah shared one common feature with Goldsmith's Village Schoolmaster: though vanquished, he could argue still.

EIGHTEEN

Processions & Rallies

The month of November became a month of competition in processions and rallies for demonstrating the strength of popular support for and against JP's movement. The main demonstrations were organised in Patna after the massive show of popular backing for the Patna March on November 4 despite the unprecedented preventive measures taken by the government.

On November 11, the CPI organised a big procession and rally with full support of the government. The processionists were allowed to come out of the Gandhi Maidan with bows and arrows, lathis and spears. A young processionist was seen even carrying a shining naked sword. He was later relieved of it by the police under orders of the District Magistrate when the latter's attention was drawn to it. They were allowed, however, to carry the lathis, spears and bows and arrows. Another procession led by the Congress President, Mr. Barooah, and the Union Defence Minister, Mr. Jagjivan Ram, was taken out from the Maidan by the Congress on November 16. Both the processions turned into rallies on their return to the starting point.

I had clocked the JP-led procession, which went to Raj Bhawan to submit 10 million signatures on petitions demanding the dissolution of the State Assembly on June 5 (which was fired upon by the Indira Brigade). The processionists marching 10 to 15 abreast on an average took one hour fortyfive minutes to pass the Dak Bungalow corner near which the PTI office was located.

The CPI procession of November 11 moved on an average 10 abreast and it took one hour fifteen minutes to pass that point. The procession led by Mr. Barooah on November 16 passed through the Patna-Gaya Road and it had to be clocked at the Kotwali crossing. The News Editor of the PTI, Mr. P. S. Kasvekar, Mr. Kaushal Manmohan, Chief Reporter of our Patna Office, a foreign correspondent (most probably representing the *Daily Telegraph*) were with me at the crossing and all four of us clocked it. The procession took only 45 minutes to pass that point. Yet when it transformed itself into a rally at the Gandhi Maidan, Mr. Barooah estimated it to be half a million strong (almost the entire population of Patna).

The CPI demonstrators had come by steamers, trains and buses without tickets while the government had turned a blind eye to free-tripping. Every facility was provided by the government to enable the CPI to collect crowds from outside to swell the ranks of the processionists. The Congress had turned the Gandhi Maidan into a city of tents to provide accommodation to the demonstrators who were to take part in the procession of November 16. On the evening of November 15 when newsmen visited the camps, they found most of them empty. By late night pro-Congress demonstrators, suspected by JP to be mostly hired men, started arriving by trucks, steamers, trains and State Transport buses from the neighbouring countryside. In spite of all this the Congress put up a poor show.

JP alleged that the CPI had been paid rupees twentyfive lakhs for organising its show while the Congress itself had spent rupees sixty lakhs for its own procession. The CPI denied the charge while the Congress ignored it.

It was a different picture altogether on November 18 when JP addressed a public meeting at only two days' notice. One could not believe it unless one saw it. JP was deeply moved. He called me and asked me to give my estimate of the gathering. It was very difficult to arrive at a figure. Almost two-thirds of the Gandhi Maidan, whose circumference is exactly one mile, was jampacked with people. I confessed that in my long career as a journalist I had never seen such a huge gathering in Patna (a gathering of almost equal size had turned out to hear Pandit Jawaharlal Nehru address a public meeting at Muzaffarpur on the occasion of the Bihar Political Conference in 1949 for which the Congress had carried on propaganda in the north Bihar villages for more than one month to ensure a mammoth gathering).

The Statesman photographer Raghu Rai climbed atop the

flag mast at the Gandhi Maidan and took a beautiful photograph which gave a clear idea of the vastness of the gathering on the 18th.

In a 120-minute speech, JP accepted the challenge of the Prime Minister to seek the verdict of the people at the next general elections to settle the issue. He said Mrs. Gandhi herself had given a call to make the elections a battlefield and he was confident that the opposition parties supporting his movement would give her a fitting reply though he himself would not contest. He said he was confident that there would be only two contesting parties when the elections came—the Congress and the CPI on one side and those dedicated to his cause on the other. He quoted poet Dinkar and warned the Congress:

"Do Rah Samayka Rath Ka Gharghar Nad Suno
Singhasan Khali Karo Janata Aati Hai."

(Listen to the rumblings of the moving chariot of time carrying the message: vacate the throne, the Janata is coming.)

JP said the country was fast moving under Congress rule towards dictatorship. The press was being gradually muzzled and the leaders espousing the cause of the people were being detained under the MISA as if they were smugglers or blackmarketeers.

"The defenders of democracy", he said, "held a Bihar rally at this very place on November 11 (CPI) and on November 16 (the Congress). They brought hired men at a huge cost. They covered the Maidan with tents and shamianas to feed and shelter the hired men they had brought to participate in the rallies. They brought men in special trains, fleets of buses and trucks. From where did the money for all this come? Today's rally is not a Bihar rally but merely a Patna rally. There is not a single tent or shamiana. Yet look at the sea of human heads. The people gathered here have occupied two-thirds of the Gandhi Maidan under the open sky. They have come voluntarily at very short notice. You judge for yourself on whose side is the Janata".

The next day in Delhi the irrepressible Mr. Barooah said that the Congress rallies at Ranchi, Patna and Jaipur had proved that the masses were with his party and that they were fully aware of the threat to democracy and were prepared to defend it.

Overcrowding in the jails of Bihar was proving to be a problem for the government. 9 central, 28 divisional and 31 district jails had a total capacity of housing 18,000 prisoners. These jails had been accommodating 36,000 prisoners in the hot summer months of May within two months of the launching of the movement. Despite many Samiti agitators having been released, the jail population had again gone up to 40,000 by mid-November. There were only 50 security prisoners when the agitation started. Their number went up to several thousand by this time.

The Congress leaders held a three-day conclave at Narora in Uttar Pradesh and on November 24 endorsed in a resolution the party's offensive against Mr. Narayan's movement and called for its intensification till the organisation emerged victorious. Mr. Barooah warned partymen against any confusion about JP. He said JP was a political leader and he should be treated on that footing.

The Prime Minister, Mrs. Gandhi, explained that it was not a question of confrontation between two individuals but over basic policies. She said: "It is a confrontation with certain organised forces. They are very small in number but they command influence because of their position in society. We have to combat them as it is not a question of the Congress alone but of the whole nation."

Mr. Chandrasekhar, MP, was reported to have disagreed with the majority assessment of the character of JP's movement. A tea party he had given some days ago to JP at Delhi at which 60 Congress MPs had participated, was discussed at the Narora conclave and it was described as a "wrong step". Mr. Barooah said whether it was intended or not, it tended to create an impression that about 60 Congress MPs were in sympathy with Mr. Narayan's stand.

As if in reply to the Narora camp, participants at a national conference of several political parties agreed to extend JP's movement all over the country. It was attended by leaders of the Jana Sangh, the Congress(O), the Bharatiya Lok Dal, the Socialist Party, the Forward Bloc and the Akali Dal. It also set up a coordination committee with Mr. Radhakrishna, an associate of JP, as convener.

On November 27, at a largely attended public meeting, JP announced the launching of a people's movement in Haryana State at Kurukshetra. He referred to the venue of the meeting and said it was good that the agitation was being launched at Kurukshetra where the battle of Mahabharata had been fought. He said UP was next on the list for launching the movement.

From his own experience, he said, of what he had seen on his way to Kurukshetra from Delhi (his motorcade was attacked and this led to an opposition walk-out from the Lok Sabha next day) and the harassment to the people intending to attend this meeting, he had ample confirmation of what he had been hearing about the redoubtable Chief Minister, Mr. Bansi Lal.

JP said: "Let me inform Mr. Bansi Lal that very soon I shall be visiting Haryana again, not for one day only as today but for more days. The people's movement in Haryana commences today at this historic place. The people of Haryana must not relent nor retrace their steps, come what may. You must see that the Chief Minister, Mr. Bansi Lal, goes as also the Central Government headed by Mrs. Indira Gandhi."

Next day JP told a meeting of lawyers in Delhi that the country was fast heading towards dictatorship. He said the Congress Government was turning a deaf ear to the legitimate demands of the people. The erosion and corrosion of the Constitution was going on unabated, the rule of law was being abridged, civil liberties were being suppressed and sinister attempts were being made by the ruling party even to bypass the judgments of the Supreme Court. What more proof was needed that democracy was now being subverted to give place to dictatorship, he asked.

The attack on JP's motorcade resulted in a clash in Gaya. The local Chhatra Sangharsh Samiti took out a procession in observance of "Black Day" on November 30 in protest against the incident near Kurukshetra. This procession was confronted by another procession taken out by anti-JP elements observing "Anti-Fascist Day" and this resulted in the clash.

JP announced on that day at Mokameh (Patna district) at

a public meeting that the month of December should be devoted to the building of Jana Sangharsh and Chhatra Sangharsh Samiti cadres by organising training camps to train them. He directed that the month should also be utilised by Samiti volunteers to fan out in the villages to educate the masses about the aims of the movement.

It is to be noted that both the Union and the Bihar Government had construed JP's acceptance of the challenge of Prime Minister, Mrs. Gandhi, to seek the verdict of the people at the next general elections as an acceptance of failure of his agitation. A note to this effect was sent by the Bihar Government to the Government of India, which concurred with it. No wonder they received knock-out shocks when the elections came!

NINETEEN

Satyagraha Again

The winter session of the Bihar Assembly was to commence on December 4. On December 1, the Chief Minister, Abdul Ghafoor told reporters at the BSF camp at Meru (near Hazaribagh) that the supporters of JP would never again be allowed to gherao the Assembly. The Samiti boys kept their plan secret till the opening of the session lest the Government foiled it by taking preventive counter measures. Samiti workers from Nawadah and Rohtas districts suddenly appeared before the residences of Ministers, legislators and the Assembly gates on December 4 and started offering dharna-satyagraha and courting arrest. In all about 300 of them were arrested that day. This programme of satyagraha continued till the Assembly session lasted and many Samiti volunteers were detained and sent to jail.

The Working Committee of the All India Jana Sangh met at Jammu on December 1 and passed a resolution justifying the party's support to JP's movement. It also decided that in view of the fact that the Congress leadership was heading toward dictatorship, the Sangh should have poll alliances to ensure direct contests between people's nominees and Congress candidates at the next elections.

On December 6, a public meeting scheduled to be addressed by the Congress President, Mr. Barooah, at Baroda at the Jubilee Maidan had to be abandoned because of angry demonstrations by pro-JP youths. Anti-Barooah slogans were raised and some chappals were reported to have been hurled on the dais.

The Working Committee of the All India Sarva Seva Sangh, which met at Ghazipur in UP on December 7, could not come to an agreement on the question of extending the Bihar type agitation in UP. Some members opposed it on the plea that Acharya Vinoba Bhave did not approve of it. JP, however, told a public meeting that the people of UP should formulate a line of action for launching a Bihar type of agitation if they felt all was not well with their State. He said he himself would not suggest any such plan as he was not familiar with the conditions obtaining in UP.

An impression had been created at the time that JP was being obstinate about his demand for the dissolution of the Bihar Assembly without delay. JP made it clear that this was not so. He said at Katihar in early December that he was extending the deadline for Assembly dissolution by one year. But if it was not dissolved by that time, he would see that a Janata Vidhan Sabha (peoples' assembly) was elected.

On December 8, speaking at a public meeting at Ballia, JP warned Congressmen against the evil designs of the communists, who, he said, wanted to share power at the Centre and elsewhere by taking advantage of the current political and economic situation. He made it plain that he did not want to break the Congress Party. He still wanted that sincere Congressmen who genuinely believed in national reconstruction and the ushering in of a new social order to work conscientiously (this had reference to men like Mr. Chandrasekhar, Mr. Krishna Kant, Mr. Mohan Dharia and others).

The Prime Minister, Mrs. Indira Gandhi, told the nation in Delhi on the same day that it should not allow forces of "chaos and destruction" to get the upper hand. A week later she was more explicit. Addressing a big Congress rally organised at Lucknow on December 15 as part of its counter-offensive, she denounced the JP-led agitation and said: "It is anti-people and it aims at gagging the common man." While she was delivering her speech at Lucknow, the police were lathi-charging students at Hazaribagh for showing black flags to the Bihar Labour Minister, Mrs. Ramdulari Sinha.

One of the aims of JP's idea of total revolution was ending the caste system. The abolition of the dowry system was another. In mid-December, while boarding a train for eastern UP, he suggested to a big crowd of youths at Begusarai railway station that if they believed in his ideals, they should prove it by giving up the sacred thread. Many youths at once tore up their sacred threads. This led to a joint protest from representatives of the State units of the Sanatan Dharma Pratinidhi Sabha, the Bidwat Parishad, the Pandit Sabha, the Deb Bhasa Parishad and the Hindu Mahasabha. They met at Birla Mandir at Patna and regretted in a resolution JP's advice to youths. The resolution quoted scriptures and pointed out that the sacred thread was not a symbol of caste.

On December 17, JP told a mammoth public meeting at Bettiah that the nation's fate was linked with the fate of the Bihar movement. He said Mrs. Gandhi's "Garibi Hatao" slogan had proved to be a cruel joke because under the Congress regime the rich were becoming richer and the poor poorer. Those who were supposed to be protectors of the people had become their oppressors.

One of the fundamental postulates of democracy is independence of the judiciary. But the Congress Government wanted a committed judiciary. And when the verdict of even the committed judiciary went against its interests, the rulers sought to bypass and nullify it through legislation. JP's Ballia speech caused concern to Mrs. Gandhi because she felt he was trying to drive a wedge among her own partymen.

She made an oblique reference to partymen who felt sympathetic towards JP in her speech at a meeting of the Congress Parliamentary Party on December 21 and said that she did not object to Congressmen mixing with members of opposition parties socially. It was a different matter, however, when they felt nearer to the opposition politically. A distinction should be made between two, she said. (By then her slips had started showing.) She took a peculiar stand on the issue of corruption, which had provided the biggest handle to JP's supporters to denounce the Congress rule. Inaugurating a Retail Dealers' Convention in New Delhi the next day, Mrs. Gandhi said that those who were raising the bogey of corruption were hampering India's exports. She maintained that the malaise of corruption existed in one form or another in every country but in India it was being exaggerated beyond all proportion. She said this at a time when the import license scandal, the rags scandal and other big scandals were rocking the nation.

Soon after her apologia for corruption, JP announced a four-phased Bihar type movement for Uttar Pradesh. It was to commence on January 2, 1975 with the submission of a memorandum of seven demands to the Chief Minister of UP. The announcement was made by JP at Varanasi on December 27. He listed the following demands: (1) safeguarding of democracy; (2) end of anti-farmer policies; (3) ending unemployment; (4) ensuring honest and just administration; (5) eradication of corruption; (6) introduction of educational reforms; and (7) removal of social evils.

The second phase was to begin on January 17 with the observance of "Anti-Repression Day" throughout the State by taking out mute processions. The demands were to be explained at public meetings to be held in every constituency in the third phase on January 30. JP suggested that at least five to ten public meetings should be organised in every constituency. Formation of Action Committees at all levels was advised in the fourth phase.

The day after JP had announced Bihar type agitation for UP, Mrs. Gandhi was greeted with black flags at Shivaji Park in Bombay when she went to inaugurate the 27th annual convention of the Indian National Trade Union Congress. Undaunted by the slogan-shouting black-flag-waving crowds, she asserted that the Bihar agitation against corruption was "bogus". She asked: "Are not there corrupt people in the movement itself? Wait for a few days, all bad things in the movement will come to light. If I cannot remove corruption, how can the Jana Sangh or the Socialist Party?"

The black flag demonstration had been organised against corruption in public life, rising prices and wage-freeze. All the opposition parties, except the CPI and the Shiv Sena, participated in it.

Mrs. Gandhi's charge that there were corrupt people even in JP's movement was possibly prompted by reports received from her intelligence sources about some bungling in the collection of donations by the Samiti boys through coupons of various denominations issued under JP's signature. JP had referred to it himself in his speech at a public meeting at Varanasi, which had been twisted and exaggerated. The Bihar Pradesh Chhatra Sangharsh Samiti met in Patna on December 31, 1974 under the presidentship of JP and directed all its members, who had been provided with coupons to submit accounts. A three-member sub-committee was also set up to enquire into these alleged bunglings. The enquiry revealed that though the head office of the Samiti had maintained proper accounts, some muffasil offices had failed to do so. The total sum involved was small and nowhere near rupees eighteen lakhs alleged in inspired reports appearing in a section of the press. JP maintained that the amount involved was not much. But to prevent any future bungling he cancelled the old coupons (which did not mention the sum donated in words) and issued fresh coupons to collect funds from donors supporting the movement.

TWENTY

L. N. Mishra's Death

After a marathon 13-hour discussion, the national conference of the Socialist Party adopted a resolution at December end at Kozhikode giving clearance to its leadership to go ahead with forging an alliance at the national level and the State levels. It stressed, however, that the alliance should not be on the pattern of the Grand Alliance of 1971 but on the basis of the existing and developing movements in each State.

While the Socialists ware deliberating at Kozhikode, over a dozen student leaders of UP arrived in Patna to study the Bihar movement and finalise way and means to launch a similar strategy in their State. They had detailed discussions with the Samiti leaders and returned after a few days.

Mr. Lalit Narain Mishra, Union Railway Minister, died at the Danapur Railway Hospital (west Patna) on January 3 of injuries sustained in a grenade blast at Samastipur. This was a signal for the Congress leaders to throw the entire blame on the agitation led by JP.

JP, who was then in Delhi, immediately demanded a thorough probe into the causes and circumstances of Mr. Mishra's death. He condemned the act of terrorism which had resulted in the Railway Minister's death. Mrs. Gandhi promptly gave her initial reaction by throwing dark hints against JP's supporters and warning the people against forces of violence and disruption. Congress President, Mr. Barooah, was more explicit. He said: "What had started with character assassination had been followed up by cruel and loathsome murder. Fascism will not stop at anything short of murder."

Yet at the time the country was agog with rumours which told a different story. Mrs. Gandhi herself referred to these rumours in her speeches. The members of the family of Mr. Mishra also had their own suspicion which did not link it at all with JP's agitation. Understandably, they dared not voice their suspicion publicly. Only after the 1977 poll debacle of the Congress the aggrieved widow of Mr. L. N. Mishra pricked the bubble. It was Dr. Jagannath Mishra, the then Irrigation Minister of Bihar and younger brother of Mr. L. N. Mishra, who came to the rescue of Mrs. Gandhi after some initial delay and issued a statement scotching all rumours about her alleged involvement in the death of his brother. Mrs. Gandhi, who had so long stubbornly refused to remove Mr. Ghafoor despite the agitation launched by JP, soon afterwards asked the Chief Minister to make room for Dr. Mishra.

Here is how Mrs. Gandhi referred to the rumours herself. Speaking at a condolence meeting held in New Delhi on January 7, she said all sorts of rumours were being spread about Mr. Mishra's death. "If I am killed, they will say I did it." Pointing her accusing finger at JP's supporters, she said Mishra's death was part of a "dangerous plan" and only a "rehearsal for a larger plan". "I know who their target is and I am not afraid of death. Everybody knows who Mr. Jayaprakash Narayan's target is."

On the same day at a public meeting at Ujjain, JP declared that despite all the calumny that was being hurled at him, he was not going to withdraw his movement. He also referred to an appeal for withdrawal of the agitation made by Mr. S. A. Dange, Chairman of the Communist Party of India, Mr. Gour Murahari, Deputy Chairman of the Rajya Sabha, and several Congress members of Parliament and said that the Bihar movement was a people's movement and it would continue till it was crowned with success.

Earlier, addressing a huge gathering of youths and students at Bhopal on January 4, Mr. Narayan had referred to rumours about a snap poll. He was confident that the Congress would be defeated. He announced that the Jana and Chhatra Sangharsh Samitis would be authorised to field their candidates. He also said that he had told a recent meeting of representatives of opposition parties supporting his movement not to interfere with the selection of people's candidates and to keep the movement above party interests.

If his strategy worked, JP said, these Samitis would later work as watchdogs over their representatives. Even though the Constitution did not provide for the right of recall, the Samitis would ensure that they behaved in the interests of the electorate or compel them to resign. Even at that point of time he maintained that winning elections could not be the end but only the means to an end. Power had a corrupting influence. A change of government alone would not solve the problems of the people born of the sins of the past 27 years.

JP stated unequivocally that the people would have to continue their agitation even after the defeat of the Congress and the establishment of a new Government for redressal of their grievances and solution of their problems.

A demand was voiced at the meeting that JP should launch a Bihar type agitation in Madhya Pradesh too. His reply was revolutions were never thrust from above or imported from outside. The youths, students and the people should themselves chalk out their programmes and submit their demands first to the Chief Minister.

On his return to Patna on January 9, JP replied to the Prime Minister's charges regarding the death of Mr. L. N. Mishra. He said that he would invite any group of impartial observers from outside Bihar to tour the State and see for themselves if the Bihar movement had done anything to create the kind of atmosphere as Mrs. Gandhi had insinuated. In a written statement, he charged her with trying, with the help of the CPI to whip up a climate of hysteria in the country. He said it augured ill for the country that Mrs. Gandhi should have worked herself up into such a pitch as she did in the course of her condolence speech. The only objective she could conceivably have in doing this was to fabricate a justification for large-scale repression and eventual imposition of her authoritarian rule.

"It is remarkable", JP said, "that in spite of the fact that the Bihar Government has let loose a reign of repression resulting in more than a hundred lives lost in police firings, over a thousand heads and limbs broken or grievously injured, and in scores of thousands of men, women and children having been jailed, many of them illegally, and also in spite of a violent campaign of abuse and calumny and character assassination that has gone on for the past months in which top Congress leaders, including the Prime Minister, have been taking part, there has been only one police constable killed by an angry crowd in the course of the entire nine months of the movement. And for this crime I have publicly apologised to the Bihar police.

"It would not be out of place", JP had said, "to point out that even in the days when I believed in violent social revolution, I was opposed to the politics of assassination and condemned it as puerile terrorism. Later when I became a democratic socialist, I rejected not only terrorism but also violent revolution. And now when I have come to believe in Sarvodaya as true socialism, violence has no place at all in my thinking and action. Therefore, to hold me responsible for creating a climate of hatred and violence is not only to insult me but also to insult the intelligence of the people."

"While it is saddening as well as frightening that the Prime Minister for her own political purposes wishes to create a dangerous situation in the country, I should like to appeal earnestly to the students, youths and the people of Bihar and of the country to keep their heads cool and refuse to be provoked into any kind of violence either of deed or speech.

"If they have regard for me and any concern for the future of their movement and that of Indian democracy and feel any sense of responsibility towards their country, I do hope they will pay serious heed to this appeal. May God guide them at this critical moment."

Long after the death of Mr. L. N. Mishra, his widow, Mrs. Kameshwari Mishra, broke her self-imposed silence at a press conference on May 27, 1977. By demanding a fresh enquiry she has nullified the enquiry held into the causes and circumstances of her husband's death and cast serious doubts about the subsequent findings of the Mathew Commission of Enquiry. She now demands that "the real culprits" be brought to book. Whether this will be done or is possible is anybody's guess.

Mrs. Mishra said the death of her husband was still shrouded in mystery. She wanted to know why the rostrum erected at Samastipur railway station, where he became the victim of a grenade blast when he went there to inaugurate a railway line, had been dismantled overnight. She said at no stage had the

CBI asked her anything about the incident nor did the Mathew Commission give her any opportunity to express her suspicions about the persons responsible for her husband's death.

Mrs. Mishra asserted that the CBI enquiry and the Mathew Commission's enquiry were meant to be only an "eye-wash". She said Dr. Jagannath Mishra (who also had been injured in the grenade blast), who was a Minister in the Ghafoor Cabinet was subsequently "rewarded". (Mr. Ghafoor was asked to step down and Dr. Mishra was made the Chief Minister sometime after he issued a statement denying the rumours referred to by the Prime Minister in her condolence speech at Delhi on January 7, 1976.)

Mrs. Mishra said that she had believed that Dr. Jagannath Mishra would put his heart and soul to trace the real culprits but everybody knew what he did or did not. She said she had remained silent because of the enquiries and the emergency. She said that in view of the changed circumstances she had written to the new Prime Minister, Mr. Morarji Desai, and his Home Minister, Chaudhary Charan Singh, to trace the actual culprits.

TWENTY-ONE

Peoples Governments

A two-day Sarvodaya Workers' Conference, which concluded at the Shekhodeora Ashram of Mr. Narayan in Gaya district on January 12, decided to set up Janata Sarkars (local people's administrations) in the villages and Panchayats and even at higher levels, if possible, within three months to demonstrate that these would be better than the CPI-backed Congress government in Bihar. It also decided to establish a 1,00,000 strong Gram Sangharsh Bahini to bring about peaceful revolution in the villages. Youths of the age group of 14-30 were to be admitted in the Bahini and they were to be trained by Mr. Pratap Rau Saheb of Maharashtra, an ex-army Major. The Bahini was established but the number of youths joining it was less than expected.

JP attended the conference, which also asked the people to boycott the official Republic Day functions on January 26 and to organise separate functions of their own. JP said the present government had ceased to represent the people and had been responsible for ruining them economically, politically, culturally and spiritually. It had forfeited the moral right to organise such functions.

Addressing a public meeting at Baroda on January 18, JP challenged the Union Government to hold a referendum in Bihar to ascertain whether the movement for the dismissal of the Ministry and the dissolution of the Assembly had the backing of the people or not. He claimed that ninety per cent of the people would support the movement.

He told another gathering at Bhavnagar on the next day that the agitation in Bihar was bound to spread all over the country because the situation in other States was similar to that in Bihar. He also predicted that the Congress would have to write off most of the States in the next elections because the people were fed up with its broken promises and misrule.

On January 20, the West Bengal Chief Minister, Mr. Siddhartha Shankar Ray, bravely declared at a meeting of Congress workers in Patna: "We accept the challenge of JP and we shall see in which State he succeeds in defeating the Congress." When this was brought to his notice, JP, who was then touring Gujarat, told reporters at Ahmedabad that the Congress was bound to lose as the people's faith in it had been rudely shaken.

On January 26, the Chhatra and Jana Sangharsh Samitis all over Bihar boycotted the official Republic Day celebrations and held separate celebrations of their own. The police interfered with them only at Katihar and also made a lathi-charge when an attempt was made by large number of youths to unfurl the national flag at the venue of the official function. In Patna three separate celebrations were organised by the Samiti at two of which poor rickshaw-pullers were given the honour of hoisting the national flag.

Since women were participating in large numbers in JP's agitation, the Congress now sought to mobilise Congress women to join the fray. JP was made the target of bitter attacks by participants in the two-day Women's Conference held in Patna organised by the Congress. Mrs. Nandini Satpathy, Chief Minister of Orissa, who presided, led the attack. She told the conference on its opening day on February 1 that JP's agitation was against the basic norms and values of the society. It sought to destroy the established practices and create chaos. She ridiculed the idea that it aimed at bringing about a revolution. On the contrary, its object was counter-revolution as it went against the progressive policies of the Congress which had nationalised banks, legislated land reforms, fixed ceilings on land and urban property. (The Janata leaders ignored the role of Mrs. Satpathy and set her up to contest the Dhenkanal seat in Orissa in the Assembly elections in June, 1977.)

Mrs. Chandrika Mahapatra (Orissa) compared JP with Hitler and described his supporters as smugglers and corrupt men. Mrs. Phulrenu Guha (West Bengal) felt JP's agitation might put the wheels of progress back. Mrs. Pratibha Singh, MP (Bihar) said: "We should fight the reactionaries till we win." Others, who spoke in the same vein, included Mrs. Harbindar Kaur (Punjab), Mrs. Sarla Sharma (Himachal Pradesh), Mrs. Renuka Chakrabarty (Tripura) and Mrs. Sumitra Kulkarni (Gujarat).

The political resolution adopted at the conference said the assassination of Mr. Lalit Narain Mishra was only an indication that fascist forces were out to destroy democracy and they had claimed their first victim. It maintained that the opposition headed by JP was trying to destroy democratic institutions and to create political and economic chaos and lead the country to anarchy. It, therefore, called upon all women, particularly Congress women, to accept and meet the challenge of anti-democratic forces and the forces of violence with courage and determination.

The Women's Conference over, a three-day Narora type Congress camp commencing February 9, was organised in the salubrious climate of Rajgir under the presidentship of the indefatigable Mr. Deb Kant Barooah. It was restricted to only 200 Congressmen of Bihar, including Ministers, members of Parliament from Bihar, presidents and general secretaries of District Congress Committees and a few prominent legislators. It discussed ways and means to counter JP's agitation after its counter-offensive had dismally failed.

Mr. Barooah threatened action against any partyman supporting or sympathising with instead of opposing JP (he was referring, without actually naming them, to Mr. Chandrasekhar and his colleagues who were pleading for a dialogue between JP and the Prime Minister). Although the camp was being organised for the specific purpose of meeting the challenge of JP's agitation, he aired his feeling of happiness over his discovery that the people of Bihar in general were not with Mr. Narayan.

JP told a mammoth gathering in Patna on February 13 that the agitation would continue even if he died. He referred to Mr. Barooah's remark and pointed his finger to the audience and asked simply: "Are you not the people?"

But Mr. Barooah had merely been echoing his mistress voice. Mrs. Gandhi loved to snub those who frequently talked of a national dialogue on issues like unemployment, rising prices, educational and electoral reforms, curbing corruption etc. Speaking at a meeting of the Executive Committee of the Congress Parliamentary Party on February 16, she had angrily asked: "Dialogue with whom and on what basis?" When this is the official attitude democracy goes down the drain and not all the Queen's men can win elections.

Earlier Mr. Satpal Kapur and Mr. K. D. Malaviya had criticised Mr. Chandrasekhar, Mr. Krishna Kant and Mr. Mohan Dharia for talking about a dialogue with JP. The Prime Minister said that in view of the stand taken at the Narora camp that JP's movement was reactionary and that it sought to push the wheels of progress back, pleas for dialogue would only create confusion within the ranks of the party.

JP was in Delhi then conferring with non-communist opposition leaders on the political and economic situation in the country in the context of their apprehension that a Bangla Desh type of dictatorship might be imposed on the country by Mrs. Gandhi and her party. The participants besides JP, included Messrs. Morarji Desai, Asoka Mehta, Chaudhary Charan Singh, Karpoori Thakur, Piloo Mody, L. K. Advani, Era Sezhiyan, S. M. Joshi and Madhu Limaye.

Though internal emergency was still to be proclaimed, JP questioned the justification of the external emergency continuing in the country, since the war with Pakistan was over long ago. Addressing Central Government employees, he outlined the steps already taken by the Union Government to subvert democracy and warned them to be vigilant in view of the happenings in Bangla Desh, where dictatorship was being established, and Pakistan, where the National Awami League had been banned.

On his return to Patna, JP repeated his warning that the Prime Minister had designs for "murdering democracy". He said she was contemplating imposition of dictatorship on the lines of Bangla Desh, where Sheikh Mujibur Rahman had banned all political parties except his own, the Awami League, curbed the powers of courts and taken other equally obnoxious measures on the advice of Mrs. Gandhi.

He told a public meeting that during the last four years Mrs. Gandhi had done everything to throttle democratic institutions and while crying wolf from time to time, she was herself out to take the country on the road to fascism following the footsteps of Hitler and Mussolini.

The radio and television were already under the control of the Government and they were dutifully blaring out false propaganda against the agitation and maligning it. The press had also been under various kinds of pressures as well as allurements. Those, who refused to toe the official line and purvey harsh truths, were sought to be marked out. The pressures were exercised not from the State but the Central level.

At the conclusion of JP's speech several thousand youths and students marched in a procession to the Patna station of the AIR shouting "Jhutha Parchar Band Karo" (stop the propagation of lies), "Indira Radio Murdabad". When they reached the outer gates of the AIR carrying black flags, they were halted by armed policemen. They continued to hold demonstration while three of their representatives, Messrs. S. H. Razi, Convener, Bihar Jana Sangharsh Samiti, Vijay Krishna, Secretary Bihar Chhatra Sangharsh Samiti, and Shankar Singh, Convener, AIR Demonstration Committee, were allowed to go inside and submit a memorandum to the Station Director. The memorandum condemned the AIR for playing the role of a "drummer" of the ruling party and the Government and demanded an autonomous status for it.

The Action Committee of the Samiti announced on February 21 the formation of the first Janata Sarkar in Chandi Block comprising 14 Panchayats in Nalanda district. Chaudary Brahm Prakash, a former Chief Minister of Delhi, who inaugurated it, said this people's government would have three functions: settling village disputes in people's courts, eradication of corruption and redressal of grievances of the villagers.

The Committee claimed that 15 other officers and 40 employees had been "appointed" for running the "Sarkar". It said the Janata Sarkar had received about one hundred complaints, which were expected to be resolved amicably through the efforts of the "Sarkar".

Mr. Morarji Desai and other leaders launched a signature campaign in Gujarat on February 23 to secure a "people's mandate" for early elections to the State Assembly. In Ahmedabad, former Chief Minister, Hitendra Desai and Mr. Babu Bhai Patel, President of the GPCC(O), went round the city collecting signatures in support of the demand. It was decided that Mr.

Morarji Desai would lead a procession to Raj Bhawan on March 6 to present the citizens' mandate to the Governor.

Bangla Desh was declared a single-party republic on February 24 with Sheikh Mujibur Rahman as the Chairman of the new national party, called the Bangla Desh Krishak Shramik Awami League. All other parties were deemed to have gone out of existence from that day. A month ago Bangla Desh had switched over from the Parliamentary to the Presidential type of government. Sheikh Mujibur Rahman had become President from Prime Minister on January 25.

Mrs. Gandhi, who was believed to be the guide and mentor of the Sheikh, ridiculed the opposition in the Lok Sabha on February 27 for their attempts to replace her at the behest of JP. In a vivid metaphor, she said they intended to replace her government with a government which would have the brain of the CPI(M), the heart of the Congress(O), the tongue and lungs of the Socialist Party and the hands and feet of the Jana Sangh.

When Mr. Jnashewar Mishra (Socialist) queried "What about Maruti", the Prime Minister asserted there was no corruption in regard to Maruti. She said nothing wrong had been done and every question on this subject had been answered fully. She maintained that no special favour had been shown to "some one" just because he was connected with the Prime Minister. She admitted that she was unhappy about the use of MISA against students but maintained in the same breath that compared to other countries student agitators were being subjected to "the minimum use of force".

TWENTY-TWO

Delhi Chalo

On March 2, the Prime Minister dropped from her Council of Ministers, Mr. Mohan Dharia, Minister of State for Works and and Housing, for advocating dialogue with JP and eulogising his movement. Another charge against him was that he had insulted the Maharashtra Pradesh Congress President, Mr. P. K. Sawant, in his reply to his letter dated February 15 in which the PCC President had warned him not to indulge in public utterances violative of the party discipline. (Mr. Sawant himself had rushed to the press with his letter of admonition without waiting for Mr. Dharia's reply.)

Both Mr. Sawant and Mr. Rajni Patel, President of the Bombay PCC, were happy over the dropping of Mr. Dharia. Mr. Patel said: "This was what we wanted. I hope disciplinary action will be taken against those who share Mr. Dharia's views on JP's movement."

JP, who was in Delhi, pointed out that Mrs. Gandhi's action had clearly shown that she was determined to destroy the Congress as a democratic political party and he called upon Mr. Jagjiwan Ram and Mr. Y. B. Chavan to give a lead to save the party from destruction. He said the people expected that they and other Congress leaders, still believing in the traditional values of their party, would give a lead at this critical juncture. If they did so, it would be in accordance with their own standing with the people. It would also determine the fate of their party and government.

Mr. Narayan said in a statement that the issue raised by Mr. Dharia's resignation was not whether he had been guilty of indiscipline or disloyalty but whether the Congress was going to be saved as a democratic party and whether Indian democracy itself was safe in the hands of the Congress as it was presently led. Mrs. Gandhi's decision to dismiss Mr. Dharia showed how hollow her desire was for discussion with the opposition. He also wondered how was it that all the five Ministers, who had been recently dropped (whom did not name), where known for their honesty, integrity and loyalty to the ideals of the Congress. (They were Messrs. Bhola Paswan Shastri, Nitiraj Singh Chaudary, Prof. Sher Singh, Prof. A. K. Kisku and Mr. Dharia.)

He repeated his warning that the people and the youths were now conscious and they would not tolerate any conspiracy to succeed in establishing dictatorship in the country.

Mr. Chavan remained Her Majesty's most obedient servant and came out with a statement ruling out any dialogue with JP. The reason? His was the voice of "a reactionary alliance in the country". As for Mr. Jagjiwan Ram, who still enjoyed his "Babuji" status in relation to Mrs. Gandhi, he reacted to JP's call by saying that the Congress alone with its all India character could hold the country together. Indeed he asked JP to ponder over the consequences of his recent attempt to bring about a combination of political parties with conflicting ideologies and diverse interests to undermine the Congress. He did not, however, indulge in any diatribe against JP.

Mr. Ram's disillusionment came later when Mrs. Gandhi refused to step down after the Allahabad High Court judgement and clung to power by declaring internal emergency and changing the Constitution to make her above the law. And to add insult to injury she kept him for sometime under virtual house arrest and surveillance. Though the disillusionment came as perhaps the rudest shock of his life, he had no option during the emergency but to swallow the humiliation and bide his time. When the time came, he levelled the score with such nice precision that Mrs. Gandhi, who had gained a reputation as a master political strategist, was completely thrown off her balance.

As was to be expected, the dutiful members of the Executive of the Congress Parliamentary Party passed a resolution unanimously on March 5 reaffirming their faith in the leadership of Mrs. Gandhi.

Undeterred by the militant postures of the Congress leadership next day (March 6) the non-communist opposition parties and youths and students organised the biggest ever anti-government demonstration in India's Capital. All the methods adopted by the Bihar Government to deter the people from joining the march to Patna on November 4 were applied by the Central Government and every possible hurdle put on the way of the marchers. But in spite of all such efforts, the procession that came out of the ramparts of the Red Fort had never before been witnessed in Delhi. Rows and rows of men and women, young and old, from Bengal to Punjab and Jammu to Mysore joined the procession led by Mr. Narayan in a jeep followed by Choudhary Charan Singh, Piloo Mody, S. M. Joshi, Madhu Limaye, Samar Guha, Madhu Dandvate, N. G. Goray, Asoka Mehta, George Fernandes, Prakash Singh Badal, Tridib Chaudhury, Atal Bihari Bajpayee, L. K. Advani and other opposition leaders. The pride of place in the procession was given to the youths of the Bihar Chhatra Sangharsh Samiti. After them came the Gujarat contingent and participants from other States. How big the procession was could be estimated from the fact that it took three and a half hours to reach the Boat Club from the Red Fort.

The processionists carried banners of their respective States and placards bearing the slogans "Singhasan Khali Karo, Janata Aati Hai", "Bihar agitation is continuing, the turn of Delhi has come now", "Janata March to Parliament is for bringing about total revolution", "The Janata has come to tell the parliament what they want", "Bring down prices", "End corruption", "We have no quarrel with the police, they are our brothers", "Whatever be the provocation we won't raise our little finger", "Leave the chairs and gaddis, you are no longer are our representatives", "This freedom is false because we are hungry". Almost entire Delhi came out on the streets to watch the progress of the procession.

A delegation on behalf of the marchers led by Mr. Narayan went from the Boat Club to Parliament and submitted a memorandum of the demands of the citizens to the Speaker of the Lok Sabha, Mr. Dhillon, and the Deputy Chairman of the Rajya Sabha, Mr. Jatti. It expressed the solidarity of the people of India with the Bihar movement, which symbolised the feelings of the nation. The time had come when the people of the entire country felt it their duty to oppose the move of the rulers to trample under foot their basic rights and to fight for justice and saving democracy.

It demanded that the Bihar Ministry be dismissed, the Bihar Assembly dissolved and fresh elections be held in Bihar and Gujarat. It also demanded that the prices of essential commodities be brought within the reach of the poorest of people, fixation of minimum wages and flooring and ceiling on incomes, redistribution of land and acceptance of the right to the tillers, assurance to provide jobs for the jobless and improvement in rural economy.

Its political demands include restoration of full civil liberties and withdrawal of the Maintenance of Internal Security Act and the Defence of India Rules, revocation of the external emergency, electoral reforms and the right of the electorate to recall representatives who failed them. It also demanded educational reforms, strengthening of Panchayats and District Boards, the decentralisation of power, eradication of corruption from public life and the appointment of Lok Pal and Lok Ayuktas with no exemption of the Prime Minister or the Chief Ministers from probes into charges of corruption against them.

Addressing a mammoth rally at the Boat Club later, Mr. Narayan described the demonstration of March 6 as a historic event and said that during its 27 years of rule, the ruling party had failed the people completely. He warned the people that the rulers wanted to incite them to violence and that they should never walk into the trap as it would enable the government to impose dictatorship through massive counter-violence. They must follow the path of non-violence shown by Mahatma Gandhi whatever be the provocation. He cautioned them that voices from the ruling party had already been heard in favour of "limited" dictatorship as if dictatorship could be restricted. Who will control the dictator? he asked. He was referring to repeated suggestions made to this effect by Mr. Sashi Bhusan, MP.

Mr. Narayan also gave a call for the observance of "Anti-Emergency Day" all over the country by holding demonstrations in every town.

The election petition filed against Mrs. Gandhi by Mr. Raj Narain in the Allahabad High Court was already causing her enough headache. The magnitude of the demonstration of March 6 brought home to her the realisation that unless she did something drastic to crush the movement led by JP, which was fast spreading in other parts of the country, her days would be numbered. The idea of proclaiming internal emergency as the first step towards saving her "gaddi" must have germinated then. Still she decided to wait for the judgment of the Allahabad High Court as she had some hope that she might win. And she remained patient though JP was making moves to escalate the movement by announcing fresh programmes of action at the Boat Club rally.

What had particularly worried the Prime Minister about the Delhi March was that the biggest contingent of demonstrators had come from her home State, Uttar Pradesh, followed by Madhya Pradesh, Delhi and her favourite Bansi Lal's Haryana. It was also disturbing that no party flag or headgear was seen in the Delhi procession in response to JP's suggestion to present a united front of the angry people. This clearly indicated that the non-communist opposition parties were fast reaching the stage when they would be willing to merge their separate identities and unite under a single banner to oust her from power. So long as they remained disunited, she could retain her whip hand. The demonstration showed that she might soon lose this advantage.

Reports had also reached her that on that very day at Ahmedabad. Mr. Morarji Desai had led another huge procession to Raj Bhawan and submitted the "people's mandate" for ending President's rule. Mr. Desai had warned the Governor, Mr. K. K. Vishwanathan, that if the Government did not announce fresh elections by March 14, a Statewide satyagraha would be launched in Gujarat. The portents were certainly ominous because JP had already launched agitations in UP and Haryana besides the year-long agitation in Bihar.

On October 18 and 19, Mrs. Gandhi had to appear personally in the witness-box in the Allahabad High Court before Mr. Justice Jagmohan Lal Sinha and undergo gruelling cross-examination. She was particularly questioned about the activities of Mr. Yashpal Kapoor, formerly an officer on special duty in her Secretariat, as her election agent. She had to plead amnesia when some ticklish questions were put. She was pinned down, however, on important issues despite her denial of several allegations. When she left the Court she must have had a premonition that her ordeal was not over but only about to begin.

TWENTY-THREE

Anniversary of Agitation

Another huge procession led by JP was taken out in Patna on March 18 by the Bihar Chhatra Sangharsh Samiti in observance of the first anniversary of their agitation. Leaders of the opposition parties, including the Forward Bloc, besides large contingents of Samiti workers from each of the 31 districts of the State participated in it. It was an unwieldy procession for which permission had been taken from the District Magistrate as a prohibitory order under section 144 Cr. P.C. was still in force.

The processionists marched from the Gandhi Maidan carrying flags of their respective districts and banners and placards bearing their demands. Many women and lawyers in their black gowns joined it. They shouted slogans demanding dismissal of the Ministry, dissolution of the Assembly, bringing down prices, eradication of corruption, jobs for the jobless and change in the system of education.

Their slogans included "Jab Se Indira Ayi Hai, Kamar Tor Mahgai Hai" (prices have been becoming back-breaking since Indira's assumption of power), "Indira Tere Samajwad Me, Bachche Bhookhe Marte Hain" (children are dying of hunger under the Indira brand of socialism), "Jab Tak Bhookha Insan Rahega, Dharti Par Toofan Rahega" (storms will rage in the country as long as the people remain hungry), "Police Hamara Bhai Hai, Us Se Nahi Larai Hai" (we have no quarrel with the police, they are our brothers), "Tana Shahi Nahi Chalegi" (we won't tolerate dictatorship), "Sar Farosi Ki Tamanna Aab Hamare Dil Me Hai, Dekhna Hai Jor Kitna Bajoo-e-Katil Me Hai" (we are prepared to be beheaded and we want to see how strong is the executioner). Groups of students and youths snake-danced and clapped shouting "Jai Jai JP, Jai Jai JP, Sab Ka Neta JP Hai" (victory to JP who is the supreme leader of the people).

After two hours it reached the Martyrs' Memorial in front of the barricaded gates of the State Assembly and stopped there and again raised slogans under the blazing afternoon sun. Volunteers of the Samiti began distributing a printed charge-sheet against the government which affirmed that the Bihar Legislative Assembly was no longer acceptable to the people. It should, therefore, be deemed to have been dismissed. It also called for election of a new Assembly without delay.

The charge-sheet read: "The present members of the Assembly have forfeited the confidence of the people and they have, therefore, no right to continue as representatives of the people. The Government, which has been surviving on account of the support of the MLAs, has attempted to destroy democracy. It has been ruling through ordinances, which proves beyond doubt that it has lost its democratic conscience. Ordinary laws should have been enough to deal with developments arising out of the movement of the students and the people but the government has been invoking the MISA and the DIR to keep itself in power. There is no administration worth the name in the State. So much so that there does not appear to be any more need even for the agitation to immobilise the government. If it had to depend on its own strength, it would have ceased to exist long ago. But it is being kept artificially alive with the help of the Central Government. The MLAs sit inside the Assembly and make speeches that the movement has fizzled out but their Central leaders have to issue appeals off and on for the withdrawal of the agitation."

It also said: "Fortytwo MLAs have resigned so far. We honour them. But others are clinging to their membership in a spirit of selfishness. This shows their lack of concern for the people. It is the people's birthright to recall and dismiss their representatives. They hereby announce that sovereign power rests in them under the Constitution. Legislators and Ministers are servants of the people. If the masters wish they can dismiss them."

It concluded with the proclamation: "You are no longer our representatives. Leave your chairs and gaddis as we are dissolving the Assembly and dismissing the Ministry."

The charge-sheet was then read out before the gathering by Mr. Mithilesh Kumar Sinha, a senior member of the

Samiti. At JP's suggestion three Samiti leaders were sent to paste a copy of the charge-sheet on the eastern wall of the Assembly. The District Magistrate permitted them to cross the barricades for the purpose. They pasted the charge-sheet and returned with the procession to Gandhi Maidan, where Mr. Narayan addressed a big rally.

JP told the rally that the journey towards the goal of total revolution would be long and arduous and the students and youths must work with determination and dedication to achieve it. They should not think that their task would be over with ensuring the victory of the people's candidates at the next elections. He pointedly told the youths that the struggle was not for power but for ending all forms of exploitation corruption and achieving social, political and economic freedom.

He said: "You agree there should be total revolution. You want to end corruption. But I want to know how can you achieve it if you accept dowry? I am told a medical graduate fetches the highest dowry. Next in order comes the engineering graduate and perhaps the lowest in the rung of the ladder is the arts graduate. If a man with four daughters to give away in marriage has to pay a dowry of Rs. 20,000/- each, how is he going to get the money without being corrupt?"

"You know", JP said, "our social and political system is such that despite all legislation for introducing land reforms, even now five per cent of the landed people in the villages exploit the remaining ninetyfive per cent. If your father owns surplus lands beyond the ceiling, is it not your duty to ask him to give up the surplus and distribute it among the poor kisans and the landless? But are you going to launch hunger-strike to persuade your father to see reason?"

"You must know", JP said, "that the path of peaceful total revolution is not at all easy. Your methods must not only be peaceful but also pure. Above all you must be fully organised and disciplined. Today's procession, though it was big, was very indisciplined. The CPI people whom we rightly criticise are much more disciplined. You must be able to set an example in discipline if you want to succeed.

Mr. Narayan said the agitation had continued for full one year and the time had come for stock-taking. He regretted that although a year had passed, the Sangharsh Samitis had not been able to set up Jana Sangharsh Samitis in every Panchayat. Janata Sarkars had been formed in only twenty out of 587 blocks. This was far from encouraging. He said he would like to see Janata Sarkars and Janata Adalats (courts) functioning in every block by the end of next June. He would be happy if Janata Sarkars were also formed in every locality in the State Capital, Patna, itself.

He also deeply regretted that the programme for fighting corruption in government offices and blackmarketing had virtually been abandoned. This must be taken up again in right earnest. He said the year-long struggle had achieved one thing however. It had dispelled the dark clouds of despair and frustration that had seized the people during 27 years of Congress rule. The agitation was no longer confined to Bihar. It had spread all over the country. The unparalled demonstration before Parliament on March 6 in Delhi was the result of the struggle. Another good effect of the agitation was that it had struck against casteism to some extent in Bihar.

The political parties supporting the agitation, JP said, must think on non-party lines if they wanted to succeed. It was not the fault of the people that the Congress was in power so long though they had voted against it. It was the fight among the opposition parties that had helped the Congress to bag the majority of seats in the Assemblies and Parliament though the majority of the electorate had disowned it.

For himself he was convinced that unless all the opposition parties other than the CPI forged into one strong unit in the fire of the struggle, it might be extremely difficult to achieve total revolution. He said the so-called left parties were the worst culprits in this regard. West Bengal provided the best (or worst) example. In West Bengal any number of left parties were fighting against one another. He regretted the role of the CPI(M) for its vacillation in joining the struggle wholeheartedly. (At this point, the Socialist leader, Mr. Ramand Tiwary, whispered in JP's ears that the CPI(M) had joined that day's procession.)

Mr. Narayan: "I am glad to know it. But they should not think that they have obliged me by participating in it." He said those who talked of revolution had no idea of mass psychology. Revolutionary programmes were evolved and accelerated through struggle and not propagating theories and coining slogans. He maintained that party politics could not solve the burning problems of the country. Had it been so, the Congress could not have ruled for such a long time. It had remained in power because of the opposition parties fighting among themselves.

Winning elections, JP said, was neither going to solve the problems nor bring about total revolution. If the Congress was defeated and the newly-elected representatives of the people started behaving like their predecessors, how could there be total revolution? he asked. The goal of total revolution would have to be pursued with vigour and determination even after the battle of the ballot was over.

For the first time, four youths, all samiti leaders, were allowed to address the meeting briefly. They were Prof. Jagannath Prasad Yadav, Shahabuddin, Narendra Kumar Singh and Raghunath Gupta (the first two won the Assembly elections held in June, 1977 but the last two lost). They called upon the people to follow the line of action chalked out by Mr. Narayan in letter and spirit.

The main burden of JP's speech was devoted to the role of the youths and the opposition parties but he also lashed out against the Prime Minister, Mrs. Gandhi, the Congress President, Mr. Barooah, and the Chief Minister of Bihar, Mr. Abdul Ghafoor, for their sustained propaganda against his agitation that it aimed at ushering in fascism.

He said: "If they have a shred of honesty left, they should go and see the victims of the police firings and lathi-charges on peaceful agitators. The charge of fascism holds good for the Prime Minister. I want to ask her, whose will should prevail, that of the 'Janata' (the people) or of the 'Tantra' (establishment)? The Gujarat Assembly was dissolved more than a year ago. Why has not she ordered elections yet? Is this democracy or fascism?"

"The emergency", JP said, "is continuing for nine years with a brief gap. May I know why the emergency should continue? Has any foreign country attacked India? Under which provision of the Constitution can she continue the emergency in the name of economic crisis? The fact is that if she feels that she is going to lose the elections, since the Indira wave is over, she will postpone the elections indefinitely in the name of emergency. If this is not fascism, what else is?"

"Today the situation in the country is so bad that even small children are raising the slogan 'Indira Tere Samajwad Me Bachche Bhookhe Marte Hain' (in your brand of socialism O Indira, children are dying of hunger)", he said.

TWENTY-FOUR

Unfortunate Chief Minister

Four days later, Mr. Ghafoor told a public meeting at Chandaus in west Patna that he was "the most unfortunate Chief Minister" because he had to contend with "attacks from within and outside" with the result that he could not do many things he wanted to do. He did not dwell upon the attacks from within but spoke on the effects of the JP-led agitation. He said that since the agitation had been launched a year ago, the government had to spend rupees five crores on tackling the law and order situation.

Fate quite often takes a hand to determine the course of history. This was demonstrated when Mrs. Gandhi gambled her political career on the election of Mr. V. V. Giri for the Presidentship in 1969 against her own erstwhile nominee, Mr. Neelam Sanjiva Reddy. Mr. Giri won by a very slender margin of votes. If the Congress-led coalition Ministry in Bihar headed by Sardar Harihar Singh had not fallen on a snap vote on a cut motion on the budget demand for animal husbandry on June 20, 1969, the result of the contest for the Presidentship might have been different. The Sardar's supporters were pro-Syndicate. (political bosses who controlled the Congress Party) If his Ministry had continued in office, an overwhelming majority of Congress legislators would have pitched in for Mr. Reddy. With the Sardar out, they gambled in favour of Mrs. Gandhi's new nominee which enabled her to consolidate her power and rule till the Lok Sabha elections in 1977 after gaining a massive mandate in the 1971 Parliamentary poll. Had Mr. Giri lost, she would have perhaps gone into the limbo of oblivion. The Syndicate leaders would have seen to it.

I have referred to this possibility because of the curious confrontation that started with Mr. Ghafoor's Ministry and

JP which ultimately led to the ouster of Mrs. Gandhi and her party from power. It may not be idle to speculate what would have happened if Ghafoor had thrown up the sponge and quit when full-throated demands for his dismissal were voiced from every corner of the State. He did resign, though it never became public knowledge, but it was not accepted by the Prime Minister.

It can now be disclosed that neither the Prime Minister nor Mr. Lalit Narain Mishra ever allowed Mr. Ghafoor a free hand to come to a settlement with JP. At the initial stages of the agitation Ghafoor went to the residence of Mr. Narayan, whom he held in high esteem, and sought his cooperation for fighting corruption within his "limitations". This did not, as it could not, satisfy JP who felt that Ghafoor's Ministry was a puppet Ministry under the remote control of Mr. Mishra who was considered to be the king-maker of Bihar. So the confrontation began. Ghafoor was a "nominated Chief Minister" like his predecessors, Daroga Prasad Rai and Kedar Pandey.

It was common knowledge that Ghafoor hated the corrupt politicians and often humiliated them openly before others by his cutting remarks. But he was fighting with his back to the wall and was in no position to deal with all corrupt politicians at a time. He unceremoniously snatched away the portfolio of one Minister. Another Minister he had to include in his Cabinet against his will was never given any portfolio and he remained without portfolio till 35 Ministers were dropped. Normally a jocular and amiable person, he became known for his irascible temper and irregular dismissal and suspension of officers whom he suspected to be corrupt. But many orders given by him were not carried out because of the machinations of some of his Cabinet colleagues.

Ghafoor had been a rebel from his youth. In 1937, as a student of Aligarh University, he had challenged Mr. Jinnah at a public meeting and had become an outcaste. He was for long in the Forward Bloc and was an ardent follower of Mr. Subhas Chandra Bose (he was not Netaji then). He had come out of the Congress when the Mahamaya Ministry was toppled by it through the expedient of encouraging large-scale defections and became one of the founders of the now-defunct Loktantrik Congress and its General Secretary.

But the lure of office still held him back from quitting in the face of the JP-led agitation because of a cussed streak in his character. I was in a very embarrassing position at that time. Everybody knew that he was one of my closest friends. This, however, was not the whole truth. My circle of close friends, who regularly visited my office, included almost all important politicians of the State, whatever be their hue. Ghafoor knew—maybe from CID reports—that I enjoyed the affection of JP and that my sympathies were with his cause. On the other hand, JP also knew of my friendship with Ghafoor. Sometimes he used to have a dig at me at his press conferences: "Aap Apne Dost Ko Keon Nahi Samjhate Hain"? (Why don't you persuade your friend to take the right course?) How could I tell him what I had been advising Ghafoor?

I did advise Ghafoor, whenever I got an opportunity on the telephone or otherwise (after the launching of the agitation he had shifted from his Chhajjubagh residence near the PTI to his official residence at the barricaded King George Avenue and I seldom had occasion to meet him), to quit instead of fighting with JP. My refrain used to be: "You are no match for JP. Now throw up your hands and quit." His stock reply used to be: "You are always siding with my Chacha (meaning JP). Why don't you persuade him to call off this agitation?"

It would be presumtuous on my part to claim that Ghafoor decided to quit on my advice. But it is a fact that as early as May 17, 1974, only two months after the agitation had started, he did tender his resignation though it never became known. Compulsions of the situation forced him to take the decision. On the one hand he had to combat JP's agitation and on the other he had to face the onslaught of his partymen out for his blood mostly because of the open insults that he hurled at corrupt politicians which led to friction with Lalit Narain Mishra.

There are two parts of the story how it came about. I had first-hand reports of both. The "pro-changers" in his party had forced Ghafoor to call a meeting of the legislature party on May 20, 1974 to seek a vote of confidence. He had made up his mind to attend it and offer his resignation. But he changed his mind after an incident that occurred at his official residence.

On May 16, the President of the BPCC, Mr. Sitaram Keshari, MP, one of the Bihar pets of Lalit and Indira Gandhi, went to Ghafoor. He was accompanied by Mr. Bhogendra Jha, MP (CPI) and Jagannath Sarkar, Secretary, Bihar State Council of the CPI. Ghafoor was enjoying the morning breeze in the open. He had some chairs brought out and offered them tea and enquired in his usual style as to what did he owe this unexpected pleasure?

Keshari replied that he and his CPI friends wanted to discuss with him the political situation in the State. Unable to contain himself, Ghafoor blurted out an abusive epithet (actually a term of endearing relationship) and said that when a friend like him was also in his enemy camp, what was the point in discussing the political situation?

Keshari tried to laugh it away and repeated his request for a discussion. When Ghafoor gave the same reply, Keshari flared up. And then for fifteen minutes there was an exchange of abuse from both sides (Keshari could outdo Ghafoor any day in this game), to put it mildly, in the language of the heart. The loud exchange drew curious onlookers. There was no dearth of such people at the Chief Minister's residence.

I had a near-verbatim report of the wordy duel from a friend occupying a ring-side berth. The next part of the story I had from Ghafoor himself. There were two dissident groups. One led by Ram Lakhan Singh Yadav and Nagendra Jha and the other led by Dr. Jagannath Mishra, the younger brother of Lalit Narain Mishra. The Ministers, who had been dropped on April 18, were mostly with the Mishra group. The first group was originally against the untrimmed Ministry. Both the groups met separately during the day. There was also a joint meeting that night at Srikrishna Gyan Mandir. Ghafoor received all these reports and became pensive. He decided that there was no point in submitting his resignation at the party meeting. He did not tell anybody what was in his mind and quietly left for Delhi by the next morning's flight alone. He met the Prime Minister and handed over his resignation. He told Mrs. Gandhi: "Madam, I am fed up with my partymen crying for my blood on the one hand and tackling the situation created by the JP-led agitation on the other. I am your nominee, hence I am submitting my resignation to you."

Mrs. Gandhi did not open the letter. She was silent for a few seconds. Then her face flushed. She angrily thumped the table: "You must stay, you must stay, you must stay." She ordered Ghafoor to go back saying that she would settle everything.

Ghafoor was taken aback. He had expected his resignation to be accepted because Lalit also wanted him to go. He had just wanted to spite the dissidents by stealing their thunder by submitting his resignation to the Prime Minister instead of creating an impression in the minds of the people that he had knuckled under at the party meeting. Since he was not prepared to leave the Congress for the second time, he accepted Mrs. Gandhi's directive to continue in office. He quietly returned to Patna and refused to tell anybody about the purpose of his sudden visit to Delhi.

At the behest of the Congress High Command, *i.e.* Mrs. Indira Gandhi, the legislature party meeting held on May 20 was changed into an informal get together. After three days a plane-load of pro-changers went to Delhi and met the Prime Minister and hurriedly returned to Patna like scalded cats chanting the refrain: "Ghafoor is our leader. We stand solidly behind him like a rock." I heard their chant at the airport, where I had gone to see the Tamasha.

It was a quirk of fate that Mrs. Gandhi refused to accept Ghafoor's resignation. Had Ghafoor resigned and elections held afresh, it is a reasonable guess that JP's confrontation with the Centre might have been averted because the edge of the agitation itself might have been blunted. Although Mrs. Gandhi later started loudly proclaiming that JP's agitation was directed against her, at that point of time she could not have thought that ultimately she would become the target because JP himself had not thought of it then. And even if she had thought so, she did not imagine that the agitation would become so powerful that she would be dislodged. She played with fire when she decided to make Ghafoor his instrument to fight JP and his followers and to cause them maximum inconvenience. Throughout the period of the agitation, the statements about JP made by Mrs. Gandhi have a spiteful, if not contemptuous, undertone. Her reference to JP staying with Mr. Ramnath Goenka and giving the cue to her Alsatians for barking loudly in unision and her invoking the name of Acharya Vinoba Bhave to slight Mr. Narayan are all indicative of her attitude.

She had summed up Ghafoor nicely. She knew Ghafoor was honest. Even JP had certified it, only to withdraw it angrily after the repressive policy pursued by his government. The students used to raise abusive slogans against corrupt Ministers by name and carried their cartoons in their processions whenever JP was out of Bihar. But they never charged Ghafoor with corruption. But honesty in her book was not a plus point in his favour because it did not give her any lever against him, but she knew that this short-tempered man would strike back if he was cornered.

Why did not she allow Ghafoor to arrest JP even at the height of the agitation? It appeared to have a sinister aspect. A legislator had been manhandled by some young agitators and Ghafoor had said in the Assembly that he would not hesitate to send even the tallest agitator (meaning JP) to his "Aasli Mokaam" (jail). I was very angry with him and telephoned to ask if he was in his senses? Was it deliberate and he meant it or was it an outburst in a fit of anger? Normally he should have responded with an angry retort. But he was unusually calm. He said in a low voice: "I can't tell you everything on the telephone. I meant what I said. Someday I will tell you why."

I was stunned. Many of us, who knew him well, had taken his threat as a mere angry outburst full of sound and fury signifying nothing, or at worst, he was merely echoing Mrs. Gandhi's voice. But what he said put an altogether different complexion to his threat.

After a long time he told me what had been happening behind the scenes after extracting a promise that I won't divulge it. I shall quote him from memory because I did not take any notes. Here is what he said: "You think you know a lot about the Bihar situation. You know nothing about what is going on behind the curtains. I had been receiving disturbing reports that anybody and everybody had access to JP's residence. Anybody could finish him off and there were reasons to suspect he might be murdered. The Samiti boys were demanding my head on a charger. On the other hand my partymen were almost daily sending telegrams or letters to the Prime Minister that I was helping the agitation and surreptitiously meeting JP at the residence of Satyendra Narain Sinha (Organisation Congress member of Parliament) at night."

His voice rose: "Can you imagine what will happen if JP is killed? Both the Samiti boys and my partymen will at once turn against me and throw the entire blame on me. Mian Ghafoor will become one of the Most Condemned Men of History like Godse, and that too *Gunah Belazzat* (for no fault of mine)."

"The irony of it was", Ghafoor said, "that people sneeringly said that I was echoing Her Majesty's voice and not mine. I was scared and I wanted to take JP into protective custody. I was never permitted. My idea was to keep him in a nice bungalow with all the amenities of life and to allow only such visitors who were confirmed friends and associates of JP. I was prepared to face whatever criticisms might be voiced. But she never permitted me to arrest JP".

"You know", he said, "what happened on November 4 when you circulated that news about JP's arrest (I did not correct him). I could never understand what was in the Prime Minister's mind. She would always advise me to 'go slow, go slow'. Neither would she come to a settlement herself nor allow me to do so. And all the while I had to face the music".

Ghafoor was asked to step down in April, 1975, when the Prime Minister decided to "reward" Dr. Jagannath Mishra, according to the widow of Mr. Lalit Narain Mishra.

TWENTY-FIVE

Agitation Spreads

The students' trouble spread in Uttar Pradesh and Orissa in the month of March, 1975. Both the Banaras Hindu University and the Gorakhpur University were closed *sine die*. The Utkal University was also closed on the eve of JP's visit to Orissa. In Bihar the Samiti volunteers showed black flags to Mr. Ghafoor while he was going to Paliganj in west Patna on March 22 to address a public meeting. The Samiti alleged that the police had made a lathi-charge on the demonstrators.

Things started moving fast. On March 25 Mr. Ghafoor again offered to be relieved (at the behest of the Prime Minister) and this time the offer was accepted. The Congress President, Mr. Barooah, announced in Delhi that he would be relieved and the Bihar Congress Legislature Party would be free to elect a leader of its choice. What was left unsaid was that Mrs. Gandhi had already decided to reward Dr. Jagannath Mishra.

Since the Prime Minister's wish was not disclosed, trouble arose on the issue of leadership when Mr. Kedar Pandey, a former Chief Minister, announced his decision to contest with the backing of the supporters of Mr. Ghafoor and the original dissidents led by Mr. Ram Lakhan Singh Yadav and Mr. Nagendra Jha. Pandey also had a substantial following of his own. He broke away from Dr. Mishra's camp on the ground that the latter had backed out from his promise to accept him as the leader of the party. Dr. Mishra denied the allegation and said it was for the party to decide who should be the leader and announced his own candidature.

Dr. Mishra had given the impression to the Prime Minister that in the event of a contest he would win hands down. But when Mrs. Gandhi became doubtful of the outcome of the contest on the basis of her own private reports, she started building up pressure to clear the deck for her nominee's election in her typical style. She still did not come out in the open. Mr. Yashpal Kapoor and Mr. Kamlapathi Tripathi started telephoning Mr. Ghafoor and Mr. Kedar Pandey to avoid contest and ensure unanimous election of Dr. Mishra.

Mr. Ghafoor had a brush with the bumptious Yashpal Kapur and told him that he was not going to take directions second-hand from a private secretary. If the Prime Minister wanted Dr. Mishra, she should say so herself. He told the same thing to Mr. Tripathi more politely. While backstage manoeuvrings were going on, Mr. Bindheshwari Dubey, Health Minister, a staunch supporter of Mr. Pandey, announced that the contest would take place since the Congress High Command had committed itself by leaving the choice to the State Legislature Party. Mrs. Gandhi had no option but to come out in the open and telephone Mr. Ghafoor and tell him that it was her wish that there should be no contest and that Dr. Mishra should be elected unanimously.

Mr. Ghafoor then came to me and issued a statement calling upon partymen to respect the Prime Minister's wish. Mr. Pandey, normally a very gentles soul, was so cut up that he rang up Mrs. Gandhi to know her mind from her own lips. When she told him what she wanted, he protested: "If this was in your mind, why did not you tell me when I met you recently in Delhi?" Such a posture from Mr. Pandey amounted to virtual revolt. Although he abided by her decision, he fell from her grace.

All this drama deceived nobody, far less the Chhatra Sangharsh Samiti. It announced: 'Our struggle will continue. We had no personal quarrel with Mr. Ghafoor. Our struggle is for the dissolution of the Assembly as it has failed to deliver the goods to the people, whose confidence it has lost completely. We are convinced that the Congress and its allies will never be able to eradicate corruption, bring down prices, provide jobs for the jobless and introduce radical changes in the present system of education. Such a task can be achieved only by a newly-elected Assembly comprising the genuine representatives of the people who would be liable to be recalled if they went astray."

Ghafoor stepped down and Dr. Jagannath Mishra replaced him and was sworn in on April 12, 1975 as the new Chief Minister.

While the infighting within the Congress was going on in Bihar, the storm-troopers of the ruling party belonging to the Chhatra Parishad and the Yuba Congress used strong-arm methods to break up a students' meeting to be addressed by Mr. Narayan at the University Institute at Calcutta on April 2. They damaged JP's car, climbed on its roof and shouted abusive anti-JP slogans and demonstrated their muscle power. JP's car was kept under gherao for twentyfive minutes while the police merely looked on. JP watched the performance of the "heroes" dumbfounded. After sometime the police made a passage for JP's car to enable him to return abandoning the meeting. In the melee Samar Guha, MP and several others had been injured and the windscreen of the car smashed.

On the previous day JP had told a convention of student representatives of the colleges of Orissa at Bhuvaneshwar that he would not hesitate to give a call to the armed forces and the police to disobey immoral orders of their superiors. He had said: "I have not given the call as the time for it has not come yet. I know the Research and Analysis Wing (RAW) is analysing my speeches to find out if I have given such a call in order to prosecute me. I have, however, appealed to policemen of Bihar not to obey unjust orders if they are asked to shoot peaceful demonstrators. I have asked them, however, to obey orders to quell violence."

A former Chief Justice of India and the then Chairman of the Law Commission, Mr. P. S. Gajendragadkar, took up cudgels on behalf of the establishment and denounced JP for his stand on the role of the army. Addressing the All India Lawyers' Conference in New Delhi on April 27, he said if JP's stand was accepted it would lead to chaos. He emphasised that dissent in a democratic country must function within self-regulatory constraints prescribed by the ethos of democracy.

The attack on JP's car led to a protest Bihar Bundh on April 6. It passed off peacefully except for a police firing at Sahpur checkpost in West Patna. It was said that violent demonstrators had heavily brickbatted and injured several policemen and officials manning the checkpost. No one was injured in the firing. Official sources alleged that attempts had been made by demonstrators at several places to interfere with the movement of trains.

The Bundh day also coincided with the observance of the "Anti-Emergency Day" throughout Bihar. Addressing a largely attended evening meeting at Gandhi Sarovar in Patna City, JP demanded the immediate withdrawal of the emergency as there was no danger of foreign aggression. He said the government was depriving the people of their fundamental rights by continuing the emergency and helping the Prime Minister to establish her dictatorship. He said the manner in which his Calcutta meeting was not allowed to be held was a clear example of naked fascism.

The Nava Nirman Samiti of Calcutta organised a silent march led by Mr. Profullo Chandra Sen, a former Chief Minister of West Bengal, on April 10 in protest against the hooliganism at the students' meeting organised at the University Institute. The marchers had their lips sealed with cotton cloth and their hands tied behind their back. The march commenced in the morning from Mahatma Gandhi's statue at Park Street corner and ended at College Square before the University Institute.

On April 7 Mr. Morarji Desai had launched an indefinite fast at his residence in New Delhi to press for the holding of elections in Gujarat within one month. The fast had commenced with a prayer meeting attended by about three hundred sympathisers (18 months ago he had undertaken another fast in Gujarat for the dissolution of the Assembly). Sympathetic fasts were undertaken all over the country.

On April 12 at a Rae Bareli seminar the Prime Minister, Mrs. Gandhi, announced that the emergency would not be lifted on the ground that "the country is still facing external and internal dangers". She said: "The atmosphere in the country is surcharged with violence. There is also drought in some parts of the country. It will be unwise, therefore, to lift the emergency in the interest of the nation."

With Morarji's health deteriorating, on the seventh day of the fast, she yielded on the issue of holding elections to the Gujarat Assembly which had been dissolved sixteen months ago.

Mr. Desai broke his fast by taking a glass of lemon water offered by Mr. Narayan (Much later, when things were slipping out of her hands, she admitted that it had been a mistake to have ordered the elections to the Gujarat Assembly in the second week of June, 1975.)

Twenty Samiti workers were beaten up on April 18 at Bodh Gaya while they were returning from a public meeting addressed by JP. They were attacked by members of a rival CPI procession. The CPI workers raised anti-JP slogans to which they protested and immediately they were pounced upon and assaulted. Several Samiti boys were also brutally assaulted at Maharaja College at Arrah at a function organised by Youth Congress boys to celebrate Kuer Singh Jayanti on April 23. The Samiti organised Arrah Bundh on April 28 in protest. Similar attacks on Samiti workers were also reported from Muzaffarpur and some other places.

Mr. Narayan charged the Bihar Government with using hired goondas against student and youth agitators for the purpose of beating them up while the police were ordered to turn a blind eye. He told a press conference on May 24 that this method had been copied from West Bengal. He said: "It is creating a problem for me because the youths are prepared to remain peaceful in the face of police repression and violence but they are fretting against assaults by hired goondas. If such goondaism leads to unforeseen consequences due to the people's wrath, the government alone would be responsible."

When the University Grants Commission then headed by Dr. K. L. Shrimali came to Patna, the University Students' Union organised a black flag demonstration on April 21 in protest against the closure of the Banaras Hindu University and the suspension of its General Secretary, Bharat Singh. They also physically obstructed the nine members of the Commission from entering the Patna University campus.

While this was the situation in Bihar, a Janta front was formed on April 26 by the non-communist opposition parties in Gujarat to fight the elections. Mr. Morarji Desai did not, however, agree to have a common symbol though it was agreed that he would lead the front. The issue was kept open for the time being. JP felt unhappy over the lack of complete unity and announced at a press conference in Patna on the same day that he would not involve himself in the election campaign in Gujarat. He, however, appealed to the opposition parties to combine against the Congress and the CPI for fighting the elections. He was persuaded to visit Ahmedabad after three days and had a 75-minute closed-door talk with Mr. Desai. He tried to convince Morarji to accept a common symbol. The talks failed. Mr. Desai is understood to have suggested that, since it was the biggest partner in the alliance, the Front candidates should accept the symbol of the Congress(O).

Mr. Narayan again paid a three-day visit to Gujarat commencing May 31, two weeks before the poll, to "meear a lot of confusion that had been created about my stand *vis-a-vis* the Gujarat elections". He said: "My main interest is with the people's struggle. But if in the course of the struggle elections come, I am certainly interested in the victory of those who are in the struggle. If *Jana Shakti* (peoples' power), *Yuva Shakti* (youth power) and *Raj Shakti* (State power) work in collaboration, it is hopeful for the struggle but the results of the elections themselves have no other relevance for the movement.

He described reports about differences between him and Mr. Morarji Desai as "totally baseless". He said the Janata Front candidates had been selected smoothly. Only twentytwo cases had been sent for arbitration to Mr. Desai which the latter had distributed quite generously.

JP said it was true that the Nava Nirman Samiti had virtually disintegrated but most of those who belonged to it had joined the Janata Front. So it was not true that they were against the Front. There was also a lot of confusion about Janata candidates. The question was posed: Who was a Janata candidate? Since Chhatra and Jana Sangharsh Samitis had not been set up in the constituencies in Gujarat as in Bihar, there was no scope for consultation with the people. But he had never said that the Janata front candidates were not Janata (people's) candidates. In the given situation it would not be wrong to say that the Janata Front candidates were the Janata candidates, he argued.

JP had not involved himself in the Nava Nirman Samiti's agitation in Gujarat in the previous year because of its violent nature though he had visited the State. He had agreed to lead the students' agitation in Bihar only on the understanding that they would remain peaceful whatever might be the provocation. During his tour of other States, he always emphasised that Gujarat type of agitation, should never be emulated. If there was to be agitation, it should be on the Bihar pattern with modifications, if necessary, in the light of local conditions. That was why JP said if elections were ordered in Bihar he would campaign for the people's candidates.

That very day (April 26), Mr. Mohan Dharia told a convention of freedom fighters in Bombay that the Congress Party had been taken over by persons having "tremendous capacity to collect black money through unscrupulous methods". He maintained that fast erosion of values and character and gradual extinction of inner-party democracy in the ruling party were posing a serious threat to democracy. According to him the present election system and the style of functioning of the party were themselves sources of gathering black money. He pointed to the sky-scrapers at the Backbay Reclamation in south Bombay and said these were living monuments of such corrupt practices.

TWENTY-SIX

Janata Sarkars

At a press conference in Patna on may 24, JP announced a three-month programme for the setting up of Janata Sarkars in all the 587 Blocks of Bihar between May and the end of July. If it took a little more time, he would be satisfied if such Sarkars were established by the end of September.

He tried to remove some popular misconceptions about the Janata Sarkars. Barring the no-tax campaign, the government, he said, could take no exception to its other functions, which were regulatory, correctional and judicial. The Janata Sarkar was meant amicably to settle village disputes out of courts. Its aim was also to keep a watch on the public distribution system to see that essential commodities were distributed equitably at fixed prices and to prevent blackmarketing and profiteering.

The Janata Sarkar would also ensure that teachers in middle and primary schools and government employess attended to their duties. It would also look after repair of school buildings, roads, etc., and prevent theft of power. Another important task of the Janata Sarkar, he said, would be to prepare land records in the villages to ensure distribution of surplus lands beyond the ceiling among the landless. He cited the case of one Mahanth who held at least 4,000 acres of surplus land in three blocks alone. The Mahanth had transferred these lands in the names of his disciples and distributed them by creating 18 trusts, only one of which was found legal by the District Magistrate and the rest invalid.

JP had given the call for the setting up of Janata Sarkars months ago. He had also reproached the Samiti leaders in his speech at the rally held on the occasion of the anniversary of the agitation for their failure to set up more than 20 such Sarkars in the Blocks. He renwed his call for establishing Janata

Sarkars in all 587 Blocks because he found the new Ministry headed by Dr. Jagannath Mishra "worse than the Ghafoor Ministry".

Addressing a public meeting at Mahnar in Vaishali district on the occasion of the four-day annual conference of the State Socialist Party, he said the Mishra Ministry was "much more repressive" towards the people's movement. He said it had gone one step ahead than the Ghafoor Ministry by "hiring goondas for assaulting peaceful Samiti demonstrators".

JP gave a call to the people of Uttar Pradesh to organise a Chhatra-Yuva Sangharsh Bahini on the lines of the Bahini organised in Bihar. He said in a statement issued on May 24 that students and youths of the age group of 11-30, who were committed to the ideal of total revolution, and who owed no allegiance to any student or youth organisation or political party should be enrolled in this Bahini. They should pledge their loyalty to the cause of "Sampurna Karanti". He also announced a five-member organising committee for the Bahini in UP comprising Messrs. Arun Kumar, Ram Datt Tripathi, Awadh Narayan, Karnail Singh and Santosh Bharatiya (Convener).

"I find", JP said, "that a need has been felt in UP for creating some kind of an organisation for those partisans of the movement, who, though active, are unable to work in concert or even to coordinate their activities because they do not belong to any political party or organised group. Therefore, I also propose the organisation of a Nirdaliya (non-party) Jana Sangharsh Manch (platform) for such persons and nominate the followikg organising committee for the setting up of the proposed Manch: Messrs. Om Prakash Gaur (Bareli), Tej Singh (Meerut), Swami Krishnanand (Agra), Lokendra Bhai (Jhansi), Vinay Bhai (Allahabad), Sarvajit Lal Verma (Faizabad), Chandra Dutt Tiwari (Lucknow), Shyam Prasad Pradeep (Varanasi), Mewalal Goswami (Gorakhpur), Mahabir Bhai (Convener) and Mrs. Sarala Bhadoria".

The Bahini and the Manch, he said, would carry out programmes of action laid down by the State level Jana Sangharsh and Chhatra Sangharsh Samitis. In addition, they would have their own programmes in furtherance of the objectives of the movement in UP.

The election tempo in Gujarat had started mounting at the

time and several meetings of the "popular" Prime Minister had been brickbatted (JP and other opposition leaders condemned such action). She too started lacing her speeches in Gujarat with her solicitude for the downtrodden Harijans and Adibasis, conveniently forgetting that the oppression of Harijans under the Congress government in Maharashtra had led to the Dalit Panther movement. She also kept silent on the murder of the Adibasi leader of Bastar in Madhya Pradesh and the brutal suppression of his followers. She forgot the burning down of the houses of three hundred Harijan families in Sherpur village in Ghazipur district in UP. Only sometime ago, a Harijan leader, Mr. Deomuni Chamar, had also been shot dead on the border of UP and Bihar. In Bihar, the oppressed Harijans fighting for their rights were being hunted down like dogs in Poonpoon, Masaurhi and Dhanaura Blocks in Patna district and in Piro, Sahar and Sandesh in Bhojpur district on the plea that they were Naxalites.

The fateful month of June arrived. The Chhatra and Jana Sangharsh Samitis jointly observed "Total Revolution Day" from June 2 to June 5 all over Bihar by holding street corner meetings to explain its basic objectives, taking out torchlight processions etc.

By the end of May Janata Sarkars had been set up in 15 out of 18 Blocks of Giridih district, it was claimed by Mr. Arun Kumar Verma, a member of the Steering Committee of the Samiti, after a tour of the district. But the same effort at Siwan ran into trouble. The Akademy Award-winner Hindi poet Nagarjun, Mr. Z. A. Zaffry, Socialist leader, and Mr. Bikram Kuer, a member of the Steering Committee of the Samiti, were arrested in Panchrookhi Block in Siwan district on June 1. It was alleged by a Samiti leader, Laloo Prasad Yadav, that a large number of policemen had been deployed at the place where many youths had assembled to set up the Janata Sarkar. He said the boys were chased and beaten up by the police.

A week before the Gujarat poll, Mr. Narayan advised the opposition parties other than the CPI to opt for an outright merger instead of forming a Federal Party or continuing a Janata Front. Mr. Karpoori Thakur, a BLD leader and former Chairman of the defunct Sanjukta Socialist Party, endorsed JP's suggestion. But nothing came out of it.

TWENTY-SEVEN

Critical Phase

The most critical phase of the agitation began in the month of June, 1975. JP charged the Prime Minister at a public meeting at Ahmedabad on June 1 with opening the floodgates of defection even before the people could give their verdict at the Gujarat poll. He particularly referred to Mrs. Gandhi's press conference at Rajkot the previous day in which she had said she would welcome into her party all legislators having faith in the Congress policies and programmes. He said it was painful to hear such utterances from the daughter of a great democrat like Pandit Jawaharlal Nehru.

JP felt if Mrs. Gandhi was to lead a party of "defectors and traitors" he did not know what kind of democracy she was going to build. On June 3, the Prime Minister denied at Navsari that she would encourage defection if the Congress failed to get a clear majority in the Gujarat Assembly. There were charges and counter-charges. At Rajkot JP said that the Prime Minister herself was a defector as she had filed the nomination of Mr. Neelam Sanjeeva Reddy for the Presidency and then worked against him in favour of Mr. V. V. Giri.

Three days later during his tour of West Bengal at Tamluk, JP charged the Prime Minister with accepting crores of black money for election expenses in lieu of favours. He said those who gave the black money received concessions for their business and industries. The result was that corruption ruled supreme in the Cabinet, the top administrative levels, and down to the lowest levels. Without giving a bribe nobody could get any work done by the government. He maintained never before was there so much corruption in the country. There were serious charges against Mrs. Gandhi's Ministers but no enquiry was allowed to be held though during her father's time enquiries had been set up against Sardar Pratap Singh Kairon and Mr. Biju Patnaik. The Lok Pal Bill to ensure enquiries against Union Ministers had not been allowed to be introduced in Parliament since 1971.

Next day JP led a mammoth march in Calcutta and addressed a rally of half a million people. Seven opposition parties, including the CPI(M) and even a section of the extremists, joined the procession. The marchers did not carry any party flag. Mr. P. C. Sen and Mr. Jyoti Basu followed behind JP. The organisers alleged that thousands of people coming from different parts of West Bengal had been prevented by the police from reaching Calcutta.

Mr. Narayan repeated his call given earlier at Tamluk for the organisation of Jana Sangram and Chhatra Yuva Sangram Bahinis from the village to the State level.

Mr. Siddhartha Shankar Ray, Chief Minister of West Bengal, organised a counter-rally at Saheed Minar on June 7 where he lashed out against JP and his "die-hard reactionary allies" and said that their attempts to bring about desruption and crush the Congress would prove futile. He discribed JP's movement as a fascist movement and said that so long as fiftyfive crores of Indians were alive the vile efforts would never succeed. If JP wanted to crush the Congress, he would have to annihilate the people of India first.

Mr. Ray pitied the CPI(M) for joining the march which appeared to him to be its funeral procession because it could not even carry its party flag and had to join hands with "reactionaries" of the Jana Sangh and the Congress(O). He maintained that the CPI(M) had invited its political death by joining the bandwagon of JP. (The same CPI(M) gained absolute majority in the Assembly poll and Mr. Jyoti Basu headed the CPI(M)-led United Left Front Government and was sworn in on June 21, 1977. Mr. Ray returned to the bar.)

TWENTY-EIGHT

The Judgment

On June 12, 1975, Mr. Justice Jagmohan Lal Sinha of the Allahabad High Court delivered judgment on the petition filed by Mr. Raj Narain against the election of the Prime Minister, Mrs. Indira Gandhi in the 1971 mid-term Lok Sabha poll.

The 55-year-old, balding judge found Mrs. Gandhi guilty under the existing law of the corrupt practice of using to further her election prospects the services of Mr. Yashpal Kapoor, Officer-on-Special Duty in her Secretariat, while he was still in Government service. The Court found Mr. Kapoor had been engaged in election work for Mrs. Gandhi from January 7, 1971, after she had held out a week earlier as a prospective candidate in Rae Bareli. The Court held that Mr. Kapoor remained a gazetted officer of the Government of India till January 25, 1971, when the President accepted the resignation he tendered on January 13.

Mrs. Gandhi was also found guilty of obtaining the assistance of the District Magistrate, the Superintendent of Police, the PWD Executive Engineer and Hydel Engineer of Rae Bareli to make rostrum and other arrangements at her election meetings during her election campaign. The judge ruled that this was corrupt practice under the election law.

As prescribed in the law, the judge debarred Mrs. Indira Gandhi from election to any House of Parliament or State legislature for six years. The judgment was received amidst wild cheering despite the court's admonition against such behaviour before the judge took his seat.

Justice Sinha then signed the order and Mr. R. J. Chatterji, his Bench Secretary, put the seal of the Court. A judgment unseating an incumbent Prime Minister from Parliament passed into history.

As was expected, from every corner of the country, the resignation of the Prime Minister was immediately demanded by all opposition leaders. Following the normal procedure all over the democratic world, the Prime Minister should have resigned without delay. But she started prevaricating. For reasons not readily understandable, rumours were spread from circles close to the Prime Minister that she was wavering but at the same time wanting to step down. She was, however, being pressed hard by her followers, including her Cabinet colleagues and members of the so-called Congress High Command, not to be in a hurry but to wait and watch. Subsequently, a lot was said again after the Congress debacle in the Lok Sabha poll leading credence to this very carefully spread rumour about her willingness to quit office after the judgment and that if she did not, it was not her fault but of others around her. Would a strong-willed woman like her be so docile, really? The myth must be a *Mithya*, a lie.

The evidence on record shows that she never intended to resign, come what may. In fact, keeping in view the possibility of an adverse judgment, the ground had been prepared well in advance to justify her continuance in office. When the opposition leaders were crying themselves hoarse demanding her resignation, readymade specious pleas were being doled out all over the country by the ruling party leaders, members of Parliament and of State legislatures, PCCs and DCCs trotting out identical arguments why she should stay on. They started asserting in chorus their faith in the leadership of Mrs. Gandhi (as if she could not remain the leader of the Congress Party if she vacated the office of the Prime Minister). The Congress Parliamentary Board itself urged her to lead not only the party but the nation in spite of the judicial verdict against her.

The more clever ones pointed out that the Allahabad High Court itself had stayed the order for 20 days. Was that the reason why the Press Trust of India, the national news agency, was pressurised to hit up in its lead the stay part of the order rather than her guilt and punishment? Not that it mattered—those who put the pressure did not realise it. No amount of camouflage could hide the fact that her political career was in shambles because of the judgment.

The PTI lead of this news read:

"Mrs. Indira Gandhi, first Prime Minister of India to be held guilty of corrupt election practices obtained today a breather of 20 days to appeal to the Supreme Court against a judgment of the Allahabad High Court unseating her in the Lok Sabha and debarring her from election to any House of Parliament or State Legislature for 6 years.

"Justice J. M. L. Sinha, who pronounced the historic judgment in Court Room 15 of the High Court at 10 this morning granted the stay of his order within half an hour in his chamber. The Judge said he was satisfied by Mrs. Gandhi's counsel that there were sufficient reasons for the stay of the operation of the judgment and order he had delivered."

Why hit up the stay part of the story? The screaming banner headlines of newspapers, including the pro-Congress dailies, ignored this lead and announced "PM Unseated" or "PM debarred for 6 years", which was the cream of the news.

As to the reactions of Congress MPs soon after the judgment was on the wires. Mr. Ram Sekhar Singh's took the cake. The sapient Mr. Singh observed: "The destiny of the country cannot be changed by a judicial verdict. Sovereignty lies in Parliament and Mrs. Indira Gandhi is the undisputed leader of the Congress Party which commands majority in Parliament. So the question of her resigning from Prime Ministership does not arise . . . It is time to think of amending the Constitution to establish the supremacy of Parliament over the judiciary."

Incindentally, this command performance also let the cat out of the bag. Since Mr. Singh is in all probability not a prophet, his statement showed that the 39th and the 42nd amendment to the Constitution had been planned long in advance. The 39th amendment came into force on August 8, 1975. It replaced Article 71 and introduced a new Article 329A. It also put in the 9th Schedule several Acts, including the Representation of Peoples Act, the Election Laws (amendment) Act, 1975, which were made immune from attack in any court of law.

The new Article 71 empowered Parliament to pass laws regulating the election of the President and the Vice-President and made a provision for deciding disputes relating to their election. It took away the jurisdiction of the Supreme Court in the matter.

Article 329(A), which was a new insertion, had six clauses. The first three dealt with elections to Parliament of persons holding the office of Prime Minister or the Speaker. These clauses deprived the courts the jurisdiction to try election petitions against such persons with "retrospective effect", a masterly or dastardly touch, as you please.

Clause 4 did away with the application of laws to disputes arising out of such elections. It also declared such elections to be valid "notwithstanding any court judgment".

Clause 5 laid down that an appeal or cross-appeal pending before the Supreme Court shall be disposed of on the assumption that the judgment under appeal was void, that the findings contained in the judgment never had existence in the eyes of the law and that the election declared void by the judgment should continue to be void in all respects.

Clause 6 provided that the new Article 329(A) would have precedence over the rest of the Constitution.

It was on the strength of this monstrous 39th Amendment, the death-knell of democracy, that Mrs. Gandhi won her appeal in the Supreme Court when the emergency was on.

It is not necessary to go into the statements made by Congressmen in detail because all sang more or less the same tune that they had full faith in her leadership and that her continuance was a must. What they did not explain was why could not they have her as the supreme leader of their party enjoying their absolute faith to the point of crawling veneration without her being the Prime Minister?

But why waste time on the inspired reaction of her sycophants? What about her own stance after the judgment? The day after the judgment her rabble-raisers brought to her residence the Delhi Transport Corporation workers to shout "jais" and demand her continuance by ignoring the judicial verdict. She told the gathering that she was not upset by the judgment. Was it because she had already made up her mind to flout it? She assured her audience that she would continue to serve the country. How? Obviously by remaining Prime Minister.

In the context of the Allahabad judgment, she had also the cheek to accuse "certain foreign powers of weakening the country". The relevance of this wild innendo has been neither explained nor challenged. The innendo apparently was that where her own agents had failed, "certain foreign powers" had been able to get at Justice Sinha. There could not have been a greater contempt of court.

That day one after another crowds of hired men were brought to her residence. In all she addressed nine such "meetings" where slogans were raised by the faithfuls demanding that she stay in office. Quite sure in her mind what she would do, she was merely going through the motions to show to the world that it was the pressure of her partymen and the will of the people that left her with no option but to continue as PM.

However, the performance of the clique emboldened her to take risk after risk. In the initial stages Mrs. Gandhi's coterie, which pulled the strings to make the puppets dance and sing to their tune, harped only on their faith in her leadership, equating the Congress with the people, though the party had lost the Gujarat Assembly elections on the very day the Allahabad judgment was delivered.

This lacuna in the approach was soon made up by a number of amenable retired High Court judges, who began to issue statements arguing that she had a legal right to continue till the hearing of her appeal in the Supreme Court. After all, had not the Allahabad judge himself granted 20 days' stay of his order, which was in the nature of a temporary reprieve? This did not touch the delicate question whether the Prime Minister also had the moral right to continue. The issue was as much moral as legal.

It was, however, argued by her partisans that both the judgment of the Allahabad High Court and the interim stay order had to be respected. It might be a different matter if the Supreme Court granted only the usual limited and not absolute stay on the Prime Minister's appeal. Did not Mrs. Gandhi have as much right to the final verdict of the Supreme Court as any other citizen? The rule of law had to be the same for the Prime Minister and the commoner (ironically, the 39th Amendment to the Constitution put an end to that). The Congress Parliamentary Party advanced this egalitarian argument in a resolution adopted by it on June 18.

Though no lawyer, JP gave a smashing reply to all this

pettifogging. He pointed out that the Congress Parliamentary Party's resolution was yet another instance of unabashed political immorality of the Congress leadership and of its mischievous attempt to mislead the people. He said: "The point at issue is not whether Congress MPs have faith in Mrs. Indira Gandhi's leadership but whether there is rule of law in this country and whether it applies equally to every one, high or low. According to the plea made by Mrs. Gandhi's lawyer, the 20 days' stay order was obtained to enable the CPP to meet and elect a new leader to function until the Supreme Court decided her appeal. But the CPP met to proclaim the indispensibility of Mrs. Gandhi's leadership, that is, her Premiership.

"Here is a clear notice given that no matter what the law of the land might say, Mrs. Gandhi, in as much as it lies within the power of the Congress, will continue to be India's Prime Minister. It is in order to buttress this modern version of 'divine right' that the hysteric rallies, the colourful processions, the slander campaign against Mr. Justice Sinha, the effigy-burning and the rest of the fascistic campaign are being stage-managed. This is the meaning of Mr. Barooah's pontific pronouncement that laws are made by the people and the leader of the people is Mrs. Gandhi's implying that what she said or did was the law, irrespective of what any court of law might say or do."

Another idea that was being fostered was that Mrs. Gandhi's offence was only of a 'technical' nature. In the first place this was but pulling wool over one's eyes. First, however polite, the court had found her lying and knowingly using government machinery to further her electoral prospects. In the second place, a great part of the law of the land is technical and the entire Representation of the People, Act deals with technicalities.

But the propaganda was so good that even a seasoned journalist like Mr. Kuldip Nayar was taken in by it. Recently he has expressed the view that it was almost like unseating the Prime Minister on a traffic offence of speeding. With due deference, it was not that simple. For, in the case of Mr. D. P. Mishra former Chief Minister of Madhya Pradesh, the High Court had set aside his election and debarred him for six years from all elective posts on the sole ground that his election expenditure had exceeded the ceiling by Rs. 249.72 only. The Supreme

Court had upheld that judgment. How much did Mrs. Gandhi spend? Mr. L. N. Mishra alone knew. But he is dead.

The opposition leaders felt uneasy when, on the day after the Allahabad High Court judgment, Mrs. Gandhi assured the Delhi Transport Corporation workers that she would 'continue to serve the country'. On June 14, Messrs. Piloo Modi and Rabi Roy (BLD), S. N. Mishra (Cong.(O), Nanaji Deshmukh (Jana Sangh) and Brijmohan Toofan (Socialist Party) began a 'dharna' before Rashtrapati Bhawan demanding Mrs. Gandhi's resignation. The President, Mr. Fakhruddin Ali Ahmed, was holidaying in Kashmir. Reports current in the capital said the President wanted to return to Delhi but the Prime Minister advised him against it till he got her signal. The 'dharna' before Rashtrapati Bhawan continued.

Surprisingly enough, when the fate of the appeal of the Prime Minister still to be filed in the Supreme Court was uncertain (the 39th Amendment was also still to come), the Chief Election Commissioner, Mr. T. Swaminathan, popped from nowhere. In reply to a question, which seems to have been planted (every newsman knows how this is done), the Chief Election Commissioner said in Calcutta that he had the power to remove any disqualification of a member of Parliament, in other words, he had superior power than even the Supreme Court. If the verdict of the Supreme Court went against her, he, Mr. T. Swaminathan, could still remove her disqualification. The occasion for the exercise of that power, however, never arose. But this assertion of Mr. Swaminathan must have helped to boost the morale of Mrs. Gandhi's discomfited supporters.

Every day Mrs. Gandhi continued to address stage-managed rallies at her residence announcing her firm decision not to succumb to the opposition pressures. Her loyal camp-followers duly burnt an effigy of Justice Sinha before her residence in the presence of many spectators.

President Ahmed on his return to Delhi counselled the opposition leaders to have patience and wait for the outcome of the meeting of the Congress Parliamentary Party to be held on June 18. Meanwhile, a section of the country's youths angered by Mrs. Gandhi's stance started burning her effigies, particularly in Bihar. To prove the contrary, that there was no dearth of youths who fanatically supported her, the Punjab

Chief Minister, Mr. Zail Singh, presented the Prime Minister with a scroll purported to have been signed in blood by 519 students belonging to the Punjab Unit of the National Students' Union of India affirming their unflinching faith in her leadership and urging her to continue in office.

To buttress her claim to stay on, Mrs. Gandhi now started harping in her speeches on external threats to the country when no such threat existed. And of course external threats could be met only by her or under her leadership.

On June 18, the Prime Minister came out in the open and bluntly told the opposition parties that she would not resign to oblige them. She made this announcement at the emergent meeting of the Congress Parliamentary Party convened specifically to raeffirm faith in her leadership (not electing a new leader as her lawyer had given Mr. Justice Sinha to understand for securing the interim stay).

She declared: "My actions depend not on what the opposition says but on my own party and the people." She took this opportunity to refer to the demonstrations and rallies organised in her support in Delhi and in the States and said: "I am overwhelmed by the affection showered on me by the poorer and weaker sections of the people. Their enthusiasm has been greater than it was at the time of the 1969 split. I feel not only overwhelmed but also very humble." No wonder, she started equating her party with the people while proclaiming herself as the defender of democracy!

To further 'overwhelm' her, a huge rally was organised at the India Gate on June 20. Cart-loads, bus-loads, truck-loads and train-loads of men and women were brought from neighbouring areas of Delhi, Haryana and Punjab and also from other distant parts of the country, including Andamans, Arunachal Pradesh, Mizoram, Manipur and Lakshadwip. India Gate was bedecked with buntings carrying slogans declaring the indispensibility of Mrs. Gandhi and proclaiming absolute faith in her leadership in "Toofan Mein, Aandhi Mein" (storm and gale).

How much money had been spent and by whom to organise this grand circus was anybody's guess. But it was indeed a pageantry of power and popularity for the success of which government vehicles, the public transport system and private buses and trucks had been mobilised. The citizens of Delhi had to go without their quota of loaf produced by the local bakeries since their entire produce had to be diverted for the consumption of the people brought from outside. The All India Radio and the TV also carried on vigorous but mendacious propaganda to collect crowds at the India Gate.

Only two days later, JP's plane from Patna to Delhi was deliberately delayed to prevent him from addressing a rally of workers of non-CPI opposition parties. After waiting for several hours at the Patna airport, JP had to leave by train. He could not address the rally in Delhi because the Prime Minister was determined to serve the country and was in no mood to be balked by the leader of the "plotters" out to remove her from the seat of power from where alone she could render effective service. Had she not declared at the India Gate rally that there was "a deep-laid plot to remove her from power"? And she had thundered amidst defeaning cheers: "I shall continue to serve the country till the last breath of my life."

It was at this rally that, amidst applause, the Congress President, Mr. Debkant Barooah, announced his egregious equation: "Indira is India, India is Indira." He also suggested that her admirers should sing "Jai" in praise of Indira "Subah Mein, Sham Mein, Din Mein, Raat Mein" (during sunrise, sunset, daytime and night). This performance earned him the sobriquet of "court jester" from JP.

Undeterred by the salvos fired by Mrs. Gandhi and her henchmen, on June 22 the opposition parties organised a massive rally of their own at Ramlila Ground, though JP could not be present on the occasion. While the rally was on, Mrs. Gandhi, who had once said that she treated capitalists like worms, was herself addressing a mini-rally of business magnates led by Mr. K. K. Birla at her residence and telling them that India needed a strong Centre to bring about stability and solve the country's problems. And who else but she could ensure this? But this of course she left unsaid. Like a true gallant, Mr. Birla assured her on behalf of the business community of their full faith in her policies and statesmanship.

The non-CPI opposition parties met in the presence of JP in Delhi on June 23 and prepared a draft programme of mass action to compel Mrs. Gandhi to resign. It deferred its decision pending the ruling of the Supreme Court to be given next day on the Prime Minister's plea for an absolute stay of the Allahabad High Court judgment and order.

The Prime Minister had contended in her petition to the Supreme Court that the balance of convenience was in her favour and that irreparable damage would be done to her and there would be far-reaching repercussions in the country if an unconditional and absolute stay of the Allahabad judgment of June 12 setting aside her election was not granted.

Mr. V. R. Krishna Iyer, Supreme Court Vacation Judge, who heard her petition, however, granted on June 24 only conditional stay and imposed conditions on her functioning as a member of the Lok Sabha but without impairing her constitutional rights as Prime Minister of India. Shorn of legal technicalities, the Court order granted Mr. Gandhi the right to address both Houses of Parliament in her capacity as Prime Minister and draw her salary as such but denied her the right to vote as a member. (Under the Constitution even a non-member can be a Minister for six months after which he has to go if he cannot get himself elected.)

The conditional stay made the opposition leaders jubilant because she had herself maintained that a conditional stay order would cause her irreparable damage. The Congress MPs naturally felt sad.

The executive committee of the non-CPI opposition parties, namely the Congress(O), the Jana Sangh, the Bharatiya Lok Dal, the Socialist Party and the Akali Dal decided at a meeting to launch a countrywide movement if the Prime Minister still refused to quit. JP presided. It met again on June 25. This time the representatives of the CPI(M) and the Dravida Munetra Khazgam (DMK) also attended. It announced its decision to launch countrywide struggle from June 29 and set up a Lok Sangharsh Samiti (people's action committee) under the chairmanship of Mr. Morarji Desai to conduct the movement all over the country.

The eight-party combine of West Bengal led by the CPI(M) did not even wait for June 29. It decided that very day to launch a Statewide campaign to press for the resignation of the Prime Minister.

Despite the conditional stay, the Union Law Minister,

Mr. H. R. Gokhale, claimed that it was now clear that she would stay because the Supreme Court had ruled that she could legally continue. The Congress leadership, Congress MPs other than the Young Turks and several Chief Ministers present in Delhi at the time decided that she should stay on. But this was not all. There were still two more acts of hubris before nemesis finally caught up with the tragic heroine.

TWENTY-NINE

The Emergency

Suddenly, at the behest of the Prime Minister, a surprised and perhaps not too willing President Ahmed declared a state of internal emergency "to meet the situation threatening the security of India due to internal disturbances" although not a single case of internal disturbance had been reported at the time. The external emergency declared since the war with Pakistan in 1971 was still continuing although its cause had ceased to exist for a long time.

It was officially announced on the morning of 26th June that the Union Cabinet had met at 6 a.m., considered the situation and approved the recommendation of the President for the declararion of emergency, which was then signed by the President at 7 a.m. The reason for the internal emergency given in the proclamation itself differed from what the Prime Minister told the nation in a broadcast to the nation. She clearly said that it had been proclaimed because of "the designs of the opposition parties" which posed a threat to national security.

The decision to proclaim emergency was certainly her own. She alone took it and informed the Cabinet after the *fait accompli* and not before. Recently Mr. Jagjiwan Ram and Mr. Y. B. Chavan confirmed this. Dr. K. V. Raghunatha Reddy, former Union Minister for Labour, told reporters at Nellore on June 21, 1977 that members of Mrs. Gandhi's Cabinet, including himself, had no prior knowledge about it.

It was a pre-emptive action. When the Cabinet was told about the declaration of emergency by Mrs. Gandhi, the process of rounding up leading personalities was already in full swing. That this was the truth is self-evident from the fact that the President's proclamation followed a pre-dawn swoop in which

JP, Morarji Desai, Chaudhary Charan Singh, Atal Bihari Vajpayee, L. K. Advani, Asoka Mehta, Samar Guha, Piloo Mody and others were picked up and whisked away in the small hours of the morning from their residences. JP was roused from bed from the Gandhi Peace Foundation at 2.30 a.m. and taken away. Even the editor of the *Motherland*, Mr. K. R. Malkani, was arrested in Delhi and M. L. Kak, *Tribune's* staff correspondent at Hissar in the early hours of the morning. Similar arrests were made of the activists of the opposition parties and workers of the Jana Sangharsh and Chhatra Sangharsh Samitis throughout the country in a nationwide man-hunt which started long before the actual proclamation. The dark days of emergency had began, the darkest chapter in modern India's history.

Pre-Censorship

The nightmare that began from the early morning of June 26 continued for 19 long months. The proclamation of emergency was a virtual declaration of war against the people. As in war, so in emergency, the first casualty was truth. This was ensured by the imposition of rigorous pre-censorship and stringent media control. Such censorship had never been imposed even in the war years during the British regime. I know because I had worked on the Reuter's desk of the Associated Press of India at Bombay since the beginning of 1945. Our desk was on the first floor of the Petit Building and the military censors had their office on the second floor. They never killed a story simply because it was critical of the Government of India. Only stories likely to be of help to the enemy were censored. I remember only one occasion when a story was killed not by the military censor but by our General Manager, Mr. John Turner, because it concerned some petty scandal about a British Minister.

But the censorship that came in the wake of the emergency was something strange and unique. Initially censors were posted in the offices of the newspapers and news agencies all over the country till the Chief Censor's Office was organised in Delhi. This office in turn organised its State units which censored almost everything that even slightly smacked of any reflection on the government. In Patna, the Bihar Government issued an order under section 48 of the Defence of India Rules on the night of 26th June imposing pre-censorship of news and information published and circulated through news agencies, newspapers, magazines, leaflets, handbills, posters and any printed material.

The order said no such thing could be printed, published or circulated unless authorised by the Director of Information, the district magistrate, the additional district magistrate or the sub-divisional officer. It made exemptions, however, in favour of the PTI, the UNI, the *Hindustan Samachar*, the *Samachar Bharti*, the *Indian Nation*, the *Aryabarta*, the *Searchlight*, the *Pradeep*, the *Vishwabandhu* and the *Sada-e-Aam*. The order was to remain in force until further notice.

Rule 69 of the DIR was invoked next day by the district magistrates all over the State banning assemblage of five or more persons, carrying of weapons, shouting of provocative slogans and playing of loudspeakers for dissemination of any information prejudicial to the maintenance of law and order with retrospective effect from the previous morning. The people were warned that any violation of the order would incur conviction and sentences upto three years' rigorous imprisonment.

On June 28, the exemptions allowed to the four news agencies and six dailies were withdrawn under directions from the Union Government.

Soon the Chief Censor's office was established in Shastri Bhawan in New Delhi. It was a full-fledged organisation with Mr. Baji, the Principal Information Officer, as in charge of the organisation. But he was replaced within a few days as he was found inadequate for the task of enforcing the type of rigid censorship that the government wanted. Mr. H. J. D. Penha, a retired Principal Information Officer, was called back from retirement and made the Chief Censor. The censors' desk at his headquarters included two joint chief censors, eight deputy chief censors and at least a dozen censor officers. The Chief Censor also set up his units in the State Capitals and other newspapers centres. A prominent signboard adorned the entrance of the Chief Censor's office bearing the legend ENTRY PROHIBITED. Journalists intending to file their stories had to submit them to a censor registry and await clearance which often took several days if the newspaper he represented was not pro-government.

Several important newspapers like the *Statesman* and the *Indian Express* and its allied language publications were harassed by holding up their stories for long. They were also required to submit their editorials, galley proofs and page proofs for clearance. On the 26th June itself the offices of the *Motherland*, the *Organiser* and the *Everyman* (JP's weekly) were locked up by the enforcement branch of the police. For two days the power supply of the newspapers in Delhi were cut off with the result that none of them could come out. The *Veer Arjun*, a pro-Jana Sangh daily was so badly harassed that it was forced to close down. Similar harassment led to the closure of important journals like the Samachar, the *Main stream* and the *Himmat*. The editor of the *Hindustan Times* Mr. B.G. Verghese, lost his job for his refusal so for the official line.

After that only statements welcoming the emergency, official handouts and innocuous news items were allowed to be published. Mr. Mundrika Prasad Sinha, one of the General Secretaries of the Bihar Pradesh Congress Committee, resigned in protest (though he did not say so in his statement). The news was duly killed by the censor.

By June 30, the number of activists of the Samiti arrested in Bihar in the wake of the emergency went up to 463 according to the Home Secretary, Mr. R. N. Dash (no names were given nor allowed to be published). This figure was obviously incorrect because the figures for Patna district alone given by the district magistrate totalled 102 (Bihar comprises 31 districts). As days passed the censorship became more and more rigid. Even the press releases of the district magistrate of Patna (who was himself one of the censoring authorities) about encounters between the police and alleged extremists were killed.

One day when the Chief Minister of Bihar, Dr. Jagannath Mishra, said something about the Bihar situation at his press conference, Mr. Rakesh, the Chief Censor of Bihar (the officer in charge of the Press Information Bureau of Patna), stood up and cheekily said: "Please make it off the record, Sir, or else I shall censor it." Such effrontery was possible only because the power of the Government of India stood behind the swell-head.

No wonder, gradually censorship was extended even to the proceedings of the Lok Sabha, the Rajya Sabha, the Supreme Court and its subordinate courts. I recall, one day the Prime Minister Mrs. Indira Gandhi, said in Parliament that some people called her a dictator and declared in a huff: "Yes, I am a dictator". The PTI creeded it. But soon a cancellation came and it was killed. I am not sure now if it was before or during the emergency. But it is a fact that even the Prime Minister's speeches in Parliament were sometimes censored for keeping up pretences. When friendly journalists went to her and pleaded for relaxation of censorship, she used to pose helplessness and say: "What can I do? Even my speeches are censored." Of course, the make-believe deceived none.

Many illegal directives, much beyond the jurisdiction and the powers of the censor, were orally given. Even the dispute over Godavari waters between Maharashtra and Andhra Pradesh was not allowed to be published. The Delhi High Court judgment on Mr. Kuldip Nayar's petition met with the same fate. Health bulletins by JP's attending physicians (after he was released) were censored.

Sometimes reports of incidents, which were yet to reach newspapers offices, were prematurely disclosed by censors in their overzealousness. One such instance occurred when there was heavy police firing on political prisoners in the Bhagalpur Special Jail in May, 1976. Some prisoners, who had come out, were shot dead on the road after dragging them from nearby houses where they had sought refuge. Mr. Jageshwar Mandal, now the Minister in charge of Cooperation and then a member of the Bihar Vidhan Parishad, was a witness to the shootings. The censor gave away the news by ringing up the newspaper and news agency offices and directing them not to publish it.

The funniest bungling occurred over a long interview given by Mr. Sanjay Gandhi, the up-and-coming man, to Mrs. Uma Vasudeva for her journal *Surge*. Sanjay, who was being projected as the heir-apparent, had aired his views on all subjects on earth, some of which ran counter to his mother's known stands. But by that time Sanjay had become a powerful figure and the Press Information Bureau thought fit to release the interview in toto for publication through the PTI and UNI. Soon there were stirrings in the higher echelons and it was suggested that if at all it was to be published, it should be published in full and not in a summarised form. The PTI and UNI had released only the summaries. When the circulation of the full text was asked for, the PTI said it would release the text the next day. But the UNI, whose daily load of wordage was much less compared to PTI, agreed and issued it in full that very day. Again there were consultations at top levels and it was finally decided to kill the story altogether. Both the agencies were asked to kill it and they obliged. But by that time several newspapers had carried it in their dak editions and the censors could do nothing about it.

A large section of the foreign press used to be highly critical of Mrs. Gandhi's action in stifling the voice of the people and the press in India and assuming dictatorial powers. But not a line of these reports were allowed to see the light of the day in our country. Only comments favourable to her were allowed circulation. Several issues of the *Time* magazine were impounded. It had published a highly critical story on the proclamation of the emergency. This could be known to the Indian readers when the subsequent issues were allowed entry. The letters to the editor published in the *Time* gave or gave away the contents of its original despatch. The censors did not apparently scan the *Time's* letters to the editor columns.

The Indian newspapers gradually became stale and unreadable because of the vigorous censorship and the people had to tune in the BBC, which suddenly became very popular, to get the real news of what was happening within the country. How the world press was fed with news relating to the underground stir and the excesses committed by the authorities following the declaration of emergency is another story. This was masterminded by my friend, Mr. Jagdish Prasad Mathur, Organising Secretary of the Jana Sangh with the help of a few intrepid newsmen. They succeeded greatly in establishing contacts with representatives of the international news media much to the chagrin of the powers that be.

Mr. Mathur established an underground information cell charged with the task of feeding the world press. He operated under different aliases. His principal associates were Mr. Satish Bhatia, editor, the *Organiser*, Mr. Bhanu Prakash, editor, *Panchajanya* and Mr. K. Prabhu of the *Indian Times*, Mr.

Subramaniam Swamy, Mr. Digvijay Narain Singh and Mr. Dina Nath Mishra.

Many foreign correspondents were expelled from India during the 19 months of emergency. The BBC office was closed down. Notwithstanding the steps taken by the authorities, the cell was able to put across most of the black deeds of the Government, including MISA arrests and atrocities committed on the people. (Mr. Kuldip Nayar's arrest was broadcast by the BBC the same evening.)

The foreign press cell was organised as a wing of the Lok Sangharsh Samiti to create world opinion against the authoritarian rule of Mrs. Gandhi. A meeting of some Jana Sangh leaders, who had escaped arrest, was held in the lawns of the Golf Club in Delhi. Nanaji Deshmukh, Kunwarlal Gupta, Radhe Krishna (Gandhi Peace Foundation) and some others participated. It was decided to have a secret telephone number, meeting place and liaison with non-Congress governments in Gujarat, Jammu and Kashmir and Tamil Nadu. Underground bulletins were started. The information from States was pooled in Delhi and utilised for the central bulletin. Jagdish Mathur briefed important foreign correspondents and fed the news pool system evolved by the foreign correspondents for sharing all relevant information.

In Bihar the propaganda section of the underground was headed by Zabir Hussain, a young lecturer in English in D.J. College, Monghyr, who was also a member of the Acharyakul founded by Acharya Vinoba Bhave. He was returned to the Bihar Assembly in June, 1977 and sworn in as a Minister in Karpoori Thakur Ministry and allotted the Health portfolio.

An impression still persists that very few newspapers resisted the powers that be. This is not quite true. Their number though not large was quite sizeable. The maximum harassment was suffered by the *Statesman* and the *Indian Express* group. The *Ananda Bazar Patrika*, which has the largest circulation in the country, also remained under pressure throughout the period of the emergency. But its proprieter-editor, Mr. Asok Kumar Sarkar, did not bend though two of his star reporters, Barun Sen Gupta and Gour Kishore Ghosh were jailed.

The Government used to stop its advertisements to the newspapers which refused to toe the line. Even the pro-CPI

Patriot of Delhi was penalised for its refusal to project Sanjay Gandhi as the Coming Hero.

After the lifting of the emergency, the *Statesman* filed a suit in which it gave a fairly long list of newspapers which had been harassed and penalised with the stoppage of Government advertisements. The Government also put pressure on big business houses not to advertise in "delinquent" newspapers.

Though the press was gagged, these defiant or courageous newspapers managed at great risk to publish some truth. But, by and large, throughout the period of the emergency, the people were fed by the radio, the television and some highly paid pressmen with pure propaganda that they never had it so good when in fact all that the nation cherished had virtually been disowned to perpetuate the personal dictatorship of a ruthless lady who would stop at nothing to keep herself in power.

Throttling of News Agencies

How the *Samachar* came into being is another story. Sometime in July-August, 1975, Mr. C. Raghavan, Editor-in-Chief of the PTI, was called by the Information and Broadcasting Minister, Mr. Vidya Charan Shukla, for "consultations". Shukla mooted the idea of "creating a Tass in India". Raghavan informed me later that he had committed an unpardonable *faux pas* by replying that "a Tass cannot be created without first creating a Soviet State". He at once became a marked man. In December, 1975, an ordinance was promulgated to create a unified news agency but this move did not succeed because Mr. P. N. Haksar and Mr. Jagjiwan Ram opposed it in the Cabinet.

Then came the mailed fist. The AIR "terminated" its contract with the PTI and UNI for the supply of news. Various Government departments and State Governments were also directed to take similar action. Meanwhile, the Samachar Society had been set up and the PTI and UNI were made to enter into an agreement with it appointing it, as the sole agent for the supply of news to the AIR and other government departments. Raghavan then committed his second folly by advising members of the PTI Board of Directors against it as it would be illegal and beyond their legal authority. Dark hints were conveyed to the Directors that the alternative they faced was detention under the MISA.

In December, 1976, Raghavan was bundled out despite his contract with the PTI without any notice of termination of his service. According to Raghavan's information the orders came from Mrs. Indira Gandhi or Mr. Sanjay Gandhi and these were conveyed by their agents. Earlier he was sought to be humiliated by posting him at Bhuvaneshwar "to report social and cultural news". When he tried to stand on his rights, he was shown the door. Mr. G. G. Mirchandani, General Manager of the UNI, also suffered the same fate for opposing formation of the *Samachar*.

THIRTY

Advent of Sanjay

The emergency also marked the emergence of Mr. Sanjay Gandhi, the second son of Mrs. Gandhi. He had already gained notoriety over his people's car project, the Maruti Ltd. He enjoyed an awesome power without responsibility. Mrs. Gandhi had started leaning on him more and more just before the Allahabad High Court judgment when she had begun suspecting the loyalty of most of the people around her.

Sanjay rose like a meteor and also alas, plumetted like one. His mother helped to project him on the Indian stage first as the new Messiah of the youth. Chief Ministers of States were rebuked by her if they went to meet her without meeting Sanjay first. Persons with youth on their side and eyes on the main chance joined the bandwagon and the strength of the Youth Congress was soon claimed to have gone up to five million. Where they have vanished after the Congress debacle at the Lok Sabha polls nobody knows. Ministers, including Chief Ministers, had to quit if they incurred the displeasure of this arrogant young man. Only in West Bengal and Orissa the authority of Sanjay was a little challenged. Mrs. Nandini Satpathy had to relinquish office of the Chief Minister of Orissa because her son had set up a parallel youth organisation in the State. Mr. Shiddhartha Shankar Ray was at the point of being booted out but he escaped because the militant youth leaders of West Bengal, who could play the role of storm troopers better than the Sanjay Brigade, came out in defence of "Manuda" (Manu was Mr. Ray's nick name and 'Da' was an abbreviation of 'Dada' or elder brother).

Chief Ministers and their Cabinet colleagues in other States started lining up to pay homage to Sanjay during his visits to their States. Although he had no official *locus standi*, government files were laid out before him for his perusal if he wanted to have a look. One Chief Minister paid obeisance along with his wife and incurred the wrath of his extremely conservative community. Another Chief Minister, at least on one occasion reportedly helped Sanjay to put on his sandals. This, in the form of a cartoon, was used as a poster during the Lok Sabha poll in a State where the Congress could not win a single seat.

Taking advantage of the situation, a coterie of seniors, who enjoyed the confidence of the Prime Minister, ganged up with the young man. After the emergency was lifted this coterie was described in the press as the "gang of four", probably on the analogy of Mao Tse Tung's widow, Madame Chiang Ching's gang. It was supposed to comprise Mr. Bansi Lal, Mr. Yashpal Kapur, Mr. Om Mehta and Mr. Vidya Charan Shukla. A few others were also active on the wings, one of whom, operated from the Prime Minister's secretariat, and another, who, besides Shukla, kept the news agencies (before and after their merger) in line. There were also two *femme fatales*.

Was Sanjay really the "small fry" that Mrs. Gandhi once protestingly described him to be? The young man is under heavy fire now and may be his future is dark. Fantastic charges have been brought against him and his mother after the Lok Sabha polls. Commissions of Enquiry have been set up to examine the charges, the truth or otherwise of which would be known for certain only after their findings are made known.

It is painful to note not so much the antics of this immature and haughty young man as the to-dos of top Congress leaders and some top journalists who boosted him was India's Man of Destiny. Here are a few specimens of what some of them said and perhaps believed:

> "The emergence of Sanjay Gandhi as the Youth Leader has electrified the atmosphere in the country. Our generation is dying out. It is time that the youth take over. In this country the youth have done a lot of things, but the old people have taken more credit for it." —D. K. Barooah
>
> "Mr. Sanjay Gandhi has emerged as a powerful leader mainly because of his forthright and down to earth policy. His advent in politics can be compared with that of Jawaharlal Nehru in the Lahore Congress." —V. C. Shukla

"I hope Congressmen of Punjab will rise to the occasion and follow the path shown by Sanjay Gandhi." —Zail Singh

"Sanjay is the future of India. His future is very bright and we are proud to have the grandson of Panditji and the son of Indiraji in our midst. Mr. Gandhi, the India of Panditji's and Indiraji's dreams will be realised under your responsibility." —Rajni Patel

"Mr. Sanjay Gandhi has all the characteristics of the Nehru family. He is above casteism, regionalism and communalism and pragmatic." —Devraj Urs

"I promise that the entire route trekked by Youth Leader Sanjay Gandhi will be metalled." —Narain Dutt Tewari

"I wish to express my sincere gratitude to Sanjay Gandhi for the part he played in resolving the political tangle in Orissa." —Vinayak Acharya (after Nandini's ouster)

"If anyone can improve India, it is the youth and workers. Who can show the youth the way except Sanjay Gandhi? Walk shoulder to shoulder with him." —Bansi Lal

Many newspapers in the grip of the emergency and pre-censorship vied with one another to give Sanjay a big build up just to curry favour with him and his mother. Wrote Mr. R. K. Karanjia in the *Blitz* of 27/11/76:

"Mr. Sanjay Gandhi's rise to power came to us as History's own answer to our prayers. Here at last was a young man, uncontaminated by the political inhibitions and spiritual decadence of the past, capable of mobilising India's neglected youth power into a million-muscled Land Army. That is the logical and inevitable corollary of the Youth Congress session at Gauhati."

As late as February 5, 1977, the weekly *Current* described him thus:

"Sanjay (30). Authentic spokesman of Young India. Trail blazer."

The stance of these two weeklies known for their fickleness was understandable. Not-so-understandable was the piece written by the editor of the *Illustrated Weekly of India*, Mr. Khuswant Singh. He wrote:

> "Sanjay Gandhi has added a new dimension to political leadership; he has no truck with shady characters or sycophants; he is a teetotaler; he lives a simple life; he speaks little; he speaks in honest and forthright manner; his words are not hot air but charged with action.
>
> "He has done excellent work in Delhi. He has electrified the country's young people and channelised their energies into constructive work. He has awakened Congressmen everywhere and put them into action.
>
> "His Youth Congress has done more work in these last two years than the main Congress could do in the last five years.
>
> "And above all, he is the first Congress leader who has taken on himself the unpleasant task of cleaning and purging the party of its ills. More power to Sanjay!"

Amazing! Didn't Mr. Khuswant Singh know that Sanjay was surrounded only by "chamchas" (flatterers), most of whom were opportunists, if not scoundrels? That most of his wonderful work had been *fatwas* (proclamations) or done only on paper? Was Turkman Gate one of the wonderful pieces of work done by him? Mr. Singh had displayed a coloured photograph of the Maruti car with Sanjay standing beside it, even though it had not come out of the assembly line.

Mr. Khuswant Singh is a widely travelled clever journalist with considerable courage and a sense of humour. One cannot think of him as a journalist gone to seed turning into a sycophant. It is a tribute to Sanjay that he could fool a person like Mr. Singh.

All the adulation must have turned Sanjay's head. He soon formulated a five-point programme, which was incorporated with fanfare in the Prime Minister's 20-point programme, which now became a 25-point programme. There was nothing new or startling in Sanjay's programme. Its emphasis was on ending the dowry system and casteism. Both these points had been hammered home by so many reformers. JP in his concept of total revolution had underlined these long before. The Sharda Act had been passed even during the British regime. The

Congress Government itself had legislated to end the dowry system before Sanjay made it a part of his programme. Ironically, Congressmen themselves, who did *salaam* before him, openly took part in lavish feasts and marriages where huge sums were paid as dowry. Before legislation some social stigma could not be avoided as dowry had to be paid before witnesses. It at least provided a safeguard against misappropriation of the dowry money. After the legislation that safeguard was gone because the transaction had to be surreptitious. It still is. Previously the payment agreed upon could be staggered. After the Anti-dowry Act, it has to be paid in full in advance.

How was Sanjay going to abolish the caste system? His followers just dropped their family surnames. Even this was not new. Before independence Mr. Sriman Narayan Agrawal had dropped "Agrawal" from his name. One wonders what would Sanjay be without his surname.

What triggered opposition most was his ruthless family planning programme, which even his sister-in-law Sonia, is said to have refused to accept. But Sanjay's family planning programme created terror both in the urban and the rural areas. A rickshaw-puller seeking to renew his license had to submit to sterilisation. And not only the rickshaw-puller. When I sent my gun for renewal of license, my man was provided with a form demanding that I, an old man in his sixties, should give in writing that I would undergo vasectomy! Those who wanted to evade the privilege had to pay bribes. But in the countryside, squads of sterilisation teams accompanied by armed policemen went into action and perpetrated untold atrocities.

Resistance led to police firings. At Muzaffar Nagar at least 25 bodies of victims could be seen lying in the streets on October 18, 1976. These were the bodies of persons who had been in the crowd which had protested against forcible sterilisation and got bullets in reply. At Kairana (near Muzaffar Nagar) protest against these firings on the next day led to a repeat performance. At Peepli in Haryana, two persons were killed in police firing and many injured for the same offence. In Agamkuan in east Patna, there was a similar firing. Fortunately, only one person was killed. Instances can be easily multiplied. Call this a free country?

Sanjay's fad for beautification of cities at the cost of slum-dwellers for the benefit of the rich led to horrendeous atrocities at Turkman Gate in Delhi reminiscent of Jalianwalla Bag. The story of the gory killings at Turkman Gate on April 19, 1976 could not be suppressed even by the Argus-eyed censors as it spread by word of mouth all over the country. Bulldozers were used to demolish the *Jhuggis* and *Jhopris* (hutments) of the poor, and when they protested, they were mowed down.

Sanjay Gandhi said recently in an interview with an obscure New York magazine (the name suggested it was of Indian origin) that he was not in Delhi at the time. This proves nothing. For, if his overzealous supporters had perpetrated the horrors, he cannot escape the responsibility. It had been done obviously to please him, as part of the policy.

With her wide network of intelligence agencise, Mrs. Gandhi was fully aware of the facts. But she turned a blind eye. Mrs. Subhadra Joshi, a Congress MP, wanted to take up the Turkman Gate affair with her. But her repeated requests for an interview were refused because Sanjay did not like her. Mrs. Gandhi had full knowledge of the range and thrusts of the activities of her son. How could she feign ignorance of the fact that Sanjay with his caucus was functioning as an extra-constitutional centre of power? After all, that power had to be delegated by her. How could the Finance Minister, Mr. C. Sabramaniam, be deprived of his banking portfolio for the benefit of a Sanjay crony, Pranab Mukherji, allegedly to facilitate the use or misuse of the huge resources of the nationalised banks? Was she ignorant of the booting out of several Chairmen of the nationalised banks who stood in her son's way?

Yet the lady, who had affectionately described Sanjay as a "small fry", commended the grand success of the Youth Congress convention at Gauhati, which, she maintained, was as big if not bigger than the AICC session itself. Amidst prolonged applause of lickspittles, old and young, she had said that "the Youth Congress (that is, Sanjay) has stolen our thunder"! (A humorous colleague once described this as one of the excesses of the emergency.)

Not only Sanjay but also his associates and flatterers, who shone in his reflected glory, allegedly minted money, according to press reports which have gone unchallenged, by misusing the official machinery in several States. Officials, who had the temerity to stand up, had to suffer. The details must await the findings of the enquiries that have been set up.

When Sanjay suddenly blossomed forth in the country's political horizon, it was an open secret that Mrs. Gandhi was grooming him for perpetuating a dynastic rule. This may not be wholly true, but she did allow Sanjay to wield more and more power. Only she could not be in a hurry to vacate her post for the benefit of her son. May be after a decade or so but not soon. It would have been quite out of character for Mrs. Gandhi, who had violated every norm of public conduct and butchered the Constitution to keep herself in power, to part with it so easily even for her pet child. But she had succeeded in turning him into the biggest swell-head. For herself what she had established in the name of saving her brand of democracy after the 42nd Constitution amendment, which was not an amendment but re-enactment of the Constitution itself, was the free and easy style of a despotic ruler, indeed an empress. The picture was complete with her beloved prince, courtiers, not to mention the court jester. The provinces were to be ruled by her Mansabdars, the Chief Ministers. In this scheme the people had ceased to be citizens. They had become subjects.

In such a scheme of things, the favourite prince must bide his time till the empress in her pleasure decided to relinquish the throne in his favour or in the event of her sad demise. Her utterances had become strangely reminiscent of Hitler and Mussolini. Ironically enough, at that time she was claiming to be fighting the "fascist forces led by Mr. Jayaprakash Narayan"!

In his *Mein Kampf* Hitler wrote that there would be no democratic nonsense and that the Third Reich would be ruled by the *Fuehrer Prinzip*, the leadership principle. Mussolini boasted that under fascism the "noxious theories of liberalism would be dumped upon the rubbish-heap". He scoffed at all talk of civil liberties and held that it was for the State to decide what measure of freedom an individual citizen should be allowed to enjoy. The fascist State, he declared, organises the nation, leaves to the individual "as much liberty as is essential but deprives him of all useless and possibly harmful freedom". Didn't Mrs. Gandhi sing the same tune? Didn't she say that the democratic freedoms, as the people understood them, would never return? Spain's dictator, Francisco Franco, called a labour strike "a crime". He maintained that the right to strike was indicative of "the law of the jungle and primitive societies". (During the emergency all strikes and lockouts were banned.)

Even Hitler did not do away with the Weimer Constitution. The Constitution itself was made an instrument for establishing his fascist regime. Mrs. Gandhi too did exactly that.

Democracy stands on four pillars known as the four estates. Fascism stands on five pillars: concentration of power in the hands of an individual or group, suppression of civil liberties, abolition of trade union rights, media control for conducting one-sided propaganda of the ruling clique and reliance on brute force for keeping the people in line. That was the picture of India during the emergency.

As to the fourth estate, was Mr. L. K. Advani too harsh on the role of pressmen during the emergency that they crawled when they were merely asked to bend? When they had much better examples to emulate, they chose to play the role of some French newspapers during Napoleon's march to Paris after his escape from Elba in 1815 though they did this only in the reverse gear.

Napoleon was variously described in headlines during his advance to Paris by the *Moniteur* between March 9 and March 22 as a beast, a monster, the Corsican horror, the scourge, the torturer, the tyrant, the liberator and finally with a salutation to His Imperial Majesty! In our country not a word was said against Mrs. Gandhi when she was at the height of her power. She was denounced only when she lost.

But were there not better examples to emulate? For instance, the role of the founder of the *New York Times*, who had battled against near-insurmountable odds against the bosses of the Tammany Hall? Didn't the *Washington Post* refuse to be cowed down by Nixon's threats? ("Bomb the *Washington Post*", Nixon had said.) Why did they forget the role played by many of our newspapers during the British regime? Did not they also have the more recent example of the *Statesman*, the *Indian Express* and several other newspapers which refused to be cowed down during the emergency?

THIRTY-ONE

The Underground

It has been suggested by some writers that the JP movement had petered out even before the emergency. This ill-informed assumption is totally wrong. The movement did not die out even during the emergency. It went underground as it had to in the given situation. The movement conducted by the Akhil Bhartiya Lok Sangharsh Samiti has been described in recent Hindi book titled "Bhumigat Andolan".

A brief report on the underground movement in Bihar will suffice. But before coming to it, it is necessary to refer to two publications, one containing the Hindi speech of Mr. Narayan after his release at a farewell function in Bombay before his departure to Patna, which the censors suppressed, and the other a cyclostyled copy of an open letter in English to the Prime Minister, Mrs. Indira Gandhi, by Mr. Janak Raj Jai, one of her former assistants. Both were circulated surreptitiously during the emergency as the newspapers won't touch them with a pair of tongs.

Mr. Narayan's speech delivered on July 14, 1976 must have helped to boost the morale of those who were working underground. Following is an English summary of his speech in Hindi:

"There is no doubt that I am alive today not because of my will power alone but also because of the will of God and the efforts of the physicians of the Jaslok Hospital. The fact that I have returned from the jaws of death, indicates that it is the will of God that I should continue to serve my country. Therefore, I shall spend every moment of my life in the service of my country. Bihar is my field of work and duty now calls me there. It is in response to that call that I am leaving for Patna.

"I shall first meet Vinobaji at Paunar. In today's poluted political atmosphere, even men like him have to take part in it. The idea is being sedulously propagated that what has happened, happened for the good. Vinobaji has the capacity to turn the table in this situation. I shall have to ask him what kind of cooperation we can give in his efforts to ban cow slaughter. It is true that the present situation is very peculiar. I had thought that the emergency would be withdrawn after one year and fresh elections held. But even the term of the MISA has been extended and my hope has been dashed to pieces. Still I have not given way to despair. I still believe that the situation will change. Mrs. Gandhi will have to loosen the screws. The people should demand fresh elections. They have the right to call for elections after every five years. This right has been snatched away by extending the life of the Lok Sabha. We shall have to struggle to undo it. The opposition parties will also have to make efforts to this end.

"You will have to go to every village and awaken the masses. Whatever be the results of the elections, something positive is bound to come out of it. The situation is not favourable but we cannot sit idle by giving up all hope. Take the help of youths and students. They can achieve a lot. The Congress has understood this and has enacted many kind of dramas to attract them. But it has not succeeded to any measurable extent. The youths are our greatest hope. Many of my Jana Sangharsh and Chhatra Sangharsh Samiti workers are now in jail. But those, who have managed to escape, will feel enthused by my visit to Bihar. The Samitis will have to be strengthened and the workers sent to the villages for mass contact and mass awakening."

It appears that at this stage JP had given up his idea of partyless government. For he continued: "I have come to the conclusion after mature thought that it is necessary for the sake of democracy to have two or three political parties. Only then can the machinery of democracy function well. A necessary corollary to this conclusion is that like-minded parties should come under one flag. That is why I am trying to unite such parties and I have also met with considerable success in my efforts. The ruling party has been propagating through the newspapers that this will never materialise. Don't believe them.

Of course, there are hurdels in the way. But I think Chaudhary Charan Singh should be able to achieve this task more easily than others. Most of the leaders of the Jana Sangh and the Socialist Party are in jail. It will not, therefore, be possible for them to give up the separate identities of their parties for the time being. It will also not be proper for them to take such a decision in haste. There are other problems too. But I am sure a united opposition party will emerge soon.

"Mrs. Gandhi and her followers have been propagating for the last three or four years that I have joined hands with fascist forces like the RSS and the Jana Sangh. This is a lie. I want to assure you that there are very few Congressmen as patriotic and self-sacrificing as the Jana Sanghis and Rastriya Swayam Sewaks. They also participated in the movement shoulder to shoulder with others."

In a statement (duly killed by the censors) issued on the eve of his departure from Bombay to Patna, Mr. Narayan had said that Mrs. Gandhi had herself admitted in an interview to the *Amrita Bazar Patrika* that the gains of emergency had been economic and not political. The economic gains had been due more to a good monsoon than anything else. But the question remained where was the justification for sending lakhs of people to jail without trial, total suppression of civil liberties, throttling of the voice of the press and the establishment of a Police Raj for paltry economic gains?

"Mrs. Gandhi", he said, "has been carrying on propaganda about the economic programme. I want democracy first and everything else afterwards. I want that the problems facing the country should be solved through democratic methods. The most important thing is to have democracy first.

"I want to make it clear that the struggle against dictatorship will neither stop nor be relaxed. To fight against dictatorship is no easy task. The struggle will, therefore, be long and continuous. The people must become fearless to tear to shreds the black laws. It will be a higher struggle than even our struggle against the British regime."

JP also referred to the atrocities perpetrated on political prisoners in jail, particularly against the brother of George Fernandes. He said the normal conditions in jails had become inhuman. But he held that the people had refused to be crushed. Their will was still indomitable. If free and fair elections were held, he was sure the Congress wouldn ever win.

Mr. Janak Raj Jai had been associated with Mrs. Gandhi for a long time as her assistant and his Open Letter to her gives a ring-side view of her performance even before she had come to power. The letter said:

Respected Indiraji,

The 26th of June, 1975, will go down in our post-independence history as the blackest day, when you, to perpetuate yourself as the Prime Minister of this country made a hash of Articles 352 and 359 of the Constitution and gave meaning to the apprehension of doom that a member of the Constituent Assembly (Shri H. V. Kamath) prophesied about a future tyrant blooming out of the Articles. He foresaw the possible end of democracy in these Articles in the form of a Hitler-like take over. You have proved his fears were not unfounded. Kamath's only omission was that he did not mention your name. Possibly he could not have divined that a person like you could take birth in the Nehru family. I strongly commend to you to read the Constituent Assembly debates and ponder what hideous sin you have committed against the letter and spirit of the Constitution.

Large-scale arrests of leaders of the vocal opposition parties including equally large-scale arrests of your own party men who do not see eye to eye with you is a real death-blow to democracy in India. The only consolation that I can draw from my present surroundings is that you have given to my countrymen a foretaste of what it means to live in a form of Government with a closed coterie of morally and physically sick leaders. Probably you have taken upon yourself the fulfilment of the task which Stalin left unfulfilled in Russia. I wonder where are you leading the country to?

The people of our country had got used to a democratic form of life but they are now suddenly plunged into the gloom of censorship, midnight arrests, brutal political persecutions, incarceration in dungeons without even the elementary right to know the hows and whys of their fate. You have denied to every citizen the right to appeal to courts, the right to plead their innocence, the right to challenge their persecutors, every right by which a civilized person is distinguished from a barbarous society. Even petty newspaper hawkers have not been spared. Poor people are deprived of their livlihood and crushed with police jackboots without mercy. Such scenes on the streets make me think you would not have spared even your old Guru, Shri Rabindranath Tagore, for his glorious and memorable words:

> Where the mind is without fear
> And the head is held high,
> Where knowledge is free, where the clear stream of reason
> Has not been lost in the desert sand of dead habit,
> In that heaven of freedom my Father,
> Let my country awake.

If he had been alive, you would not have shirked from wringing his neck and to consign him to some electric crematorium as an unclaimed body. You are doing no less to Lok Nayak Jayaprakash Narayan. Do you think history will pardon you, even if by some mischance your guilt is not adjudged by the present generation?

In your present political posture, every idea, every thought that does not fit in the stream of your scheme of things sounds blasphemy to not only you, but also your coterie of henchmen and stooges, and you have now turned the calender back to thrust down the throat of this developing country the stench of inquisitions and witch-hunt. The only difference being that your version of medieval savagery is dressed up in new garbs. The contents are the same only the package is different . . .

For most of the people, their difficulty is that they do not have sufficient first-hand information and knowledge about you to understand and appreciate your conduct and character in personal and impersonal affairs. Your bards have published your pen portraits from hosannas sung by your sycophants and your biographers. Without doing any research they had published books on the basis of interviews given by you or some articles or news items appearing in the press. The tragedy is that nobody who had an opportunity to know you closely, had dared to write about you. I am happily placed in a position to provide an objective and factual backdrop into your life and character so that it may not be the continuing misfortune of my countrymen, henceforth, to single you out not either as a lady in difficulty or a leader hampered in her lofty ideals by the machinations of evil persons. Having watched you from so close quarters, I feel a sense not of awe, guilt and fright, what common clay has been raised to so high a pedestal . . .

You know Mrs. Anie Crishna who was officially designated as the personal assistant to your late father, Shri Jawaharlal Nehru, the then Prime Minister of India. She was actually working for you for many years even though you had no official position in the Prime Minister's house. You utilised her services even though your late father neither needed nor had any use of the services of this lady . . .

Miss Uma Bhagat worked as a private tutor of your son, Sanjay Gandhi, and that too without remuneration. You paid no salary out of your pocket to Miss Bhagat for the services she rendered to your son, but you got her fixed up in some government post from where she used to draw her monthly salary. Later you appointed her as your Social Secretary. To me it looks like a *quid pro quo* for services rendered in another capacity. But this exchange of favours was, it will be agreed by one and all, dishonest. Public money was spent for rewarding services rendered in private capacity.

Sanjay needed more than one teacher. You know the reasons. You got Gopal Gupta out of the Air Force School for teaching science to him. The services of Gopal Gupta were also taken gratis. You favoured him with other facilities, including the use of the Prime Minister's house car. For these services rendered in private capacity to you by Gopal Gupta, you made him a Producer in the Television Centre, New Delhi, and thanks to your patronage he has on a number of occasions been abroad at public expense.

I was amused to read your statement regarding Yashpal Kapur when you were deposing before the Allahabad High Court. We know (you and me) that I relieved him in 1957 when he was working with the Personal Secretary of the then Prime Minister. Then he was sent to you as a whole-time assistant, though not designated as such, for in 1957 you held no official position. He was drawing salary from the public funds while rendering private service to you and that too with your knowledge. All your dirty political work was entrusted to him and

I am not aware if you were so ignorant then of the Government Service Conduct Rules. You cared two hoots for the Rules just as you cared two hoots for the Allahabad High Court Judgment.

Mr. H. O. Mathai was the Special Assistant to Pandit Jawaharlal Nehru. He was then staying in the Prime Minister's house. A post of a personal assistant to the Special Assistant of the Prime Minister was created in which Yashpal Kapur was fitted in so that in that garb you could avail of his services. This is precisely what you did. All this was done in 1957 at your instance . . .

After you became the Prime Minister, one of the major beneficiaries was Swami Dhirendra Brahmachari who was given the most precious piece of land at a most strategic place for a song. Abuse of authority could not have been more gross than this favour done by you as Prime Minister. At your instance some grant was sanctioned by the Ministry of Education to Swami who was then teaching, it was said, Yoga at Jantar Mantar Road. You also used to take lessons from him. He used to visit the Prime Minister's house for the purpose. But the Swami did not keep account of the grant properly and Dr. K. L. Shrimali, the then Education Minister, stopped the grant. You got Dr. Shrimali sacked. The grant was ultimately restored and you know how it was restored . . .

In the name of God, please step down. Release all leaders and do not make a mockery of democracy, which you have already derailed.

Yours sincerely,
Janak Raj Jai

In Bihar, apparently there was lack of coordination on the propaganda front of the underground. This was understandable because most of the activists were in jail and the rest were being hunted by the police. That was why the State Jana Sangh had its underground publication, the *Lok Bani*, the Sarvodaya workers their *Tarun Kranti* and other leaflets and pamphlets edited by Prof. Zabir Hussain and one wing of the Jana and Chhatra Sangharsh Samiti, the *Mukti Sangram*. This last one was published by several underground workers including Nitish Kumar, Akhtar Hussain, Bajrang Bahadur and Surendra Akela.

It had a short life. There was another underground weekly *Hamara Sangharsh.* It was brought out by Narendra Kumar Singh, Mithilesh Kumar Sinha, Asok Kumar Singh, Dineshwar Singh Daddan, Sachchidanand Singh (present Irrigation Minister), Munsi Lal Rai, Rambilas Paswan (who won by record number of votes in the country in the Lok Sabha poll), Bhavesh Chandra, Rameshwar Sinha and Abdul Bari Siddiqui (who defeated the Speaker of the Bihar Assembly, Pandit Harinath Mishra, in the Assembly poll). This long panel was necessary to enable any one who was free to devote his time to publish this weekly.

These activists also kept liaison with their comrades in Phulwari Camp Jail where Chaudhary Brahm Prakash (a former Chief Minister of Delhi), Chhotan Singh, Vidyanand Tiwary, Sachchidanand (JP's Private Secretary), Siddhraj Dhadda, (former President of All India Sarva Seva Sangh), Rudra Pratap Sarangi and others, who had been lodged there. This contact was maintained from outside by Asok Kumar Singh, Jagannath Yadav and others through the milk contractor of the jail.

On Independence Day on August 15, 1975, the political prisoners in Phulwari Camp Jail hoisted a black flag. This led to the ringing of alarm bells and a lathi charge inside the prison in which Ramakant Thakur Bhim Yadav, Suresh Yadav and a few others were injured. There was trouble again in this jail when Mr. Shankar Singh, General Secretary of the Bihar State Socialist Unity Centre, started vomitting blood and the prisoners demanded his removal to hospital, which the jail authorities were at first reluctant to do. The alarm bell rang when Sivanand Tiwary, Rudra Pratap Sarangi, Ramanand Srivastava, Chhotan Singh and some other political prisoners angrily damaged some furniture and the telephone. The cases instituted against them for this offence were still pending even after the Janata Ministry was installed in office, they complained.

When JP was to return from Bombay to Patna, apparently on a signal from Delhi, warrants of arrest on criminal charges under the MISA were issued by the Bihar Government against Dr. Vinian of JP's Shekhodeora Ashram, Ajay Kumar, Govind Achari and Dineshwar Singh Daddan. Only the last two could be arrested. Daddan was the President of the Nava Nirman

Samiti of Patna, which functioned as a wing of the Samiti. He had organised blood donations for the victims of lathi-charges and police-firings. In all youths had given 35,000 CCs of blood to the Patna Blood Bank.

(After the police-firings at Gaya on April 12, 1974, JP had sanctioned Rs. 20,000 out of the Samiti funds for starting the nucleus of a blood bank for the victims. Gaya did not have a blood bank at the time. JP's donation enabled Gaya to have a permanent blood bank.)

On the eve of Mrs. Indira Gandhi's visit to Patna on May 1, 1976, the Bihar Government was so scared that it ordered the immediate transfer of several prisoners, who were lying sick in the Prisoners' Ward of the Patna Medical College Hospital. The prisoners to be transferred out of Patna included Messrs. S. H. Razi, Convener of the Bihar Jana Sangharsh Samiti, Tripurari Prasad Singh (present Speaker of the State Assembly), Sushil Kumar Mody, General Secretary, Patna University Students' Union, Laloo Prasad Yadav, Gopal Saran Singh and Raghunath Gupta. The last four were activists of the Chhatra Sangharsh Samiti.

The day after the emergency was promulgated, representatives of the political parties supporting the movement and the Jana and Chhatra Sangharsh Samitis met at Kadamkuan in central Patna and decided to record their protest by holding a meeting at the Gandhi Maidan. It was also decided that Mr. Ramanand Tiwary, President, Bihar State Socialist Party, Mr. Jagbandhu Adhikari, General Secretary, State Jana Sangh, Mr. Shankar Singh, General Secretary, State SUC, and Mr. Mahamaya Prasad Sinha, a former Chief Minister, would violate the prohibitory orders along with youths and court arrest.

When the demonstrators led by Mr. Tiwary approached the Gandhi Maidan on June 27 in the afternoon, they found that about 500 armed CRP jawans had surrounded the flag staff in the centre of the maidan, from where leaders used to address public meetings. When they proceeded towards it, shouting slogans, Mr. Tiwary was bodily lifted by the police and whisked away. The police also chased the demonstrators and arrested 28 of them.

Another meeting of the activists was held at the residence

of Mr. Bipin Bihari Sinha, Socialist leader, at Srikrishna Puri on July 1, where it was decided to coordinate underground activities under a Director or Sanchalak. Mr. Tripurari Saran, President, Bihar Sarvodaya Mandal, was appointed Sanchalak and Prof. Jagannath Yadav, a Samiti leader, as Coordinator. In pursuance of an earlier decision Bihar Bundh was organised on June 27. Chhotan Singh, another Samiti leader, was arrested while persuading shopkeepers to close their shops in east Patna. The Bundh was only partially successful.

Representatives of the Jana and Chhatra Sangharsh Samiti met again at Rajgir in the month of August. It decided to give a call to paralyse the government on October 2, 3, 4. The programme was carried out and about 3,000 participants were arrested all over the State. Censorship ensured the news to be blacked out.

The police raided a meeting of the underground leaders of the movement held at Gaya on October 13, 1975, on information possibly supplied by a turncoat Samiti activist. The Sanchalak, Mr. Tripurari Saran was arrested with sixteen others. The rest managed to escape. These included Ram Sundar Das, MLC, General Secretary, State Socialist Party, Jagannath Yadav, the Coordinator, Amarnath Bhai, a Sarvodaya worker and Bhavesh Chandra.

Mr. Amarnath Bhai was made the Sanchalak of the underground movement after the arrest of Mr. Saran. Jagannath Yadav eluded the police for a long time. He was arrested at Kazipur locality in Patna on May 9, 1976.

The underground observed "Black Day" on November 4, 1975 on the first anniversary of the lathi-charge on JP. Fifty youths, representing all the 31 districts of Bihar, went to the site near the Income-tax building where JP had been lathi-charged, wearing black badges. They raised slogans and distributed some leaflets. The police suddenly swooped on them and arrested 13 of them. The rest escaped.

On December 7, 1975, on the last day of the three-day International Conference Against Fascism jointly sponsored by the Congress and the CPI in Patna, some "anti-fascists" parading the main road shouting anti-JP slogans were beaten up by angry youths near the Bihar National College. The police rushed to the scene brandishing lathis and arrested some of the pro-JP youths. College students immediately came out from the university area in protest and took out a procession defying the prohibitory order in force. They also shouted anti-Congress and anti-CPI slogans. For reasons unknown, the authorities got scared and did not interfere with them.

On March 12, 1976, the underground student workers organised a Universities' Bundh, which was successful in Patna, Arrah, Gaya, Muzaffarpur and Chapra. As they observed the Bundh just by boycotting their classes, no arrest was made.

Such movements continued all over Bihar during the period of the emergency but thanks to censorship the general public could not know about them. During the emergency, to my knowledge, there were lathi-charges at least on two occasions and heavy firing once, inside jails. Gopal Saran Singh, a Samiti activist, who was victim of the lathi-charges in Buxar and Arrah jails, informed me of this after his release. There were four MISA and 33 DIR prisoners in Buxar jail. When they protested against the mysterious death of a prisoner, the DIR prisoners were locked up and the MISA prisoners—Sachchidanand Singh and three others—were assaulted with lathis in September, 1975. The firings occurred inside and outside Bhagalpur in May, 1976.

Earlier in July, 1975, there was heavy lathi-charge inside Arrah jail. Half a dozen prisoners were injured and 60 political prisoners were locked up in a room and not allowed to come out for four days. Some of them became sick and they were not even given medicines.

There were also protests against Mrs. Gandhi's style of functioning and against the two Black Bills—the 39th and the 42nd Constitution Amendment Bills in Parliament and State legislatures. Only members of Parliament and of State legislatures and reporters knew of them. The general public had no idea of such criticism because of censorship. Mr. Bhola Paswan Shastri, a Congress member of Rajya Sabha (a former Works and Housing Minister) had denounced the 42nd Amendment.

A little first person singular may not be out of place. As a member of the Bihar Vidhan Parishad, I had questioned the right of the Parliament to change the basic structure of the

Constitution by an omnibus amendment as was sought in the 42nd Amendment. I was processed under the MISA under orders from the top. Many of my anti-establishment speeches were sent to the Home Secretary (Bihar) for processing. It was mischievously suggested that I should be detained under the MISA on the ground that I was recipient—of all things—of "foreign money". Be it said to the credit of the Home Secretary, Mr. R. N. Dash, that he opposed this move when he found out that it was my son, a doctor in New York, had been sending remittances through the New York Branch of the State Bank of India. It was hard earned tax-paid money and the government should have been grateful for getting a portion of this foreign exchange without any effort on their part. As to the speech, I am told, Mr. Dash took the stand that these were privileged since these had been delivered inside the legislature. Therefore, he did not think it would be advisable to detain me under the MISA. Meanwhile, the move became widely known and the matter was ultimately dropped.

Here are some excerpts in English of that Hindi speceh delivered on December 1, 1976 when the Bill came up for ratification:

"It has been said by protagonists of the Bill that Parliament is sovereign and that it has supremacy over the Constitution. Therefore, it is contended that it has the right to amend the Constitution in any manner it likes. True, the Constitution-framers gave Parliament the right to make minor amendments to rectify minor mistakes. But the question is, can Parliament change the basic structure of the Constitution. Commonsense will tell you that you cannot. This Bill is not an ordinary amending Bill since it seeks to change the fundamental character of the Constitution. We shall be making a mockery of the Constitution if we adopt it.

"We had been taught in our childhood that creation cannot be greater than the creator. Parliament is the creation of the Constitution and not the Constitution of Parliament. I, therefore, fail to understand the claim that Parliament is fully competent to recast the Constitution and change its basic and fundamental character . . .

"It is being argued that this omnibus amendment is intended for the benefit of the people. Am I to take it then that our founding fathers like Dr. Rajendra Prasad, Pandit Jawaharlal Nehru, Sardar Vallabh Bhai Patel, Dr. Ambedkar and others lacked intelligence or that they were not sincere to the people and that those in power today alone are the true friends of the people?

" . . . You are committed to a committed judiciary and executive as also the supremacy of Parliament over the Constitution. Yet you talk of democracy! May I ask why you have throttled the voice of the press and denied freedom of expression, which anywhere in the world is a fundamental right of the people in a democracy? Very recently I was reading a speech delivered abroad by our redoubtable Information Minister, Mr. V. C. Shukla, claiming that India has the freest press in the world. I want to know from you if this is the truth, then what is a black lie? The shocking truth today is that one can speak out the truth only at his own peril. The lips of the people have been sealed. The daily *Statesman* is a liberal newspaper which does not indulge in intemperate language in its criticisms. Even when it is critical of the Government, it uses sober and dignified language. The Government, as you all know, has stopped the advertisements to this newspaper for not falling in line.

"The *Patriot* of Delhi is a pro-CPI newspaper. The CPI is an ally of the Congress. But even this newspaper has been deprived of Government advertisements for committing the crime of not displaying news relating to a particular young man . . . What is there to read in the newspapers now? You can never know the truth. They only publish the speeches and pronouncements of those in power or their hangers-on who blow their trumpets.

"I wonder if our people and our leaders had suffered and sacrificed during the freedom struggle to see this day . . . I am an independent. I do not belong to any party. I try to take an objective view of things. I cannot but take note of the fact that for nearly three decades the Congress has been in power. If in spite of it, your party has failed to deliver the goods, must you blame your predecessors in office and absolve yourself of your own failures? By blaming your predecessors, some of whom were the tallest men of our land, are you not by implication insulting their memory . . ."

The 42nd Constitution (Amendment) Bill was sent by the morning plane with a directive that it should be adopted by both Houses and returned by the afternoon flight. That was how the rulers in Delhi treated the State legislatures.

Man-hunt

Two important Bihar leaders, Mr. Karpoori Thakur, a former Chief Minister, and Mr. Basawan Sinha, ex-revolutionary socialist leader and associate of JP, remained underground throughout the period of the emergency. Mr. Sinha had experience of underground activities during the British regime and had in all served more than 15 years' rigorous imprisonment. He was first convicted and sentenced to 10 years' hard labour as far back as in 1929 in the Motihari Conspiracy Case, an offshoot of the Lahore Conspiracy Case in which Bhagat Singh, Rajguru and Bismil were hanged. While in jail he undertook a fast for 57 days. He was the person who had made arrangements for hiding Mr. Jayaprakash Narayan when the latter escaped from the Hazaribagh Central Jail. It was Basawan Babu, who used to do the gun-running from the trans-border tribal areas of the North West Frontier Province for the Azad Dasta, which, led by the late Suraj Narain Singh, Stormed the Hanuman Nagar jail in Nepal and rescued JP, Dr. Ram Manohar Lohia and others.

While underground, Mr. Sinha had to move from place to place all over the country during the emergency. But his main bases of operation were Varanasi, Gorakhpur and Calcutta. During this period he met Karpoori Thakur at Madras at a conclave of underground leaders. His wife Kamala Sinha MLC, a Socialist labour leader in her own right, was detained under several sections of the Cr. P.C. and the IPC shortly after the proclamation of emergency. A fantastic total bail bond of rupees three lakhs was demanded for her release when the lower court was moved. The Patna High Court ordered her release but she was kept in illegal detention for three more days and then a fresh order of detention was served on her in her prison cell under the MISA. The High Court again ordered her release. Soon after her release, MISA detentions became non-justiciable.

Mr. Karpoori Thakur had been to jail several times since 1942. But he had to make attempts to elude the police when he had something on him that might implicate others. During the movement before the emergency, one day he came to me with Mr. Indra Kumar, MLC (SSP) and sought refuge. He was running high temperature and also had very high blood pressure. The Police were after him with a MISA warrant. I hid him in my house.

Thakur had left for Raj Biraj in Nepal to attend a marriage ceremony on the night of June 25, 1975. When he reached Raj Biraj at midday the next day, he was told "dictatorship has been proclaimed in India". He came to know of the declaration of emergency only when he heard the AIR news bulletin. The same evening he left for Birpur on the Bihar side of the Bihar-Nepal border and stayed with a friend. There he came to know from a BBC broadcast the news of the arrests of JP and other leaders. He re-entered Nepal and remained there till September 5, 1975. Within three days the Nepal police were after him when he had already established contacts with workers of opposition parties and Chhatra Sangharsh Samiti boys of the north Bihar districts of Muzaffarpur, Darbhanga, Purnea and Saharsa. He was ordered to report his movements before hand to the Nepal police.

I had asked Thakur why he had gone underground and his reply was: "To blast the Indira Raj." He told me that soon the Government of India started pressurising the Government of Nepal to hand him over. The Nepal Government was willing to oblige provided the Government of India handed over Bishweswar Prasad Koirala, Nepali Congress leader and a former Prime Minister of Nepal living in voluntary exile in India, in return. India did not agree. So, he remained in Nepal. In the second week of July he was flown from Nepal terai to Kathmandu in a government plane and interned. He was ordered not to meet the press, issue any statement for publication inside or outside Nepal, meet any Nepalese political leader and not to communicate with any foreign mission. He was also forbidden to meet any foreigner or to visit any foreign embassy. He stayed in Kathmandu with a friend, Prof. S. N. Verma. After some time he got fed up with his shadowers and started announcing that he intended to stay permanently in

Nepal since the Indira Raj was not likely to end. He did this to put his shadowers off their guard. In this, it seems, he succeeded. Vigilance was somewhat relaxed. On the night of September 5 he shaved off his three months' growth of mustache and beard, donned a Nepali dress and decamped with the help of a top official, by a Thai Airways flight to Calcutta. He was travelling under the name of Mohan Singh. Because of his escape, his host, Prof. Verma, was kept in detention for 10 months. Some barbers and businessmen with whom he had got acquainted during his stay in Kathmandu were also harassed and belaboured by the Nepal police. This he came to know much later.

After a brief stop-over at Calcutta, he flew to Madras to attend a conclave of underground leaders about which information had reached him through the grapevine. The underground meeting at Madras was attended among others by George Fernandes, Snehalata Reddy, Basawan Sinha, Lakhan Lal Kapoor, N. G. Goray, Era Sezhnyan and C. G. K. Reddy. After a week he went to Bangalore where he met Virendra Patil, K. S. Hegde, Ramkrishna Hegde and several other leaders. He changed his disguise from that of a Nepali to that of a Maulavi and flew to Bombay to attend a meeting of the All India Lok Sangharsh Samiti. Those who attended this meeting included Sundar Singh Bhandari, Subramaniam Swamy, Ravindra Verma, Surendra Mohan, Loknath Joshi and Digvijay Singh. It decided to bring out an underground newspaper and to make preparations for launching a satyagraha movement.

From Bombay he went to Delhi, where he met other underground leaders. The situation arising out of the emergency and the brutal repression let loose by the Government was discussed threadbare. Two courses were open to the underground leaders: to prepare for a revolution or to launch satyagraha in which those who believed in doing everything above board like Mr. S. M. Joshi and Mr. N. G. Goray were to participate. From Delhi he went to Lucknow and met Mr. C. B. Gupta in the garb of a coolie because the former was under police surveillance. Then he committed the mistake of returning to Kathmandu via Gorakhpur and Bhairawa. At Kathmandu he was spotted by the Nepal CID and he had to flee in a taxi to Janakpur straight from the Gochar airfield.

By early October, Thakur had reached a village on the Bihar side of the Indo-Nepal border, where he called another meeting of underground workers of north Bihar and chalked out a plan of action for them, including training for armed revolution. He went to Calcutta again and contacted Messrs. P. C. Sen, Jyoti Basu, Asoke Krishna Dutta, Vijay Singh Nahar, P. C. Chunder and leaders of the Forward Bloc, the RCPI, the Socialist Party, the BLD and the Jana Sangh. Here also plans for gingering up the movement were formulated. Thereafter he undertook a hectic tour of Hyderabad, Madras, Ahmedabad, Bardoli, Surat, Baroda etc. contacting underground workers and reached Delhi on November 1, 1975, to attend a meeting of the Lok Sangharsh Samiti to be held on that day. In pursuance of a decision taken at this meeting a nationwide satyagraha was launched on November 11 which concluded on November 26. Several thousand supporters of JP courted jail but this never came out because of censorship.

Karpoori Thakur had a narrow shave when because of some intuitive feeling he did not accompany Mr. Rabindra Verma (both of them were similar in stature as well as in unkempt beards) to Bombay from Baroda though tickets had been purchased. This happened in January, 1976. The train was stopped at midnight when it entered Maharashtra and Mr. Verma was detained and interrogated in the belief that he was Thakur. The police did not realise that he was another much-wanted absconder and let him off only when they became convinced that he was a south Indian and not a Bihari.

During his travels, while underground, Mr. Thakur met Mr. Chaudhary Charan Singh and Mr. Babu Bhai Patel several times. He also met Mr. Mohan Dharia and Mr. Nilmany Routray and stayed at the latter's Cuttack residence for one night. He came in contact with Mr. Rabi Roy, who is now one of the General Secretaries of the Janata Party, in Calcutta. He also sought refuge in the Delhi residence of Mr. Erasmo De Sequira, a BLD leader, for a week.

Thakur used to be in touch with JP (after his release) through Raja Babu (JP's younger brother), Sachchidanand and T. Abraham, JP's private secretaries, and others. He also used to correspond with him. Both agreed that the resistance should continue. They also agreed that the non-CPI opposition parties must merge.

He met JP in January 1977, at the Gandhi Peace Foundation in Delhi and was advised to come out in the open on January 30 and not before. He surfaced on that day in Patna at an election meeting addressed by Mr. Narayan at the Gandhi Maidan. While he was returning from the meeting, he was nabbed by the police but released soon after.

On his assumption of office as Chief Minister of Bihar after the Assembly poll in June 1977, the first congratulatory telegram he received was from King Birendra of Nepal.

THIRTY-TWO

JP Released

JP was released on November 12, 1975 when, as he put it, the Indira Government was convinced "I am a guest in this world for a few days only". In his Open Letter to the People of Bihar, he said: "I was half dead when I was released."

After he had been arrested in Delhi, JP was taken to Sohna Rest House in Haryana and kept in solitary confinement. Mr. Morarji Desai had also been taken there and JP saw him for a few minutes. After that in spite of his requests he was not allowed to meet Mr. Desai even duriug lunch or dinner. Because of sudden heart trouble, after three days he was taken to the All India Institute of Medical Sciences in Delhi. After two days he was again removed. This time to the Post Graduate Institute of Medical Education and Research at Chandigarh. He stayed there till November 12, the day of his release.

Here too he was kept in solitary confinement. The officials, doctors and nurses and attendants only discussed with him his health and nothing else. There was no one with whom he could talk. He pined for company and he requested the Government to send some one with whom he could at least exchange views. But the Government refused.

JP said in his Open Letter, which was printed and circulated by the Bihar Jana Sangharsh Samiti, that in this respect the behaviour of the Indira Government was worse than that of the British rulers, who had allowed him the company of Dr. Ram Manohar Lohia at least for an hour every day during his detention in the Lahore Fort in 1943. The Government of Mrs. Indira Gandhi agreed only to allow him the company of his personal attendant, Gulab Yadav, on the condition that he too remain a prisoner with him. Naturally, JP declined.

On September 23, 1975, JP started suffering from

excruciating pain in the stomach, a thing which had never happened to him before. Medication relieved him temporarily of the pain which appeared again next month. Only when it became apparent to the Government that JP could not be cured and that he was going to die that he was released on November 12. Even then the official announcement suggested that he was being released on parole for one month though he had never asked for parole. The order for his detention was withdrawn unconditionally on December 4, 1975. At the time he was undergoing treatment in Jaslok Hospital in Bombay.

Only a week before his release JP was told that both his kidneys had been totally demaged. Mr. Subhas Chandra Bose had been taken seriously ill at the Tripuri session of the Congress in the late thirties. Mr. Bose had written an article later in the *Modern Review* captioned "My Strange Illness" in which he had hinted at the introduction of occult powers for bringing it about. But JP's kidney damage had nothing to with the occult even though the use of Tantriks was not foreign to those around Mrs. Gandhi. Either JP's kidneys had been damaged by design or by natural causes.

JP had never suffered from kidney trouble. It would have been detected long ago because he used to have thorough medical check-ups from time to time. During the first four months of his detention at Chandigarh, the Government doctors never told him that he had any kidney trouble. It was on November 5 that all of a sudden they announced that both his kidneys had been damaged beyond cure. But how and why?

JP said in his Open Letter: "I have not been able to understand till this day when, how and where did I develop this disease? At Chandigarh I took whatever medicines were given to me. I ate whatever food was served to me. Therefore, I could not understand what had happened to me. My friends have expressed their apprehension that my kidneys were deliberately damaged. Sometimes this doubt has also assailed me. The doctors of Chandigarh had behaved with me very well. Therefore, I do not suspect them. No doctor would commit such a heinous crime. But it is true that they took a long time to diagnose my disease. The doctors in Bombay felt that if I had been released 15 days earlier, it might have been possible at least to partially restore the functioning of my kidneys. God alone knows how my kidneys were completely damaged. But one thing is certain—the Government of Mrs. Gandhi released me only when it felt sure that my days in this world were numbered."

When his condition started deteriorating, swellings appeared all over his body. He had reached a moribund stage. It was only the Herculean efforts of the doctors of Jaslok Hospital that brought JP back to life. The doctors themselves held that it was JP's willpower that revived him. JP himself feels that it was the grace of God that saved him.

The Janata Government has set up a Commission of Enquiry to probe into the causes and circumstances of the damage to his kidneys. Its findings alone would determine whether it was due to natural causes or something more sinister.

JP's condition had caused widespread anxiety all over Bihar. Shortly before his return to Patna from Bombay, a rumour spread one day that JP had died and that the news was being suppressed by the Government. The students came out of their classes demonstrating angrily. Large number of policemen posted in the university area at once swung into action. The police could be seen chasing the students with lathis, beating them up and arresting them.

On instructions from the Centre the Bihar Government had reportedly made elaborate police 'bandobast' for JP's funeral as they expected his 'body' to arrive. Since this did not happen, the policemen arrangements remained to prevent the people from going to the airport to welcome him home.

Thousands of people, particularly youths, had come from different parts of Bihar on July 20, 1976 to receive JP at the airport despite the emergency. But they had to return disappointed as armed police stopped them at every point. Here in JP's own words is what happened:

"I deeply regret that those who wanted see this sick man had to return disappointed. The Government was responsible for it. It promulgated a prohibitory order under section 144 Cr. P.C. in Patna and went on announcing that those who would go to the airport to welcome me would be arrested under the DIR and made to suffer rigorous imprisonment for two to three years. Despite this Hitlerian order, many people could be seen proceeding to the airport. The police either chased them away or arrested them.

"Nobody was allowed to stand on the roadside along the route to the airport. That day even my relatives were taken into custody and kept in detention for several hours. Their fault was that they were proceeding to the Patna airport to welcome and receive me. I have heard that if groups of young men showed the courage to defy the prohibitory order and proceeded towards the airport or shouted 'Jayaprakash Zindabad', they were beaten up by the police. Such things never happened even when we were a subject nation. Even Hitler would have felt ashamed at such demonstration of brute force.

"I believe that this shameful action of the Government will only unite the people and the youths to carry on their struggle with greater vigour. What has happened only confirms, if any confirmation is necessary, that in free India the people and the youths are treated as slaves. Greater sacrifices will be necessary from them for freedom from this new slavery at a time when the whole country has been brought under the heels of dictatorship and entire Bihar has been transformed into a jaii."

Concluding his Open Letter, JP said: "I want to tell you, particularly my student and young friends that it was you who launched the struggle against the established government. I joined it later at your request. Even at that time I had told you that you will have to lead this struggle and this revolution. I became your charioteer only at your repeated requests. Now I am a wounded soldier. How much can I do in this condition? You need more strength for carrying on this long struggle for total revolution. From village to the State and national level new leadership is needed.

"People having faith in the ideal of total revolution have to rise in every village, every city, every college and school and every factory and fight for the cause of a new Bihar and new India for the restoration of democracy and civil liberties by giving up narrow and selfish interests. As long as I am alive, I shall be with you for discussions and giving advice. But you must understand that you must be prepared to pull the chariot of revolution. The struggle, as I have told you before, will be long and arduous. Its object is not merely change of government. We have to bring about a systemic change in the entire society. Therefore, you must prepare for a long struggle. The forces of history are with you. March ahead with complete self-confidence. Victory is yours."

THIRTY-THREE

Indira's Secret

I was not impressed by Mrs. Indira Gandhi when she was the Congress President. I saw her for the first time at close quarters when she came to Patna in 1959 to address a Congress workers' meeting. I had heard she was very pretty. I saw but a pale woman with sunken cheeks and decaying teeth. She looked like a faded flower. Nor did she have the gift of the gab. Her ideas were confused. When after the meeting I asked her for clarification, she only made the confusion worse confounded.

But when she took up the gauntlet thrown by the Syndicate, I turned into an admirer. I used to have frequent quarrels with Karpoori Thakur, George Fernandes, Madhu Limaye and Pranab Chatterji (former Chairman of the State SSP), who looked upon her and considered her as incarnation of evil. My admiration knew no bounds when she successfully manoeuvred the liberation of Bangla Desh and beat Pakistan hollow.

Disillusionment came slowly but surely. Doubts started creeping in when I found pressmen being won over through inducements by men known to be close to her to sing her praise. Years later, as a member of the Ganga Bridge Committee of the Bihar Legislative Council in May, 1973, I met her again at her Delhi residence. Oh, the difference. She looked like a flower in bloom. When she smiled, I was surprised to find she had teeth like a set of pearls. A nagging doubt assailed me.

But I forgot that too. I used to ghost write a column on behalf of my wife (the PTI did not permit its staffers to write for others) for a Patna daily for many years. When Mrs. Gandhi's slips started showing, I became a little critical. When in my writings I was more critical of some members of her coterie, I found the pressures mounting against me. At least on two occasions my articles were not published. This had never happened in the past 16 years. In disgust and as a protest, I stopped writing that column. JP's agitation and her ambitious and anti-democratic stance made my disillusionment complete.

But what was the secret of her hold on a large majority of her partymen? This has never been properly explained. She was feared beyond reason. Most Congressmen, Ministers, MPs and legislators felt tongue-tied in her presence. Pandit Nehru, her father, the tallest leader of our country, was respected, even held in awe, but never feared. Not in the same way.

Pandit Nehru never treated his Cabinet colleagues or State Chief Ministers as his subordinates. Dr. B. C. Roy sometimes behaved as if he was superior to Nehru. Congress MPs and State Ministers never played the role of abject sycophants. He did not allow anybody to touch his feet nor did he allow the performance of 'Arati'. He accepted only garlands which he used to give away to children.

So long as Mrs. Gandhi was dependent on the Syndicate for making her position secure she played the role of a helpless, fatherless widow. She had not gathered any sycophant, not publicly, then. Even after the Congress split she seemed to lean on two "Babujis". Yes, there were two Babujis and not one as is commonly believed. This I came to know quite by chance on December 22, 1970.

Mr. Nityanand Kanungo, the Governor of Bihar, used to consult me, I do not know why, whenever there was a political crisis. That morning I had gone to Raj Bhawan on receipt of an urgent summons from him. He was very unhappy over the pressures he was being subjected to from Delhi for delaying the formation of the ministry after the Daroga Rai Ministry fell on December 15. He told me that he had been offered the bait of another term of Governorship if he would just delay the formation of the Ministry obviously to enable the Prime Minister's men to do some political horse trading. He said he was fed up with it and was going to invite Mr. Karpoori Thakur, who enjoyed majority support as the leader of the Sanyukta Vidhayak Dal, to form the Ministry.

I asked: "Have you invited him or are you still waiting?" He said: "No. Karpoori is waiting downstairs." I advised him to extend the invitation at once and arrange for the swearing in of the new Ministry that very evening. He did. As soon as he had signed the necessary, papers his Secretary, Mr. Sukhen Chakrabarty, came running. He said Babuji was on the phone from Delhi. Mr. Kanungo took the call.

I could hear only one side of the conversation. He was saying: "Babuji Pranam. Wo Kyase Hoga? I have already invited Karpoori to form the Ministry and invitations are going out for the swearing in this evening . . . Yes, Babuji, Yes . . ." But the other side had banged the phone angrily.

Mr. Kanungo came back a little crestfallen. I asked if it was Jagjiwan Babu and if so what was he saying. He replied it was Jagjiwan Babu all right and he was suggesting postponement of formation of the Ministry.

After we had talked for about ten minutes, another phone came from Delhi. Mr. Kanungo took the phone and repeated his performance: "Babuji Pranam . . . Wo Kyase Hoga . . . etc. etc." The other side banged the phone again leaving an unhappy Kanungo holding the line.

I was piqued. I asked him how was it that Babuji, who had cut him off just ten minutes ago, rang up again? Mr. Kanungo nodded his head: "It was the other Babuji, Mr. Satya Narain Sinha."

Mrs. Gandhi had shunted Satyanarain Babu, a member of the Central Cabinet since independence, at the first opportunity as Governor of Madhya Pradesh. Jagjiwan Babu was a much tougher proposition. He could not be disposed of that easily. Moreover, he was still needed. So Jagjiwan Babu remained. Gradually she started building up her own power base after the mid-term Lok Sabha poll in 1971 when, in the wake of the liberation of Bangla Desh, her popularity was at the peak.

Most candidates, who were given tickets for Lok Sabha, were hand-picked men and women and loyal supporters. Most of them were gradually corrupted through devious means by men supposed to be close to her. Some mild critics with radical images had, of course, to be retained even if they could not be made to bend to all her wishes, to keep up the show. They were also needed because she herself had to take up radical postures if and when it suited her. But by and large many of her supporters were encouraged by her loyal Ministers and men of her inner circle to soft living beyond their means. Temptations were put in their way in the true KGB style. Such MPs wined and dined and feted their friends in five-star hotels. The lecherous among them led the life of gay Lotharios. Under the law of demand and supply, the institution of call girls became a fact of life in Delhi. In short, many of them lived much beyond their known sources of income. A sizeable number of them also amassed wealth by peddling influence. Tulmohan Ram was only the tip of the iceberg.

Mrs. Gandhi must have carefully assessed the dossiers on her colleagues and Ministers in the States from her own sources of intelligence besides information supplied by the Central Intelligence Bureau, the RAW and the Governors of States, who maintained their own dossiers, copies of which were supplied to her. In Delhi a close watch was kept on MPs and Ministers by surveillance through wire-tapping and bugging. In an expansive mood one of her most loyal "Bhaktas" once told me how the car in which he had been travelling had been bugged to test his loyalty. She had the secret bio-data of all important politicians and journalists on her finger tips.

Mr. R. D. Bhandare, Governor of Bihar, had once invited some of us, all editors of important local dailies and news agencies, for morning tea and told us jubilantly that he was updating the dossiers maintained by his predecessors on all Ministers and important officers. He said their misdeeds were known to him. He even made public speeches later at Poona and Nagpur while on a holiday that he had enough materials to send some Ministers and bureaucrats to jail. His allegations received countrywide publicity. When he was pulled up, he simply denied having made such allegations and said he had been misreported.

The conclusion is inevitable that Mrs. Gandhi kept herself informed of the indiscretions of her partymen. She knew of every skeleton in every cupboard. And the people around her knew that she knew. That was the secret of her strangle-hold on the party. There can be no other valid reason or explanation for the strange power she wielded over a large section of her partymen. She has herself provided an indirect proof that she maintained every bit of evidence that could be used as material to silence her critics within the party. She gave herself away when she threatened Mr. Siddhartha Shankar Ray, once considered to be her right hand man, with releasing the letters that he had written to her before he broke away from her after her defeat at the polls. That was the only lever she had against Ray and she hurled the threat to silence him when he turned into a critic. Ray also had her letters. So there was no showdown, fortunately for both.

She had her spies everywhere. They had infiltrated even the Sangharsh Samitis. Her remark that there were corrupt men even in the movement (this related to some minor bungling involving a small amount of money collected through coupons) gave her away. She did maintain dossiers against her political rivals. Those against whom she did not have a handle, she sent them to her dungeons during the emergency. She was not only ruthless but also very vindictive. This characteristic became more evident after she started projecting Sanjay as India's Coming Man and when her authority was being challenged by Mr. Narayan and his followers.

Mrs. Gandhi's personality has been more enigmatic than charismatic. It is difficult to imagine why the lady, who was virtually worshipped at the height of her glory after the liberation of Bangla Desh, should have cast away the love and esteem of her own people, which every human being pines for and cherishes, and invited a precipitate fall. To keep herself in power? She already had absolute power. Then why have elections?

Power corrupts, absolute power, absolutely. How right JP was! "Vinash Kale Biparit Buddhi." If the Constitution is to be amended, it should be amended to limit the term of office of the Central Ministers, including the Prime Minister, and of State Ministers, including the Chief Ministers.

There is another ancient explanation:
Striyah Charitram, Purusasya Bhagyam,
Daibo Na Jananti, Kuto Manusyah?

(The character of a woman, the fate of a man are not known even by the gods in heaven, what to speak of ordinary mortals?)

Even when all the facts are known, the mystery will remain, the triumph and the tragedy.

THIRTY-FOUR

Lok Sabha Poll

Mrs. Gandhi announced dissolution of the Lok Sabha and fresh elections in a broadcast to the nation on January 18, 1977. It came as a surprise because she had already got the life of the Lok Sabha extended. Many explanations have been offered, convincing and otherwise. Mr. Zulfikar Ali Bhutto claimed that he had forced her hands by holding elections in Pakistan. It has also been suggested that she wanted to secure legitimacy for her dictatorship because she liked to demonstrate to a world already highly critical that she and her party and not the parties in opposition, who had combined under the umbrella of Mr. Narayan, truly represented the people. All told, she alone knows the reason that prompted her to take the decision. Maybe not even she.

It is plain that she had become a victim of her own propaganda. She had genuinely started believing that Indira is India and India is Indira. The refrain in all her speeches before and during the emergency was that she alone represented the people, who had absolute faith in her. Therefore, she must be allowed to continue to serve them "till the last breath of my life".

This is also what her admirers dinned into her ears day in and day out. She wondered in public (and wonders will never cease), how was it that there had been no reaction among the people to the arrests of so many leaders and workers of the opposition. Since there was "not even a ripple", the people must be with her. Thanks to her flatterers and the Sanjay Brigade hordes, actually her lines of communication had choked up. The censorship that she had imposed, prevented her from knowing the true feelings of the people. Her intelligence agencies had also apparently stopped sending her correct reports because such reports containing unpalatable truths were frowned upon. In a sense it is the emergency that saved the nation.

Before the emergency she used to get the correct reports. I myself had been interviewed more than once by the top brass of the Central Intelligence Bureau. I do not know why they picked on me. Possibly because they had information that quite often JP's private secretary, Mr. Sachchidanand, used to send foreign correspondents, who went to JP's residence, to me for getting the detailed background (JP's telephone was tapped round the clock). The gentleman, who used to come from Delhi (I suspect he did not give me his correct name and designation), was obviously very high in the echelons of the Central Intelligence because CBI officers of the rank of DIG and SP were asked by him to take notes of what I said when he felt that the point was important enough. They met me at least twice. Every time I used to ask them why didn't they suggest to the Prime Minister to come to a settlement with JP because his demands were legitimate. In fact these very demands were voiced in slogans raised by Youth Congress and CPI workers when they took out counter-processions. The only demand they opposed was the dissolution of the Assembly, which had been added to the demands of the Chhatra Sangharsh Samiti only after the government let loose repression. I asked them if they themselves hadn't been hit by the soaring prices? Were they not worried about the prospect of unemployment of their sons and wards? Did they not know that corruption had become all-pervasive because most Ministers and their favoured bureaucrats were corrupt as hell? Why didn't they report on them?

They assured me that they submitted truthful reports but they were not the policy-makers. It was for the Prime Minister to decide the policy. I was most surprised when an officer of the Directorate of Military Intelligence, a splendid young Lt. Colonel, a Sardar, fixed up an appointment with me from Lucknow and came to interview me accompanied by an army Major. I wondered what had JP's agitation to do with the military intelligence. And I did ask him what was his angle? He put a counter-question. He asked: "Have you realised what will happen if this kind of discontent spreads in the country if there is foreign aggression?"

I scoffed at the idea and said: "Who will attack us? China?

It is having hell of a trouble with Russia and its armed forces are massed on the Soviet-Manchurian border. Moreover, a Chinese attack may lead to a global war." He quietly said: "What about Pakistan?"

Here I slipped. I had been given to understand by Harpal Nayar, a senior PTI Delhi staffer, who had undergone training as a military correspondent, that it took twelve years to build an effective squadron. I repeated what I had been told and said Pakistan was licking its wounds after the war over Bangla Desh. How could it attack us?

The Lt. Colonel said: "Forget it, Sir. Pakistan was never more strong than now. It is armed to the teeth. Its army and air force have been fully trained and armed by some of the Western powers (whom he named). It has an endless supply of petrol and aviation fuel of which we have such shortage. Money is no problem for Pakistan. Its allies have seen to it. If we are attacked our country may be crippled for many years. That is why we want to know how bad the situation is."

I gave him my assessment of the situation and said that so long as the causes of discontent were not removed, the agitation would spread even if JP was not there. I repeated my suggestion that he should report the truth and advise the powers that be to come to a quick settlement and at least remove the Ministers who had become notorious symbols of corruption. He gave the stock reply that policy-making was not his business.

This happened before the emergency. From their talks I got the impression that their job was to report the unvarnished truth of a given situation as they saw it. But after the emergency, Mrs. Gandhi's aides, out to build the personality cult, started frowning upon reports containing unpleasant truths. The people's anger against forcible sterilisation, for instance, were not liked. In Bihar Central Intelligence Officers were posted in all the 31 districts and it was part of their duty to report on the populist support for the government, particularly the Prime Minister. I have heard quite a number of them started sending garbled, euphoric reports, which had no relation to reality. As a result an impression was given to the Prime Minister that she still enjoyed overwhelming popular support.

An extreme instance was the punishment inflicted on the Inspector General of Police of Bihar, Mr. Ambica Prasad Mishra, and the Additional Inspector General of Police (Special), Mr. S. K. Chatterji. They were both summoned on March 17, 1977 by a top politician in power on the day Mrs. Gandhi arrived and stayed overnight in Patna. Dhawan was also with her. They were asked about their intelligence reports on the poll prospects of the Congress. Both the officers were reluctant to say anything because the truth was quite unpalatable. But they were forced to disclose what they knew. When they said that, according to their reports, the chances of the Congress were bleak, the boss became red in the face. That very night the intelligence wing was taken away from the I.G. and the A.I.G., C.I.D. transferred to the Vigilance Department. It is not difficult to imagine that if such high officials could be treated in this cavalier fashion, what fate awaited comparatively junior Central Intelligence Officers who dared to tell the truth. If they indulged in *suppressio veri suggestio falsi* to please the masters, nobody could blame them.

As has been stated earlier, JP was fond of saying "Vinash Kale Biparit Buddhi" whenever Mrs. Gandhi's government acted foolishly and wantonly. The Gita is more explicit. It says:

Krodhad Bhavati Sammohah Sammohath Smriti Bibhramah,
Smriti Bhramshad Buddhi Naso, Buddhi Nasad Pranasyati.

(From anger comes delusion, from delusion springs loss of memory, from loss of memory results loss of intelligence from loss of intelligence there is complete ruin.)

Anger against opposition to her rule, especially by the agitators led by JP clouded Mrs. Gandhi's vision; this in turn made her forget her own misdeeds; forgetfulness led to loss of intelligence, which led to her.

Speculation is useless why she had ordered the elections. But it is dollars to doughnuts that her clouded vision made her believe that she would sweep the polls. She was confident of popular support because she had little idea of the real feelings of the people and the result of her misdeeds. Moreover the opposition was in total disarray, with all its leaders in jail or underground. They had no resources while her War Chest was full to the brim. Didn't JP charge her with having amassed crores of rupees through dubious means? And JP is not a person who levels charges of this sort in an irresponsible manner.

What did the Nagarwala case indicate? The deaths of Nagarwala and some others connected with the case are the subject of an enquiry but not what happened to the money that was collected nor how was it collected. The fact that rupees sixty lakhs could be taken out from the vaults of the State Bank of India tells its own tale. That such a huge amount was withdrawn cannot be disputed. The counting of the money after its recovery by police officers was photographed and published in the newspapers. It proved that the vaults of the State Bank were being used for keeping a private fund for which there was no accountability. It also proved that money from this fund could be withdrawn just by the word of mouth by giving some coded signal. Nobody can normally withdraw even a four-anna bit from a bank without producing a valid document. (There was some hush hush talk that it was secret fund money meant for some "high State mission" Bullshit. Money from even non-voted secret funds cannot be withdrawn like that.)

The money that had been withdrawn must have been only a small portion of the contents of the private war chest. What happened to the balance? It must have been quietly withdrawn and removed after the Nagarwala case gained worldwide publicity. This too has to be probed as is being done in the case of collection of crores of rupees through advertisements to Congress souvenirs at fabulous rates (quite a number of these souvenirs were not published at all).

The fact that she ordered the Lok Sabha elections is being emphasised now by Congressmen to prove that she was not a dictator. This is how they are trying to make the best of a bad bargain. She must have been confident of victory. Unfortunately, here she badly slipped. And—as in tragedy—that one slip was her undoing. The opposition parties, which she thought were in disarray, lost no time in joining forces and fought the elections as one party with a common symbol. The people too were on their side. She made the fatal error of misjudging the mood of the people. She no longer knew the pulse of the nation. Power had not only corrupted but alienated her.

In urban areas, particularly in northern India, in almost every locality some young man or political worker was away from home in jail. The atrocities were no secrets. The fact that there were few public protests was due to the fear psychosis generated in the country. How long could she expect to get the votes of the people by holding them in the thraldom of fear? The Jana and Chhatra Sanghash Samiti workers as also workers of the opposition parties, who had gone underground during the emergency, had fanned out in the countryside and carried on their campaign against the Government of Mrs. Gandhi. Stories of atrocities fanned the fire of the people's indignation. There were no doubt imaginative, overblown accounts of the Government's wickedness. Attempts at forcible sterilisation added fuel to the fire. The Government, it seems, did not arrange for the after-care of even those who volunteered for sterilisation. When complications arose, there was none to attend on them.

The working class was angry because bonus was no longer obligatory but their right to strike had been snatched. The bank employees were sullen because their emoluments were suddenly slashed substantially. The kisans in the villages found that they had to pay bribes for getting agricultural inputs while the prices of their daily needs soared. They did not understand what suppression of freedom of expression or of civil liberties meant. Nor did they understand the implications of the amendments made to the Constitution. But what they clearly understood and knew was that the Garibi Hatao (away with poverty) slogan was a hoax and the detention of leaders who espoused their cause was a reality. The credibility of the Indira Government had reached its nadir.

When the elections came, they avenged themselves, and proved to the hilt Munro's famous dictum that the people vote their resentment and not their appreciation of anything. It can never be said that all that Mrs. Gandhi had done was bad. She had also done some good. But for everything she had used autocratic methods ruthlessly. JP's stand was different: Democracy first. It must take precedence even over economic gains claimed by Mrs. Gandhi. JP realised that the masses did not understand these finer distinctions. That was why he had called upon intellectuals and the educated classes, including the Samiti workers, to go to the people and explain to them and educate them on what was meant by democracy and dictatorship. He suggested this long before the elections at a seminar held in the Hindi Sahitya Sammelan Bhawan in Patna on November 7, 1976, when censorship was at its peak.

The power of money on which the ruling party put so much reliance was also one of the contributing factors for its debacle at the Lok Sabha poll. In 1971 mid-term Lok Sabha poll each Congress nominee had been advanced on an average rupees one lakh to meet the election expenses. In special cases the figures were substantially higher. In the Banka Lok Sabha by-election in 1973, the Congress spent more than rupees twenty lakhs to ensure the defeat of Mr. Madhu Limaye (Mr. Raj Narain was also one of the contestants) as Mrs. Gandhi did not want to see his face in Parliament. (I learnt this from one of her cronies.) But barring the CPI rival of Madhu Limaye, all the three other rivals forfeited their security.

In the last Lok Sabha poll Congress candidates received on an average rupees four lakhs. In special cases it was much higher. The sky was the limit for ensuring the defeat of Mr. Jagjiwan Ram in Sasaram. Jagjiwan Babu himself alleged that the Congress was spending rupees one crore to get him defeated. Only such Congress nominees, who had bigger stakes, fought valiantly. Many others, who could gauge the people's wrath and found the situation hopeless, only went through the motions of contesting the elections and saved as much as they could for their own benefit. Not all were that fortunate. Some middlemen, through whom the money passed, kept a substantial chunk for themselves. Too much money instead of proving a boon, proved a bane.

Although her partymen used to think of her as a master strategist, it is apparent that she could never imagine the predicament in which she was placing herself and her party when she ordered the Lok Sabha poll. She would have never ordered it if she had the least inkling that the Congress might face an utter and ignominious defeat, and because of her. She genuinely thought that she had given peace and stability and her thankful countrymen would, therefore, vote for the Congress as they used to do in the past. She never realised the truth of Henry Van Dyke's saying: "A peace which depends upon fear is nothing but a suppressed war." Such was the thoroughness with which she had immunised herself from the feelings of the people!

Empiricism lays stress on reliance on facts while pragmatism stresses facts and their usefulness to human life. Thanks to her yes men and her own style of functioning, she got most of her facts wrong. Lobbying for the colonies in London before they revolted, Benjamin Franklin had written a satiric piece: "Rules By Which a Great Empire May Be Reduced To a Small One." Mrs. Gandhi wrote her own rules by which, she, once the idol of her people at the pinnacle of her glory, had reduced herself to an ogre. It is a pity it is true, it's true it is a pity.

She had ensured for the nation the peace of the grave, a totalitarian State. But she never realised that the people had gone dumb with anger. Anger becomes most potent and dangerous when it is most mute. The coiled energy of that dumb anger burst when the people went to polls. JP not only stole Indira's thunder but also snatched her sceptre and gave it to the leaders of the true representatives of the suppressed and oppressed people. No wonder JP, who had been contemptuously treated and mentally tortured by Mrs. Gandhi, became the people's hero, the saintly saviour.

THIRTY-FIVE

Nixon & Mrs. Gandhi

The Watergate scandal saw Mr. Richard Nixon out of U.S. Presidency on August 9, 1974. Mr. Gerald Ford, who assumed the Presidency, told the American nation: "Our great republic is a Government of laws and not of men" (almost the exact words uttered by Pandit Jawaharlal Nehru when he inaugurated the All India Lawyers' Conference at Patna one and a half decades ago). That was the first thing the Janata Party promised the nation when it assumed office at the Centre. By enacting the 39th Amendment Mrs. Gandhi had placed herself above the law.

When Nixon took tearful leave of the White House and a devastated Presidency, he told the men and women who had served him that "only a man in the deepest valley can know how magnificent it is to be on the highest mountain". Mr. Nixon's Watergate scandal was nothing compared to what had happened in India due to Mrs. Gandhi's bid to remain on the top of the mountain she had ascended 11 years ago.

Nixon accepted that his political career was in shambles and he had no defence for his actions. No quitter, all the same he quit the White House without fuss. Mrs. Gandhi is still reluctant to accept that her political career too is in shambles. She stuck to her 1, Safdar Jang Road residence as long as she could and even offered to pay a fabulous rent to continue living in it. She didn't express a word of regret for all that happened during the emergency. She merely accepted her responsibility for the party's debacle at the polls. (Six months after the Janata Party's assumption of office at the Centre, she gathered up enough courage to even justify the emergency in a speech at Srinagar.)

In a statement issued on July 15, 1977, in reply to the charge of the Union Home Minister, Chaudhary Charan Singh, that she had even thought of shooting some opposition leaders during the emergency, Mrs. Gandhi denied it and went on further to say that she did express her regret in her election speeches at the excesses committed during the emergency and promised that it would never happen again. Public memory is not that short. What she did was to gloss over the atrocities and apologetically own them as "some mistakes". The excellent under-statement will not deceive even a child. Had Hitler been alive and confessed that Belsen, Dachau and Jadiga were "mistakes" how would the Nuremburg judges and the people of the world at large have taken it?

The lady protests too much! Let her memory be refreshed. May one ask why she did not utter a word of condemnation, when the Indira Brigade opened fire on a JP-led procession in Patna on June 5, 1974? Can she explain her silence on the attempt on JP's life at Ludhiana when a hefty ruffian tried to hold him in an iron embrace, broke one of his ribs and fled away only when Mr. Narayan cried out in pain? Again, why didn't she say a word deploring the attack on JP's motorcade near Karnal while he was going from Delhi to Kurukshetra to inaugurate a Bihar type agitation in Haryana? There were many witnesses to the attack. Some of the persons in the motorcade included Madhu Limaye, Maniram Bagri, Jagabandhu Adhikari and Jagannath Yadav. Karpoori Thakur, the present Chief Minister of Bihar, was in JP's car.

The fact is that she is unrepentant and is still waiting on the wings after installing her puppet (no longer a puppet) as the President of the AICC. She is extremely fond of puppets. Somewhere she wrote or said that as a child she used to play with dolls while her father was away in prison. It needs no psychiatrist to point out the reason why she became so fond of human puppets when she grew up. Mr. Brahmanand Reddi, former Home Minister, who cannot escape the responsibility for the rapacities that were committed during the emergency along with Mrs. Gandhi, himself gave the game away after his election as Congress President when he declared that it was not his victory but of Mrs. Gandhi, "who still remains our esteemed leader".

Mr. Nixon could at least foresee his political doom because the Watergate scandal dragged on and the world press was full of it. His angry outburst "bomb the Washington Post" neither silenced the press nor the members of the House of Representatives and the Senate. Mrs. Gandhi had muzzled the press. She had also silenced the opposition (most of whose leaders she had sent to jail or underground) as well as her own partymen. The AIR and the Television were manned by her stooges. She heard and read only what Indira Gandhi had to say of the wonderful achievements of Indira Gandhi while the silly and the wily sycophants sang her praise and the praise of her *Shahzada*.

The fact that she started pulling the strings soon after her ignominious defeat clearly indicates that' she has learnt no lessons nor does she intend to do so. On the contrary, she plans to remain in power politics. It means that if she is again able to capture power, she will not only do it again but do it more effectively. The implications are awful and it is in this light that the "forgive and forget" stand of some Janata stalwarts has to be examined. The issue is more than personal.

Kshama Hi Paramo Dharmah (to forgive is divine) is all right for the few who genuinely believe in it. They may even frown upon India's ancient *Danda Niti* (the law on crime and punishment) and be prepared to forgive the worst crime perpetrated on the people in India's long history. That is understandable though ill luck may once again make them the victims of a more tyrannical regime if Mrs. Gandhi and her cohorts manage to stage a come back to power. They may become Saheeds again for upholding the principle of forgive and forget. But have they the right to jeopardise the lives of millions of their countrymen at the alter of a high-falutin personal ethics? The answer must be a resounding "No".

Is there no way out to kill the snake without breaking the stick, as a Bengali saying goes? There is. Without being vindictive, the government can still deal effectively with Mrs. Gandhi and keep her out of mischief. Here again comes the analogy of Mr. Nixon. The government has to bring home the crimes she had committed and then grant pardon. President Ford granted such a pardon to Nixon and the acceptance of that pardon by Nixon meant acceptance of his guilt. Similar pardon may be granted to her. If she accepts it, it will mean she accepts her guilt, which will make it impossible for her to return to power again. The Janata Party leaders at least owe this much to the people who voted them to power. But will it be possible? She is making even such an easy way out for herself difficult by her present stance in which she has started justifying all the crimes she perpetrated on the people and the Constitution.

If she is unrepentant, Mr. Brahmanand Reddi, like his "esteemed leader", has not so far expressed a word of regret for all the excesses of the emergency nor held out any promise that there would not be any repetition if the Congress, which has a "great future", is returned to power. True, more clever Congress politicians with lingering hopes of turning the tables, have been faithfully promising to the people that what had happened during the emergency would never happen again. It should not be forgotten that they had all kept mum when the Attorney General, Mr. Niren De, had justified before the Supreme Court the powers that the Indira Government had assumed to detain anybody it liked, to kill anybody it liked and even starve to death anybody it liked and accepted the position that the victims would be allowed no remedy against such action. Even Hitler, notorious for his atrocities on the Jews, did not have the gumption to declare assumption of such powers though the horrors he perpetrated have now become part of history.

The promises of these Congress leaders do not stand a moment's scrutiny. These are the very people, ex-Ministers and members of Parliament, who had sworn in the name of God or solemnly affirmed their loyalty to the Constitution and pledged themselves to protect it and uphold it. Yet they did not hesitate to butcher the Constitution. If they could treat their sacred pledges with such contempt, where is the guarantee that they would not break their promises and give the go by to the pious intentions they are mouthing today? After all, the road to hell is paved with pious intentions. More so, when their "esteemed leader" is biding her time to re-enter the stage in the role of the leading lady once again. It should not be overlooked that they have not lost their teeth despite the crushing defeat they suffered at the hustings for their misdeeds. After slaughtering democracy they are now cheekily pointing the accusing finger towards the Janata Party for "trampling democratic norms". Father forgive them for they know not what they do!

Congressmen have suddenly become solicitious for the Naxalites forgetting that it was their government which had suppressed them and even liquidated many of them. When I tried to defend in the Bihar Vidhan Parishad the release of George Fernandes and the withdrawal of the Baroda Dynamite Case, I was continuously interrupted. I pointed out that even if he was involved in the case, the Janata Government was fully justified in releasing him because Mahatma Gandhi, the apostle of non-violence, had interceded on behalf of Bhagat Singh for clemency. I said even if it was argued that what was pardonable during the British regime could not be pardonable in free India, such argument did not hold water. For, tyranny was tyranny and it did not become more bearable becauss it was indigenous. When in a letter I enquired from George about it, he replied: "Tyranny is tyranny. In fact, it is worse when the tyrant is a native."

Mrs. Gandhi's sarcastic comment on JP for staying with Mr. Ramnath Goenka was revived with vengeance following the dispute over payment of interim relief to the employees of the *Indian Express* group of newspapers. Those now in the opposition could not even tolerate a sick man, a lifelong social worker who had never been interested in power, staying with a friend. How it was twisted! The Express Tower in Bombay had become a centre of extra-constitutional authority! That was why Mr. Goenka was not conceding the legitimate demand of the employees and the Janata Government was silent about it. The dispute has now been happily settled.

Although Mr. Y. B. Chavan, the Leader of the Opposition in the Lok Sabha, had admitted that mistakes had been committed during the emergency, which should never be repeated, a sizeable number of important Congressmen have not taken their cue from him. They are still ardent believers in "dinner diplomacy". You have only to listen to their speeches to find that the attacks on JP by the Defenders of the Faith (in Mrs. Gandhi) have not ceased. They forget that JP is not in the Janata Party though he is its founding father. Even so, he is its strongest support while the lady, whose voice they are echoing, is now proving to be their weakest reed.

THIRTY-SIX

JP & Janata Party

This journal is mainly a record of events, especially JP's role in the movement. In whichever State he went to campaign against the authoritarian rule of Mrs. Gandhi before and after the emergency, the Congress was swept off its feet in the Lok Sabha poll. He was the main architect of Janata Party's victory. The issue was simplified for the people by JP as a conflict between democracy and dictatorship. If the people did not stand up against dictatorship, they would remain slaves for a long time to come. Maybe for good. Mrs. Gandhi's Garibi Hatao gimmick having totally failed, her party had no answer to JP's criticism, except to discredit and denigrate him. The Janata wave swept and toppled the strongest bastions of the Congress in north India and Maharashtra.

After the Lok Sabha poll, the apologists of Mrs. Gandhi pointed out with pride the performance of the party in the south. There were some cogent reasons for it. First, the impact of Mrs. Gandhi's tyrannical rule had not been felt so much in the south though local tyrants had tortured many a Snehalata Reddy and Rajan and butchered Naxalites in arranged encounters, which had not come to light thanks to the emergency. There was also deep distrust of some stalwarts of the Janata Party for their zeal for Hindi. And language is an explosive issue. Unfortunately, mercurial men like Mr. Raj Narain have not helped to dispel it. But the most important reason of all was that JP could not campaign in the south because he suddenly fell ill while on election tour. Had he campaigned the results might have been different.

The extraordinary impact of JP was felt in June Assembly elections even when he was away at Seattle in USA. The Congress, which had been JP's target for its misrule, lost heavily everywhere. The Janata Party won by thumping majority in Bihar, Orissa, Uttar Pradesh, Madhya Pradesh, Rajasthan, Haryana and Himachal Pradesh. In Punjab the Akali Dal-Janata combine won and the CPI(M) in West Bengal. The Akali Dal had supported JP's movement. So also the CPI(M), which had invited the derisive comment from Mr. Siddhartha Shankar Ray, the West Bengal Chief Minister, when Mr. Jyoti Basu joined the procession led by JP in Calcutta on the occasion of one of the biggest rallies organised in that city of processions that it was the "funeral procession of the CPI(M)".

It is a fact that the popularity of the Janata Party had waned within three months between the March Lok Sabha poll and the June elections to the State Assemblies. In Bihar, for instance, where the JP-led movement started, the percentage of votes polled in March by the Janata Party was 64.88. In June it dropped to 43.14 though it still won a two-third majority. This was a significant drop, which the Janata Party can ignore at its own peril. The signs are not encouraging.

Even "lamp posts" had romped home on Janata tickets in the Lok Sabha election. There was, therefore, a scramble for party tickets for the Assembly seats which surpassed the Congress wranglings in the past. Caste and group factors had been totally buried at the time of the Lok Sabha poll. Casteism and groupism, which JP's concept of Total Revolution seeks to liquidate, had full play in most States. In Bihar the rush for party tickets can be imagined from the fact that there were more than 22,000 applicants for the 324 Assembly seats. Persons who had never participated in JP's agitation, and even opposed it, and did not have a good public image got party tickets while tried and tested men, who had suffered and sacrificed were ignored. The youth power, which JP had built and which had been largely responsible for the victory of the Janata nominees in the Lok Sabha poll, got representation for 42 seats only (27 of them won). Understandably, there has been much criticism, protest and misgivings. Sivanand Tiwary, a member of the Steering Committee of the Samiti, refused his ticket. The situation became so ludicrous at the time of distribution of tickets that the Bihar State Election Committee of the Janata Party had to seek *Agyatbas* (go underground).

Loud protests were heard from every other State against the manner in which the party nominations were being made.

It was perhaps fortunate that JP was then away at Seattle. Had he been in India he would have received one of the worst shocks of his life. But he was treated any better on his return? He made only one request to the Janata leadership: To withdraw Mrs. Nandini Satpathy from contest against Mrs. Malati Choudhary in Dhenkanal. The Janata leadership could have politely replied that it was too late because the nomination had been made during his absence in USA. But what was their response? "JP is not God!", "JP is not Janata Party". Janata stalwarts declared that she was the party nominee, and she must, therefore, be backed. JP didn't give the reasons for his request as he did not want to raise a controversy. But did not those who backed Mrs. Satpathy know what JP had said how her victory in the Orissa by-election was assured when she was sent from the Centre to the State to become its Chief Minister? Didn't they know what she had said about JP and his agitation while presiding over the Eastern Zonal Regional Women's Conference organised by the Congress and held in Patna on February 1 and 2 in 1975? They are all on record.

I had my differences with JP when he propounded his theory of "partyless democracy". When the Secretary of the Bihar State Council of the CPI, Mr. Jagannath Sarkar, criticised JP's stand and suggested that there should be a public debate on it, I had written a piece suggesting that JP was trying to put the clock back. After the Nandini episode I realised with some bitterness that JP was possibly right though his ideal of partyless democracy might never be realised. Will one day, JP also have to say at the fag end of his life like Mahatma Gandhi that "I have become a counterfeit coin"? For some his usefulness is over. Such is the irony of history.

After the elections to the Assemblies, same bickerings started over the composition of the Ministries and the representation that the units comprising the Janata Party before the merger should get. The formation of the Ministries had not been completed in several States a month after the Assembly election results were out because manoeuvrings and palavers were still continuing. The CFD for one, received the worst end of the stick both in the distribution of party tickets for the elections as well as in the formation of the Ministries. Nobody can deny that Jagjiwan Babu had played a significant role in turning the table on the Congress by timing his exit from it with the precision of a master strategist. His Congress for Democracy, which had merged with the Janata Party, deserved better.

The Janata Party suffers from some built-in drawbacks. The Jana Sangh, the BLD (itself a conglomeration of several parties), the Congress(O), the Socialist Party and the CFD merged not before but after the Lok Sabha poll for sharing power and not because of identity of interests and ideological affinity. It was a merger of disparate elements holding divergent and often contrary views on several important matters of policy. Had the merger been achieved during the progress of the movement itself, for which JP had made consistent efforts, the unity forged in the fire of the struggle might have produced a more cohesive party. It would have become more durable with a larger measure of identity of views on policies and programmes. But this did not happen, with the result that every unit is still thinking and behaving as a separate unit as before.

What is holding them together is the common fear of Mrs. Indira Gandhi, who, instead of waiting on the wings, has now entered the political scene apparently to stage a come back. Had the hold of Mrs. Gandhi on the Congress gone and a new composite leadership emerged, the cracks within the Janata Party would have grown wider by now and ultimately at least one or two units would have broken away. That the Janata Party has not cracked up is no credit to the leadership of the party. For that the credit goes to Mrs. Gandhi.

Though the actions and utterances of some of the Janata stalwarts may have the semblance of kicking the ladder, the fact remains that JP continues to be the party's only hope and strength. JP realises how sad and delicate the situation is and that is why he has not come out openly against the Government's style of functioning in the States and at the Centre. The horns of a dilemma in which he has been placed becomes plain when one recalls his recent remark that nobody now consults him. His hasty but halting explanation only underlines the stirrings of a noble soul. JP's idea of a total revolution for building a better and healthier society, free from exploitation, is still a far cry. Even his idea of recall of MPs and MLAs, who fail to give a satisfactory account of themselves, has not yet been given any concrete shape through legislation and the indications are that it will never be. Mr. Madhu Limaye has gone on record that the idea is good but there are practical difficulties. Among Janata stalwarts, Limaye alone has shown some sense of humility by being apologetic.

Crimes are on the increase. The prices are rising, though this was one of the main reasons that sparked off the students' agitation. There has been no overhauling of the bureaucratic set up responsible for a lot of mischief during the Indira regime. Many bureaucrats, who were hand in glove with corrupt businessmen, traders and industrialists with the connivance of or as stooges of the Ministers, are occupying the same positions. They know all the guiles how to twist some of the new-comers round their fingers at the Centre and in the States without their realising it.

The prices cannot be brought down by praying with folded hands. Crimes also cannot be tackled unless the government gives proof that it means business and authority shows its teeth. Many criminals detained under the MISA and the DIR have been thoughtlessly released without proper screening and they are now playing havoc with the lives of peace-loving and law-abiding citizens. Some are even alleged to be enjoying the support of undesirable elements that managed to get Janata Party tickets and won the elections.

Student indiscipline is reaching new heights almost everywhere. In Patna students go to attend their classes or examination halls armed with daggers and pistols. A student was caught recently with a strange weapon which could be used as a boomerang at a distance of two or three yards. Even when they are caught, no action is taken against them while invigilators are abused and threatened with reprisal by hooligans. The higher-ups themselves maintain goondas and do nothing. How they get admission to the colleges is a mystery. It is not a new development but a continuing one. But there is no doubt that liberty is being taken as license by a section of youths.

The Janata regime may rule out police action even in such a situation to tackle the Mastan type of students. If the Janata government means to control the situation on this front, it would have to take the help of youths to mend youth. But the party has alienated a large section of the genuine Chhatra Sangharsh Samiti workers while many young hoodlums and strong-arm boys of the Youth Congress have heavily infiltrated the Samiti itself and are parading as Janata Party champions. This is not an isolated phenomenon in Bihar alone. It exists in some degree or other in other States too. It is for the Janata Party and its Government to control the situation.

It is no use blaming the Congress for making an issue of the ruling party's failures. Being in opposition, it is their business to do so. They will also not shy away from hitting below the belt when it suits them. They have already started instigating the students and workers to launch strikes and demonstrations, which they themselves banned during the emergency. They will no doubt continue in their efforts to drive a wedge between the constituents of the Janata Party. Such developments are inherent in the situation. So far, the Janata leaders have been busy in politicking and soon they will again get busy in electioneering in some States. One can only hope that they will also seriously settle down to business and start tackling some of the crucial problems that affect the masses most on priority basis.

Our national debt is colossal. The economy of almost every State is in hopelessly bad shape. For instance, the Bihar Government owes to the Union Government Rs. 984 crores. Its overdrafts with the Reserve Bank of India is of the order of Rs. 116 crores. The concessions mischievously made by the outgoing Congress Ministry would cost Rs. 69 crores. All these legacies are there. These cannot just be written off. It may not be fair, therefore, to expect the new governments to cure the accumulated ills of the past thirty years with a magic wand. Cleansing the Augean stable will indeed be a Herculean task. But rightly or wrongly too much hope has been aroused in the minds of the people who have voted the party to power in the belief that it is their own party and it will provide them with immediate relief. They have been patient so far and they will remain patient for a reasonable period of time. But how long?

Even after the bickerings within the party came to the fore before the Assembly elections, the attitude of the masses reflected in their talks was "we have provided it with a Kamiz (shirt) in the Lok Sabha poll, now let us also make a gift of a dhoti or pajama so that it will be fully dressed". But it should not be forgotten that the Janata (the people) have tasted blood. It is for the Janata Governments now to establish their bonafides by proving that they are earnest in their desire to help. Above all, Janata leaders must respect JP's wishes if and when he expresses them.

A resolution adopted in JP's presence in Bombay in the last week of June, 1977, by the Prabandhak Committee of the Sarva Seva Sangh said:

"It is painful to note that active supporters of the Emergency and corrupt persons are being allowed to occupy positions of power in the Janata Party even before they have proved their bonafides. The Prime Minister and some other Ministers have set praiseworthy examples of austerity but others are still lagging behind in this respect.

"There has been a perceptible drop in the percentage of votes in favour of the Janata Party in the Lok Sabha and the Assembly elections. The Harijans seem to have withdrawn support to the party to a considerable extent. The Samiti hopes that the Janata Party will take note of these developments to put its house in order."

In his Open Letter to the people of Bihar JP had described himself as a "wounded soldier". He had also held the view that he could no longer, and indefinitely, be their charioteer. At the time of the controversy over the withdrawal of Mrs. Nandini Satpathy, he had made an observation which had gone unnoticed. "Our struggle", he had said, "against the evils of the system that brought in the emergency has not ceased and will continue till our goal is achieved".

Will the goal be achieved and JP's dream of total revolution realised? Dreams rarely are. For himself he will continue to plough his lonely furrow. Those who had once rallied round him may one day leave. The rift between him and the Janata Party may widen. How many share his deeper dream, the "higher struggle"? And though this is what has naturally drawn more attention, the crusade itself was more than a clash of personalities. Who will know and measure the dreamer of dreams, of distant truths yet to be realised?

Is JP-esque mass movement the right method for such a

goal? Perhaps the only cause that could save man and society are lost causes. JP's idea of a Total Revolution, the echo of a noble soul, is at least a reminder that nothing short of everything will do, that politics is not enough.

History will blend with pathos and move on what lines who knows? Must then a Christ be sacrificed in every age for those that have no imagination?

Index